I0764052

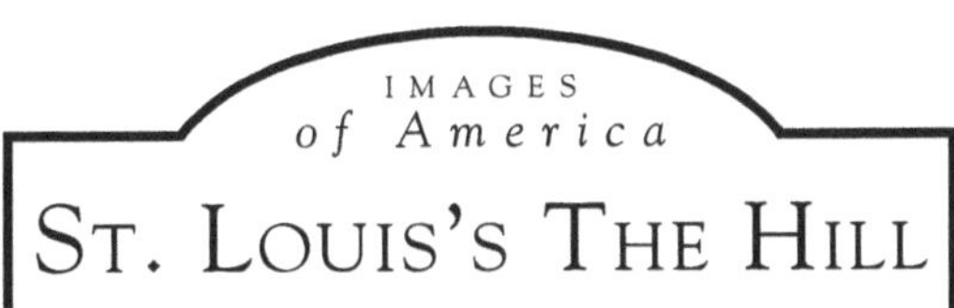
IMAGES
of America
ST. LOUIS'S THE HILL

On the Cover: John Viviano Sr. arrived in St. Louis in 1926 and married an American-born daughter of Italian immigrants who understood life on the Hill. In 1950, they opened a small grocery store on the Hill, where it remains family owned and operated. (Courtesy of John Viviano and Son's Groceries.)

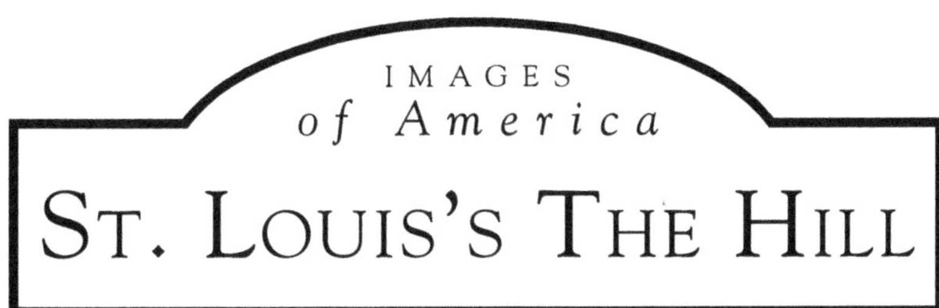

Rio Vitale

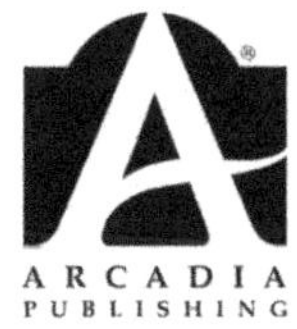

ISBN 978-1-4671-1221-5

Published by Arcadia Publishing
Charleston, South Carolina

Library of Congress Control Number: 2014932921

For all general information, please contact Arcadia Publishing:
Telephone 843-853-2070
Fax 843-853-0044
E-mail sales@arcadiapublishing.com
For customer service and orders:
Toll-Free 1-888-313-2665

Visit us on the Internet at www.arcadiapublishing.com

Contents

Acknowledgments 6

Introduction 7

1. Early Arrivals 9
2. Building a Community 17
3. Building a New Church 29
4. Population Growth 35
5. Industrial Growth 45
6. Education 61
7. World War II 71
8. Clubs, Social Organizations, and Sports 75
9. Weddings 91
10. Life after World War II 99

Acknowledgments

First and foremost, I would like to thank all of the people who left their beloved homeland to come and establish a better life on the Hill. These immigrants faced hostility and widespread discrimination in housing and employment. They united and created new-world societies, giving birth to Italian newspapers, theaters, churches, mutual-aid societies, and recreation clubs. They created a wonderful neighborhood that still thrives today. They defended our county in World War I, World War II, and the Korean War, and their descendants continue to serve in the US armed forces.

I would like to give special thanks to Barbara Torretti, Faye Berra Venegoni, Tim Valli, and Angelo Sita. These individuals supported me with photographs and stories. They have been instrumental in preserving the history of the Hill. Another special thank-you goes to Gino Mariani, an amateur photographer who took many of the photographs provided. He documented the Hill in photographs for decades and was an involved member of the community and Italian clubs in St. Louis.

INTRODUCTION

The Italian Risorgimento united the different states of the Italian peninsula into the single state of the Kingdom of Italy in 1871. At the end of the unification, the rural economy was near collapse, mainly because agriculture was still a manual job and because of the excessive demands of landowners, many of whom were absentee owners who did not even reside in Italy. As a result, production was low. The lack of agricultural development and excessive taxation left little pay for the peasant workers. Living and working conditions were poor, allowing little opportunity for a better life. Conditions in Italy were so bad that the Italian government encouraged young men to emigrate. This state of affairs forced people to leave their homeland in the hope of a brighter future.

Before 1890, most Italians immigrated to Europe or South America. Many began working in the mining areas of France and Germany. The first Italian settlement in St. Louis, located downtown, became known as Little Italy. These early Italian immigrants were mainly from the region around Genoa. This group began the Società Unione e Fratellanza Italiana in 1866. Now called the Fratellanza Society, it is currently the oldest continual Italian American organization in the United States. Members of this organization banded together to help and assist Italians with settling in St. Louis and assimilating in America.

The Hill, known as the Fairmount District in 1890, was on the western edge of St. Louis. The district had few homes, but it was settled because of its proximity to brickyards, clay mines, and other industries. Mining companies needed laborers, and the immigrants worked hard for low wages. Foreign shipping companies opened agencies run by local personnel in rural areas around Milan; one in particular was in the city of Cuggiono. These agencies helped people obtain tickets, complete forms, and comply with emigration regulations. The Hill area was settled mostly by Italians from Lombardy who lived in rural areas. The Hill saw a massive influx from Cuggiono, Inverno, Maccolo, and other towns near Milan. The rate of emigration from Cuggiono exceeded the whole province of Milan and was greater than the national average.

Many of the Lombard immigrants who settled on the Hill had previously worked in Herrin, Illinois, a coal-mining town approximately 100 miles southeast of St. Louis. When the first Italian immigrants settled on the Hill, there was no public transportation to visit the city to the east, and there were few conveniences. Many of the Lombard immigrants worked in the brickyards and clay pits. When family and friends arrived later, they also found work in the mines, foundries, and brickyards. Mining work was harsh and dangerous, and the pay was meager. Streets were not paved, and most travel and deliveries were conducted with horse-drawn wagons that had to trudge through the dusty and muddy streets. These immigrants came to make a better life than the one they had left behind. Despite harsh working conditions and discrimination, they were determined to succeed.

By the 1910s, immigrants from Sicily were arriving on the Hill. One city in particular, Casteltermini, was a source of Sicilian immigrants. Differences were recognized in the beginning, with minor problems sprouting up between people from Northern and Southern Italy, as Italy had only become a unified state in 1871. The Lombards and Sicilians continued to have their distinct identities. These differences, overcome through the intercession of St. Ambrose Church and from dedicated civil leadership, became nonexistent with the immigrants' children. St. Ambrose Church was very influential in the Hill community and became a unifying force in the neighborhood. It served as a focal point where social and religious organizations could meet and worship. This improved relations between those from Northern and Southern Italy.

Msgr. Cavalliere Cesare Spigardi was born on August 31, 1858, in Pomponesco, a community in the province of Mantova, Italy. In January 1900, he came to St. Louis, where he led numerous Italians, with whose cooperation he opened a small, simple church on Nineteenth and Morgan Streets downtown, in St. Louis's Little Italy. This church was dedicated to Our Lady Help of Christians. The second church opened by Monsignor Spigardi was St. Charles Borromeo, inaugurated on November 2, 1902, also in Little Italy. One of the most important aspects of the Hill has been the influence of the Catholic Church. Monsignor Spigardi, along with Rev. Ottavio Leone, would preach to the large colony of Italians who settled on the Hill in 1903, in the basement of St. Aloysius Church. As this colony grew, its members wanted their own church. With the assistance of Monsignor Spigardi, they founded the third Italian parish, on the corner of Wilson and Marconi Avenues. They choose to name the church after the fourth-century bishop of Milan, St. Ambrose. The first Italian school in St. Louis would be open by Spigardi with the support of the sisters known as the Missionary Zelatrices of the Sacred Heart of Jesus, who arrived in 1913 at the Our Lady Help of Christians, located at Tenth and Wash (now Cole) Streets. In 1939, the sisters helped establish the Sacred Heart Villa, and in 1943, they began teaching students at St. Ambrose School.

As the Italian population grew and developed economic opportunities in the area, the immigrants sent word to friends and relatives in Italy. Immigrants working on the Hill sent money to Italy to help cover the cost of transportation. Men would arrive first and work to save enough money to bring over the rest of the family. Some young men came to build their fortunes and return to Italy. Few returned, recalling the living conditions they had left behind. Women who came over would marry men from their hometown.

The Hill, while largely uninhabited in 1890, grew into a well-planned community between 1900 and 1920. As the Italian population increased, community organizations developed. Italian immigrants formed mutual-aid societies, which provided sickness and death benefits to families when a tragedy occurred. Many of the societies were named for towns in Italy and Sicily. Italians in St. Louis founded associations and clubs and built churches and other meeting places. They united in order to help each other observe their traditions, speak Italian and their particular dialects, and maintain memories of their shared past. The wide-open spaces of the Hill gave way to additional affordable housing and new employment opportunities. Some Italian immigrants would become shop owners and provide services and goods that previously required travel into the city of St. Louis.

One

Early Arrivals

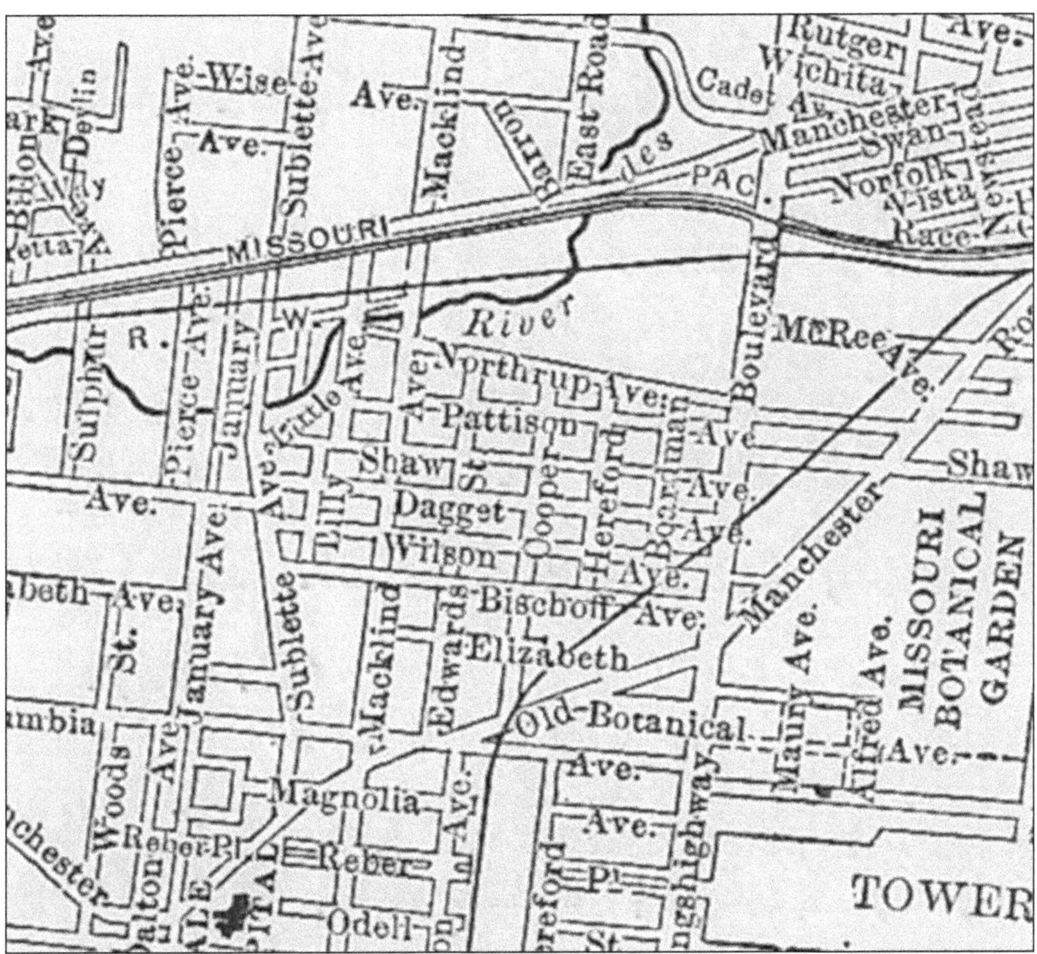

The Hill was originally part of Cheltenham, which covered a large section of southwest St. Louis. Later, it was called the Fairmount District—a small Irish, then German settlement. As the Italians moved in, the Irish and Germans moved out. A small number of African Americans lived near Northrup Avenue and South Kingshighway Boulevard, working in the clay industries. They had their own school and Baptist church on Pattison Avenue. The first Italians who came to the Hill lived mainly on Northrup, Pattison, and Shaw Avenues, the northernmost point of the Hill. Housing was scarce, so many existing homes took in boarders. Unmarried young men would come from Italy to work and save money, then return to Italy to marry and bring their brides to America. Married men would send for their families when they secured a job and a home. On January 7, 1892, a meeting of the Società Unione e Fratellanza Italiana initiated 26 new members. Of these, 23 were from Lombardy and were living on the Hill. (Author's collection.)

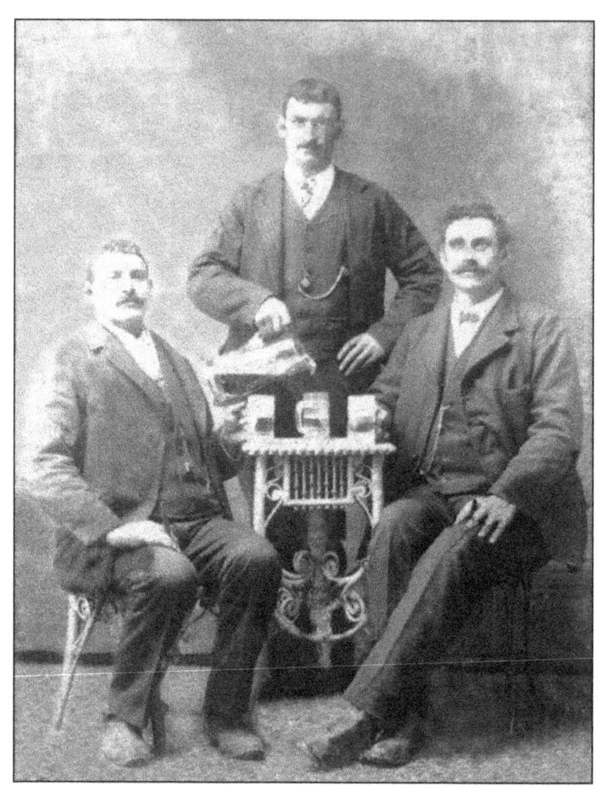

The three Barbaglia brothers came to the United States from Cuggiono, Italy. Paolo (center) immigrated on July 20, 1891. He worked as a laborer in the brickyards and married Angelina Agnes Calcaterra in 1882. Giovanni Natale Barbaglia (left) immigrated in 1893 and married Antonetta Calcaterra in Italy. Vittorio Barbaglia immigrated in 1893 and worked in the clay mines and married Virginia Pelligrini in 1894. Before families started to settle in the Hill, railroad boxcars were often used as houses. In the early 1890s, there were a number of shacks at the north end of the Hill. (Courtesy of Tonette Mugavero McArthur.)

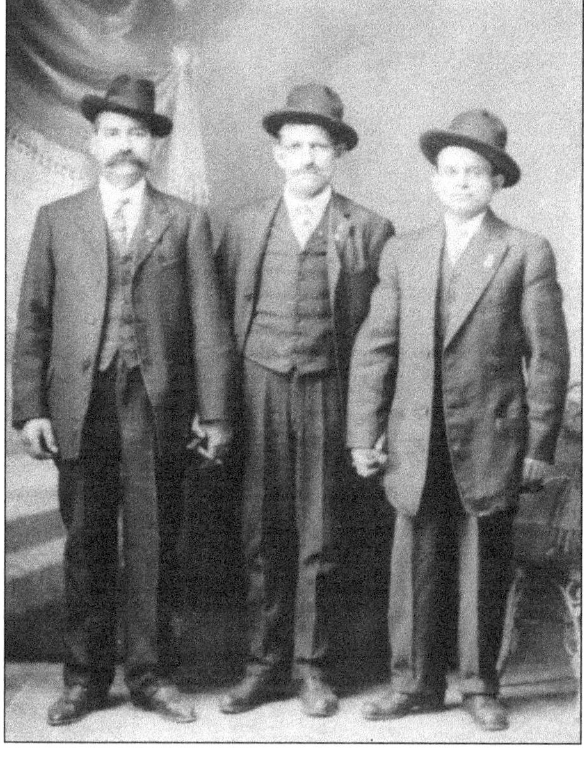

The Colombo brothers—from left to right, Carlo, Giovanni, and Battista—eventually brought their families from Italy to live on the Hill. There were a few boardinghouses, and each held about a dozen men. Often, two shifts of men would share the same room. Life was harsh for the early immigrants, as most were crammed into these homes without any utilities or conveniences. (Courtesy of Evelyn Colombo Nettemeyer.)

The groom shown here is Ferrante Ruggeri, from Buscate, Lombardy. He arrived on Christmas day in 1900 and worked as a day laborer at various jobs in St. Louis. In 1904 he wrote home, asking his family to find him a bride. They arranged a marriage with another family from Buscate. Ruggeri and Filomena Balossi, a 22-year-old seamstress, were married by Msgr. Cesare Spigardi on April 2, 1905, at St. Charles Borromeo Church. (Courtesy of Frances [Ruggeri] Stephens and Chris Stephens.)

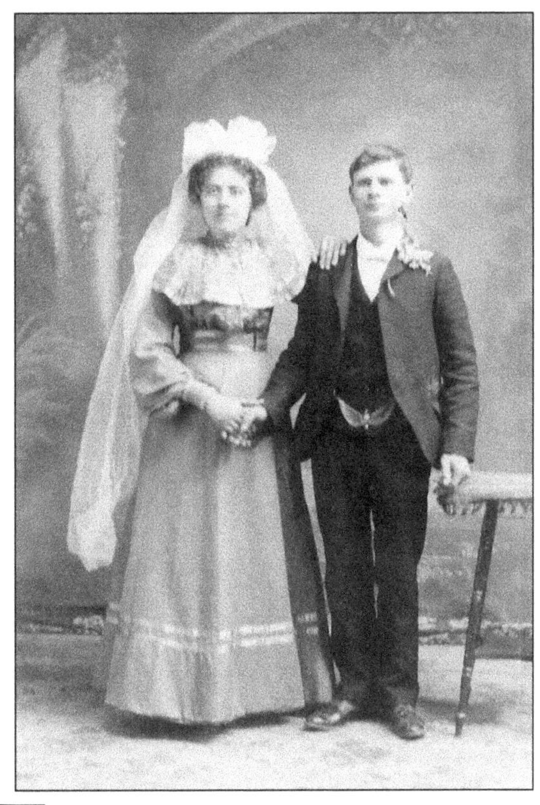

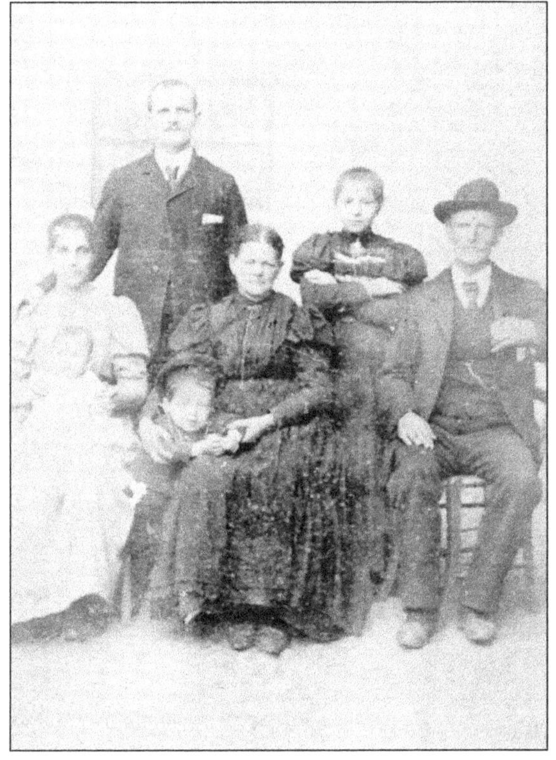

Shown here are members of the Ambrosio and Della Ruggeri family. On the left are Angelo Ruggeri (standing) and his wife, Angela. Their children are daughter Giovanina Ruggeri (second from right), son Angelo (in front) and infant Maria Ruggeri (Barbaglia). On the right are Ambrosio Ruggeri and his wife, Della. It was not uncommon for an entire generation of family members to leave the surrounding towns near Milan to come to America. For example, the population of Cuggiono fell from 6,105 people in 1881 to 4,970 in 1911, due to migration. (Courtesy of Toni Mugavero McArther.)

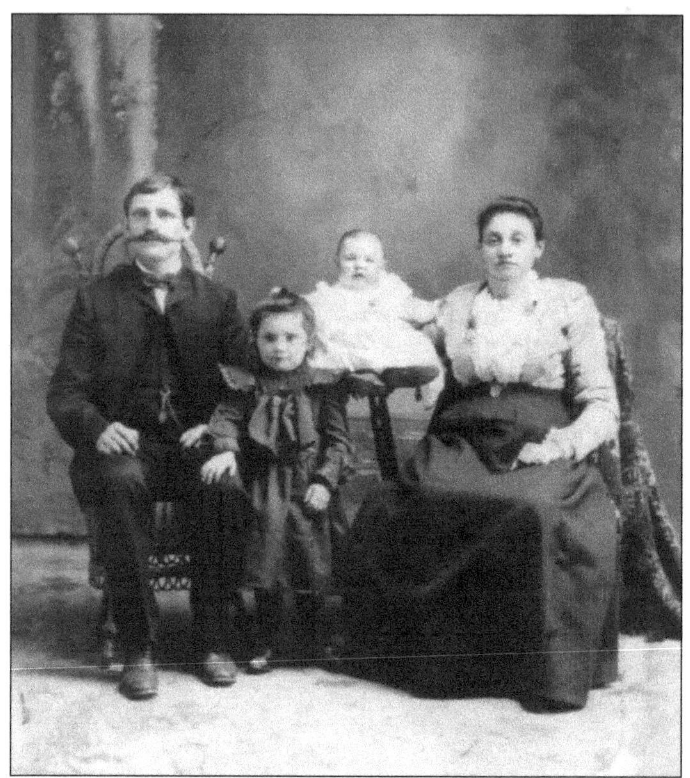

Giovanni Colombo and his wife, Luigia Cucchi Colombo, immigrated from Cuggiono. The 1910 census indicates that Maria Colombo, the older daughter shown here, was born in 1901 in Italy. Angelina Colombo, the infant, was born in 1904 in St. Louis. After the turn of the 20th century, one-story, three-room homes began appearing on the Hill. (Courtesy of Evelyn Colombo Nettemeyer.)

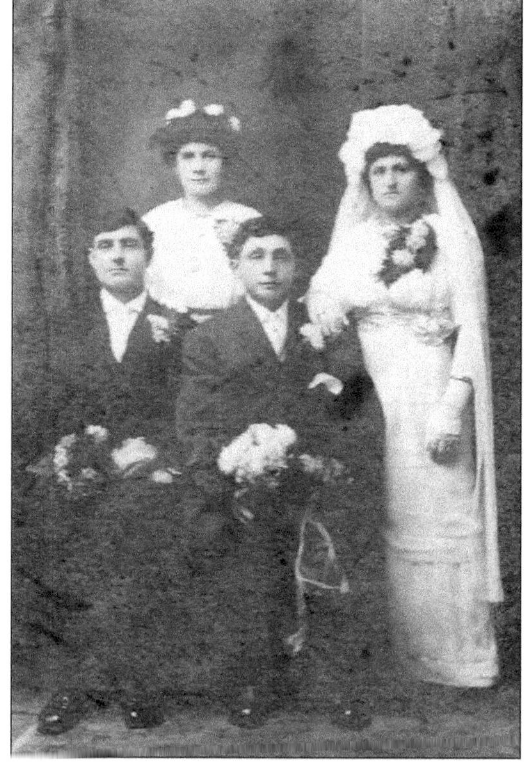

The groom is Raffaele Colombo from Castano Primo, Lombardy. He arrived in New York on November 12, 1905. The ship's manifest lists him as a mason; however, he worked in the clay mines under the Hill. The bride is Teresa Colombo from Castano Primo. She arrived on November 22, 1913. The ship's manifest lists her as a weaver. They were married by Rev. Fiorenzo Lupo on November 30, 1913, at St. Ambrose Church. The others are unidentified. (Courtesy of Frances [Ruggeri] Stephens and Chris Stephens.)

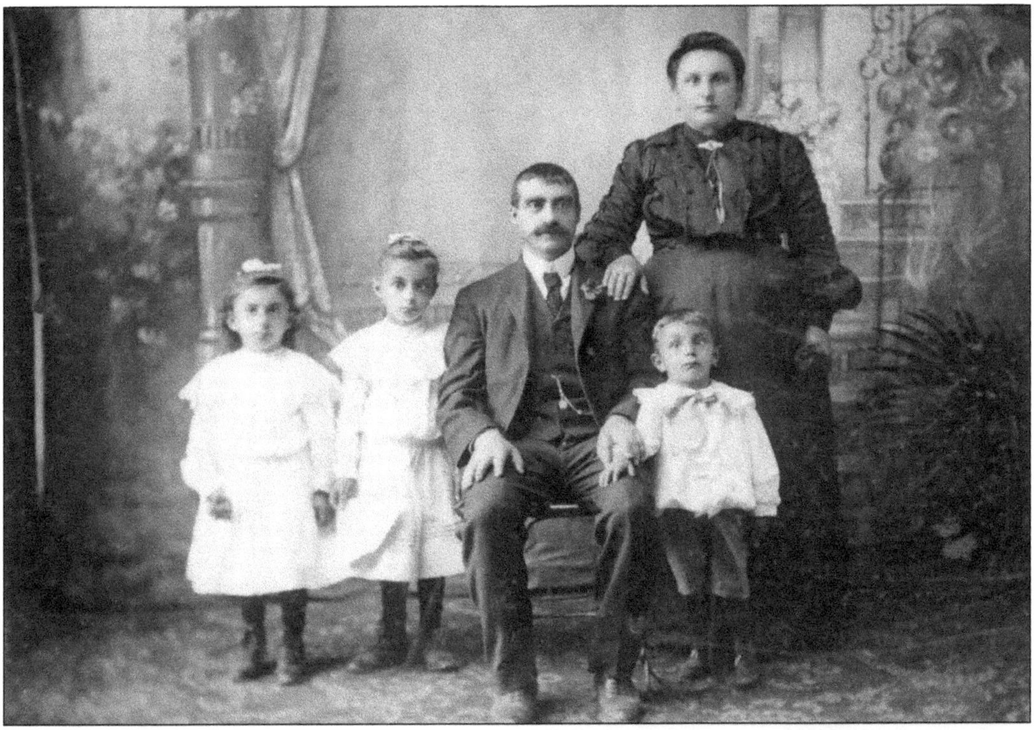

Shown here in 1905 are Henry Puricelli and his wife, Caroline. Their children are, from left to right, Mary Purcelli (Aiazzi), Josephine Puricelli (Tedoni), and Frank Puricelli. The 1900 census shows Henry, Carolina, and Josephina living at 5258 Daggett Avenue. Their three boarders were also listed: Louis Puricelli, John Puricelli, and Charles Ravetta. The occupation of each man was listed as brickyard laborer. (Courtesy of Dave Tedoni.)

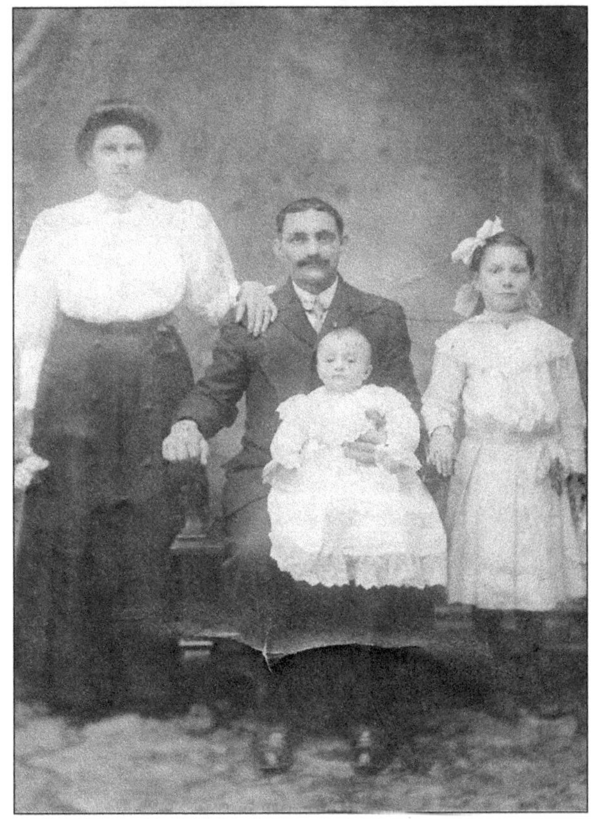

Domenico Belloli worked in the United States for seven years before sending for his wife and daughter, who had stayed behind in Cuggiono, Italy. His wife, Rose, and daughter Luigia were reunited with him on the Hill in 1907. The 1910 census lists Domenico Belloli's occupation as a laborer in the brickyard and shows him living at 5243 Bischoff Avenue. Shortly after 1910, Daggett, Wilson, and Bischoff Avenues east of Macklind Avenue would become populated. (Courtesy of Barbara Torretti.)

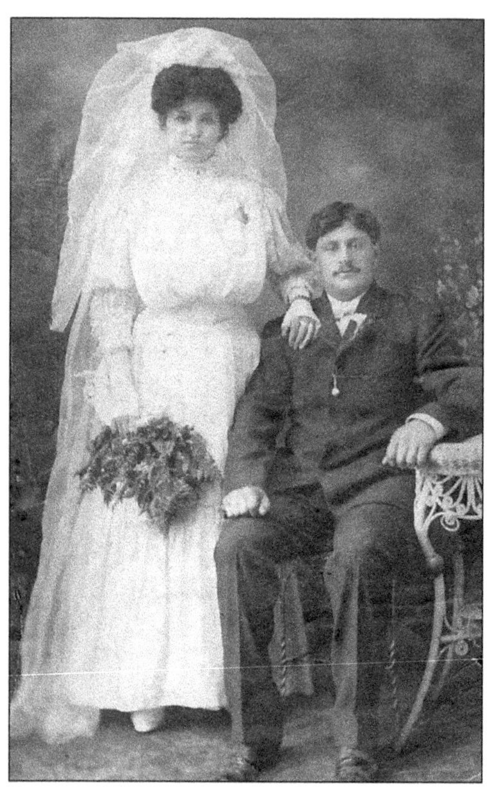

Angelo Berra from Malvaglio, Italy, and Maria Alberti were married on October 28, 1906. Reaching for new horizons and a better way of life, Angelo came to America when he was 23 years old with just $15. In St. Louis, he used his talents as a cement finisher and tile-setter to support his ever-growing family. For a time, he had the privilege of working on the mosaics for the Cathedral Basilica of Saint Louis. Angelo's greatest pride, like all Italians, was his family. He considered Maria and their 10 children a gift from God, and his nurturing of them as his gift in return. (Courtesy of Faye Berra Venegoni.)

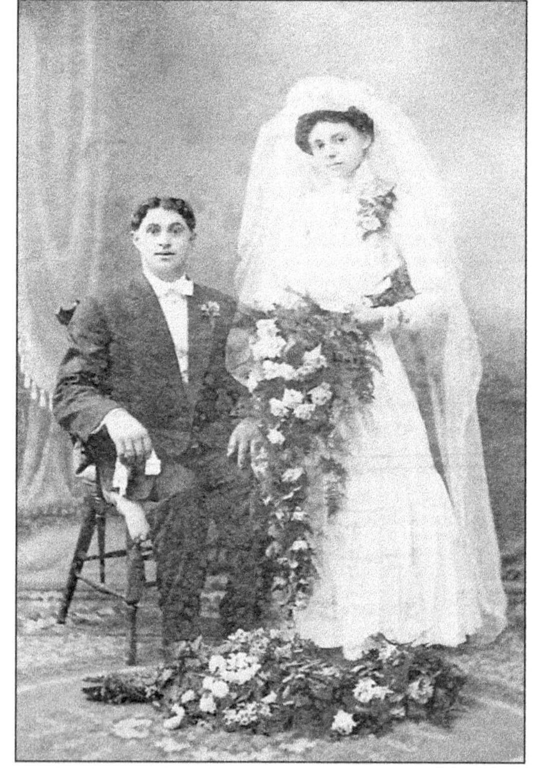

Louis Venegoni and Carolina Casiraghi were married on April 7, 1910. He was born in Cuggiono, Italy, in 1885 and immigrated to America in 1901 at the age of 16 with only $50 in his possession. He quickly declared his allegiance to his new country, becoming a US citizen in 1908. Upon arriving in St. Louis, he lived as a boarder in his brother's home and worked as a bartender. Around 1910, he began working at the Enno Sanders Mineral Water Company. While working there, he conceived the idea of starting his own carbonated beverage business. A few years later, in 1919, at the young age of 34, Louis Venegoni became co-proprietor of his own business. Along with a coworker, Isadoro Oldani, he began Blue Ridge Bottling Company. It went on to become the largest annual producer of carbonated beverages in St. Louis. (Courtesy of Fay Berra Venegoni.)

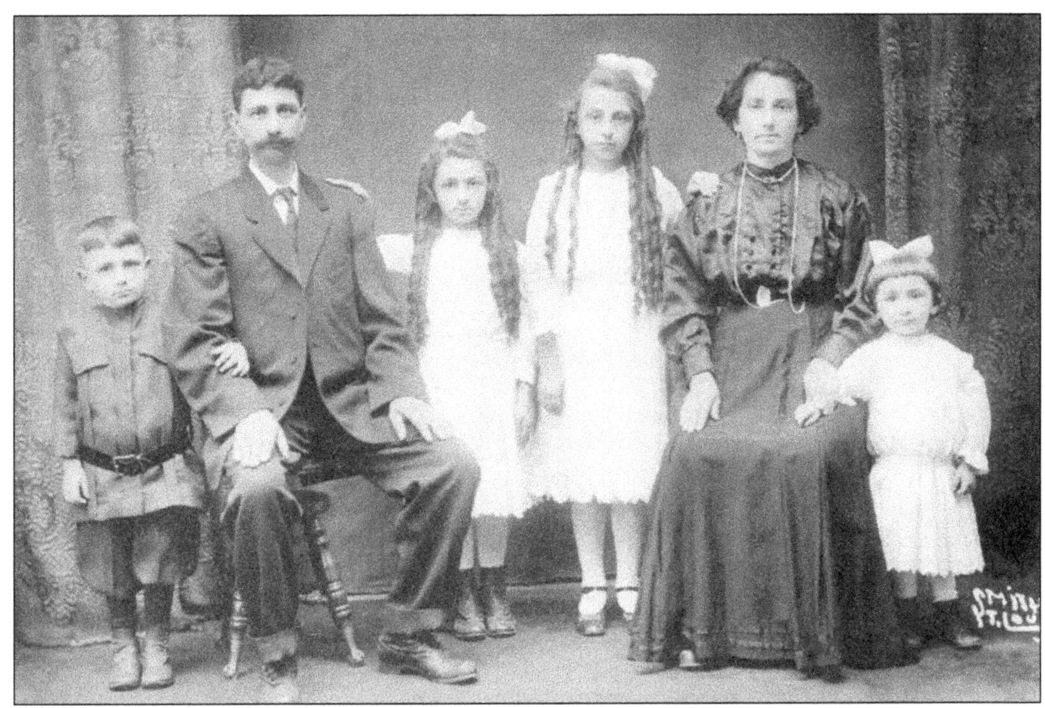

Angelo and Maria Torno and family lived on Edwards Street. Immigrants came to the Hill because of its proximity to factories and mines, which provided a modest living in a part of St. Louis that enabled them to purchase land and build a home. Small bungalows were constructed with three rooms, commonly referred to as shotgun houses. Many of these were wood-frame homes, but a few residents could afford brick houses of similar size. (Courtesy of Martha VanLeuven.)

Angelo Colombo and his family pose on the front porch of their home on Edwards Street, built from lumber from the 1904 World's Fair. Among the various buildings erected at the fair was the Italian Building, which attracted the Italians who settled in St. Louis. The Columbus Day celebration at the fair was a magnificent demonstration; the entire Italian colony turned out. (Courtesy of Martha VanLeuven.)

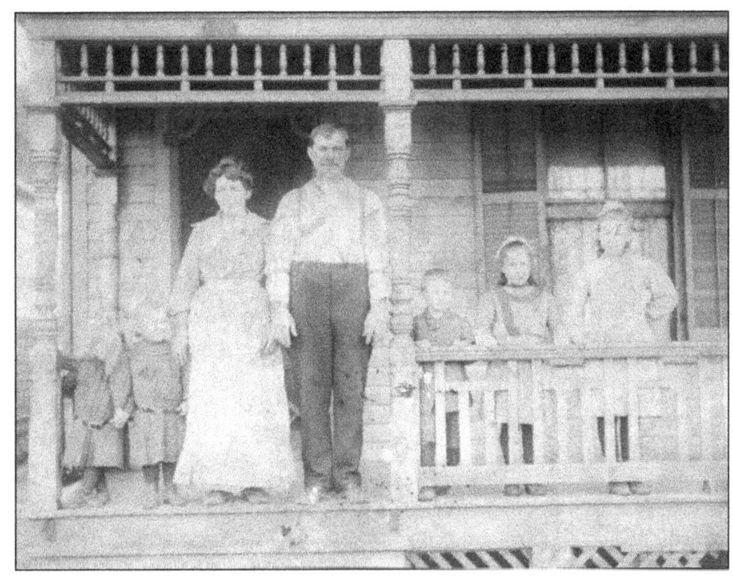

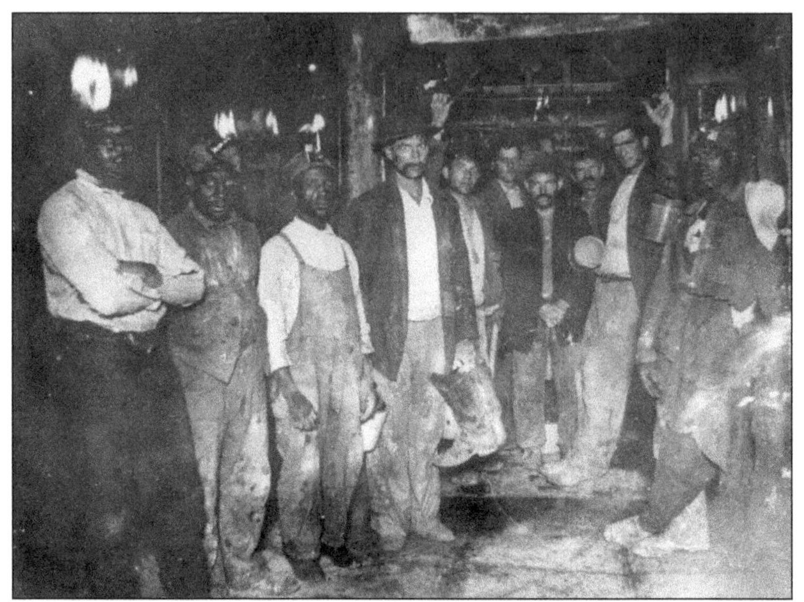

Italian and African American clay miners work together in a mineshaft on June 9, 1907. Many Italians came to St. Louis via Illinois coal-mining towns like Herrin, replacing German and African American clay miners. (Courtesy of Missouri History Museum, St. Louis.)

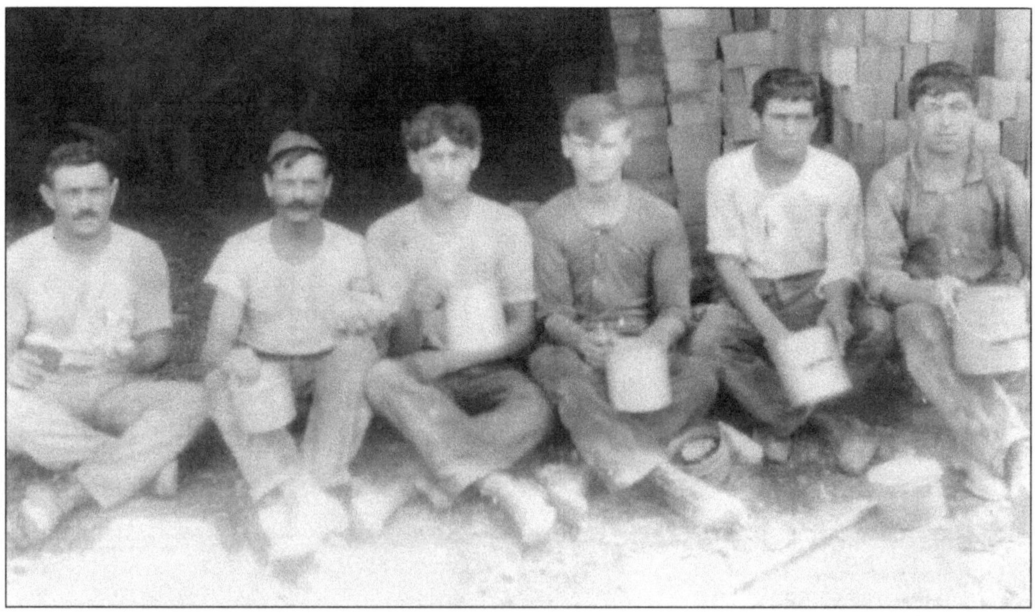

The man on the far right is Ernesto Cucchi, from Cuggiono, Italy. The mines at the base of the Hill provided work for the immigrants, but conditions were difficult and dangerous. The pay was poor, and most men worked 12-hour days, six days a week. Workers were paid by the tons of clay extracted and were required to provide their own pick and shovel. The *St. Louis Globe-Democrat* described the mining operation this way: "Half-naked bodies . . . seemed as shadows in the feeble light" in a mine that was the "scene of several calamities." (Courtesy of Evelyn Colombo Nettemeyer.)

Two

BUILDING A COMMUNITY

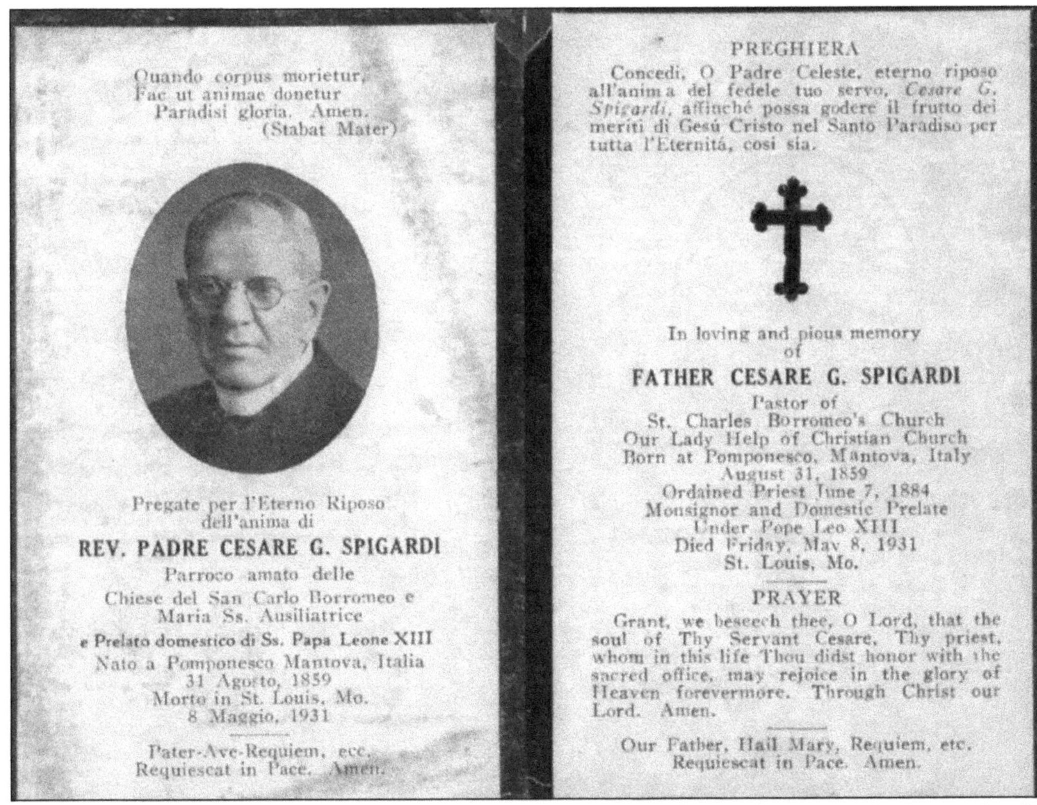

Quando corpus morietur,
Fac ut animae donetur
Paradisi gloria. Amen.
(Stabat Mater)

Pregate per l'Eterno Riposo
dell'anima di

REV. PADRE CESARE G. SPIGARDI

Parroco amato delle
Chiese del San Carlo Borromeo e
Maria Ss. Ausiliatrice
e Prelato domestico di Ss. Papa Leone XIII
Nato a Pomponesco Mantova, Italia
31 Agosto, 1859
Morto in St. Louis, Mo.
8 Maggio, 1931

Pater-Ave-Requiem, ecc.
Requiescat in Pace. Amen.

PREGHIERA

Concedi, O Padre Celeste, eterno riposo all'anima del fedele tuo servo, *Cesare G. Spigardi*, affinché possa godere il frutto dei meriti di Gesú Cristo nel Santo Paradiso per tutta l'Eternitá, cosi sia.

In loving and pious memory
of

FATHER CESARE G. SPIGARDI

Pastor of
St. Charles Borromeo's Church
Our Lady Help of Christian Church
Born at Pomponesco, Mantova, Italy
August 31, 1859
Ordained Priest June 7, 1884
Monsignor and Domestic Prelate
Under Pope Leo XIII
Died Friday, May 8, 1931
St. Louis, Mo.

PRAYER

Grant, we beseech thee, O Lord, that the soul of Thy Servant Cesare, Thy priest, whom in this life Thou didst honor with the sacred office, may rejoice in the glory of Heaven forevermore. Through Christ our Lord. Amen.

Our Father, Hail Mary, Requiem, etc.
Requiescat in Pace. Amen.

In 1903, Msgr. Cesare Spigardi, pastor of the two Italian churches in downtown St. Louis's Little Italy (Our Lady Help of Christians and St. Charles Borromeo) came to the Hill and began holding Italian Mass in the basement of St. Aloysius Church with Rev. Ottavio Leone. Several Italians on the Hill helped collect $5 from each family in hopes of building an Italian church for the residents. Msgr. Spigardi was able to purchase a small plot of land at the corner of Cooper (now Marconi) and Wilson Avenues. On May 1, 1903, construction on the new church began, and it was completed and dedicated on August 3, 1903. St. Ambrose Church remained under Spigardi's leadership for three years. During this time, Rev. Russo of St. Charles Borromeo would come to the Hill to celebrate Mass. (Courtesy of Marianne Peri-Sack.)

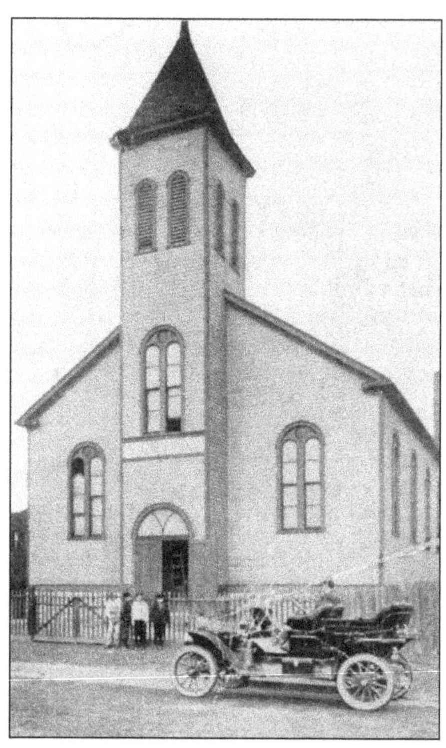

Rev. Luciano Carotti was appointed pastor of St. Ambrose and was the first residential priest in 1907. This was the official separation from the other Italian churches, as St. Ambrose was established as an independent parish. In August 1915, Reverend Carotti purchased a home from Joseph Lo Castro at 5128 Wilson Avenue, next to the church. This is the location of the rectory today. In 1915, he purchased a 60-by-170-foot parcel at the corner of Wilson Avenue and Hereford Street and erected a new school and a convent for the sisters. (Courtesy of Missouri History Museum, St. Louis.)

Mariano Deluca (seated, right) and his wife, Catherine Randazzo, pose with Mariano's brothers. This family lived in Little Italy and came to St. Louis during the 1904 World's Fair. This area was largely populated with Sicilians who worked in the produce industry or for clothing, shoe, or furniture manufacturers downtown. There was little interaction between Little Italy and the Hill until Monsignor Spigardi arrived. The Catholic Church and the Fratellanza Society became a common ground for Italian immigrants. (Author's collection.)

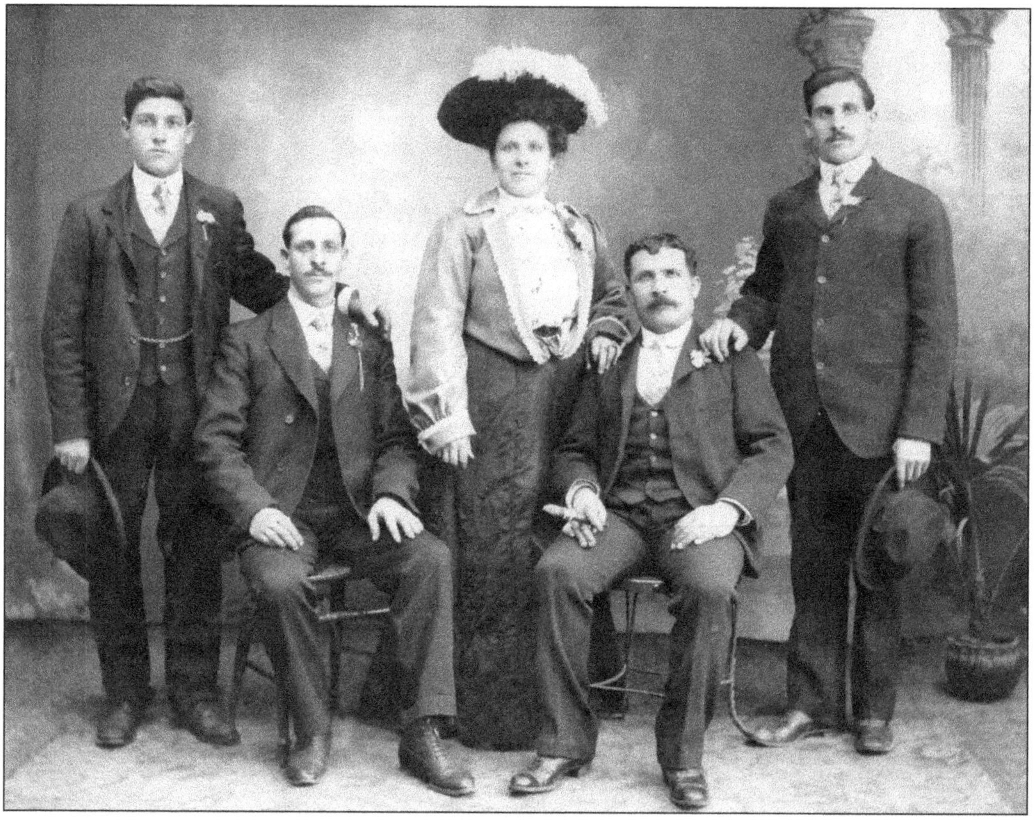

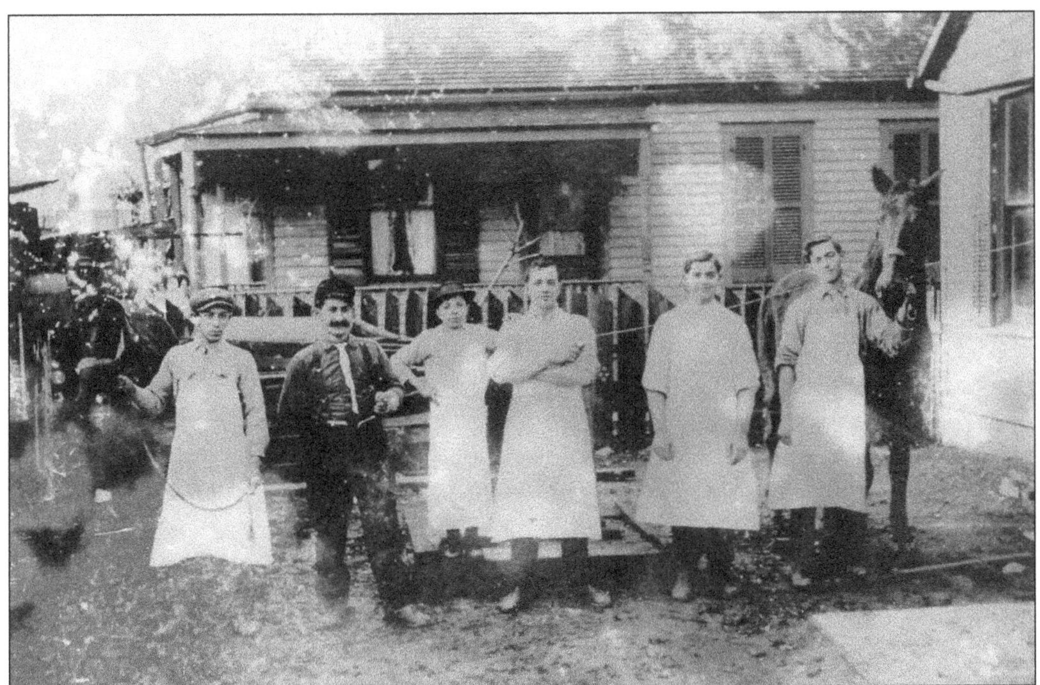

Shown here are employees of Martin Garavaglia's market on the Hill and the horses used to make deliveries. The streets of the Hill were not paved until the 1920s, and most travel was conducted by horse-drawn wagons that had to trudge through the mud of the streets. (Courtesy of Anthony Garavaglia.)

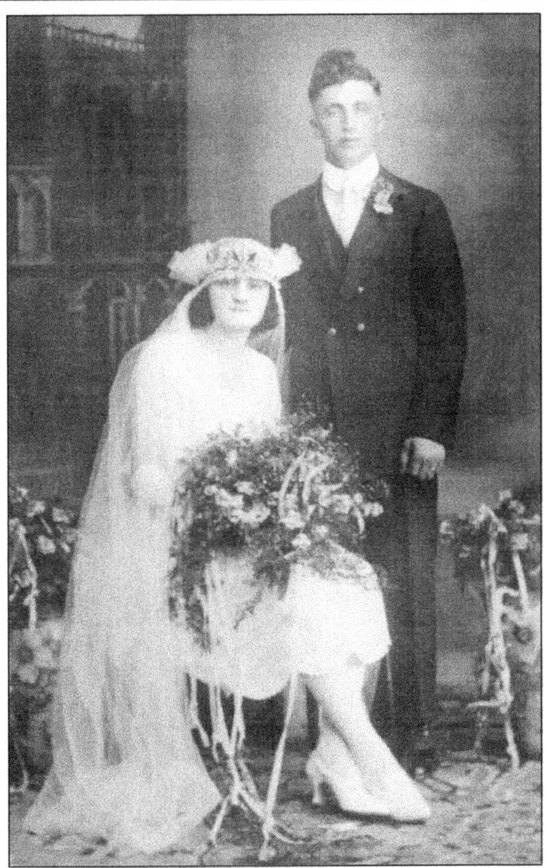

Maria Colombo, daughter of Giovanni and Luigia "Gina" Colombo, married Ernesto Cucchi. Ernesto was born in Cuggiono, Italy, and was employed at a clay mine and factory in St. Louis. They had two children, Lou Cucchi and Gloria Cucchi (Clavenna). These early immigrants banded together, largely as a response to a society that was hostile toward them. Industries located on the Hill gave residents employment opportunities, allowing them to remain in the neighborhood but also to help create a barrier to any interaction with the rest of St. Louis. (Courtesy of Evelyn Colombo.)

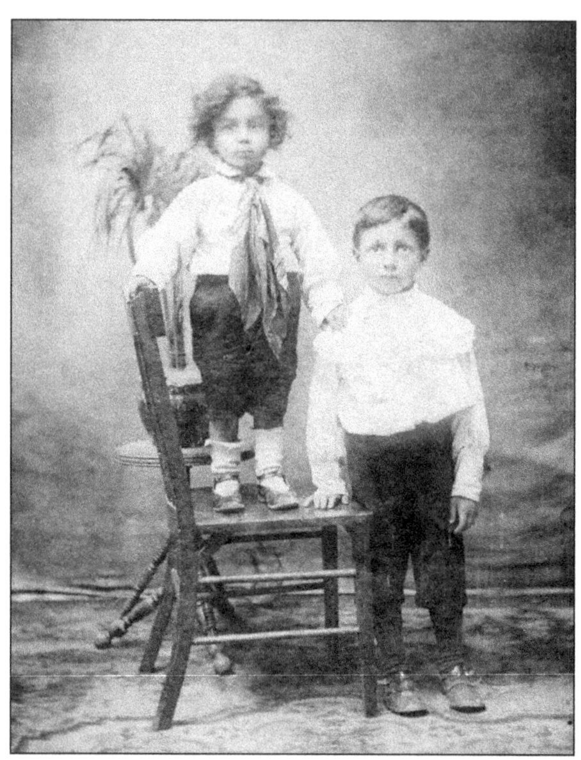

John Tornetto (left) was born on the Hill to Sicilian immigrants. Sam Tornetto (right) was born in Villagrazia di Carini, outside of Palermo, before his family came to St. Louis. Their father, Ciro Tornetto, worked at Carondelet Foundry. Northern Italians had "Big Club Hall" at 5200 Shaw Avenue, and Southern Italians had the Unione Sicilanna Principeda Piedmonte on Daggett Avenue and the Palma Augusta on Marconi Avenue. In 1907, the Mutual Aid Society imposed a $2 fine for fighting between those of Italian and Sicilian descent. Despite these residents' differences, their common belief and loyalty to St. Ambrose would eventually ease tensions by the 1920s. (Courtesy of Paula Tornetto Gusmano.)

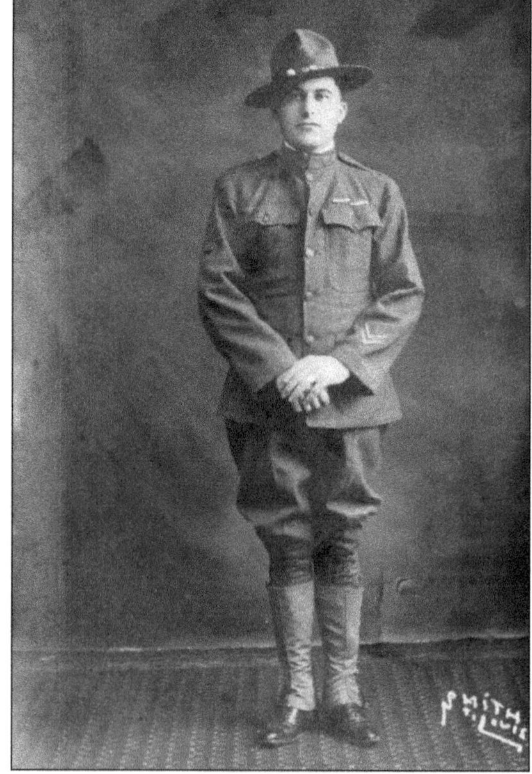

Santino Tedoni served the United States in World War I after immigrating here. In the 1930 census, his occupation is listed as clay miner. His wife, Josephine, son Thomas, and daughter Caroline were all born in Missouri. (Courtesy of Anthony Garavaglia.)

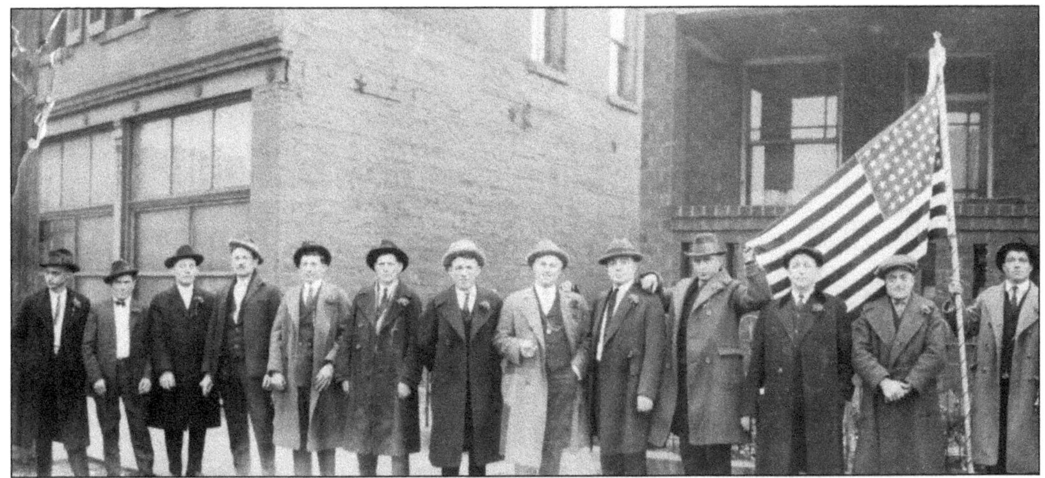

In the 1920s and 1930s, the Hill would be faced with anti-immigrant feelings and a negative image. Following the flood of immigrants before World War I, the United States implemented the Emergency Quota Law of 1921, imposing limits on immigration, including an annual limit of 42,000 Italians. The act favored people of Northern Europe, who were perceived to share the culture of the majority of Americans. The feeling of isolation that resulted would strengthen the development of the Hill's institutions and activities. Hill residents displayed the love of their homeland and their new country by proudly displaying the flags of each. (Courtesy of Marianne Peri-Sack.)

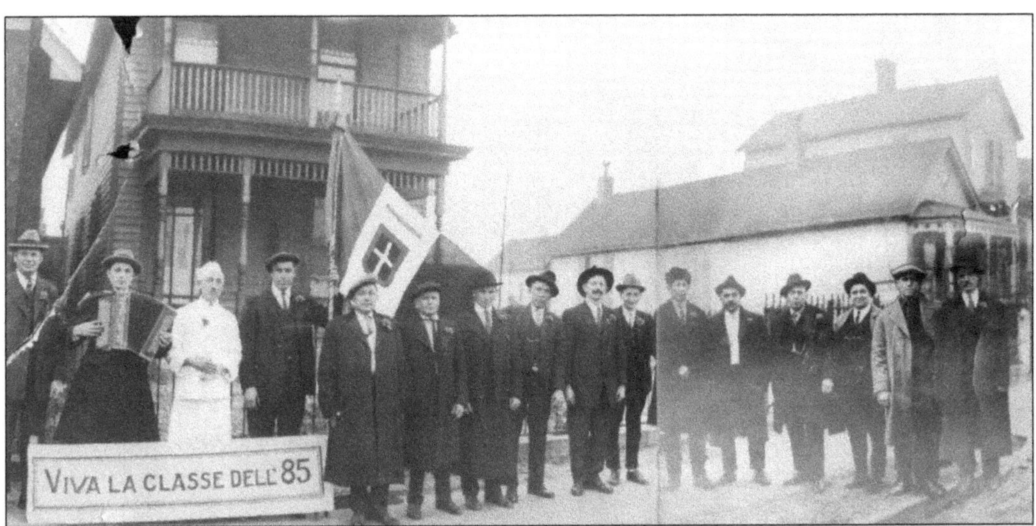

World War I offered an opportunity for residents to manifest their patriotism for their motherland as well as for their adopted country. A percentage of Italian reservists joined the Italian Army, with the majority joining the American forces. A number of Hill residents, as well as Italians from downtown's Little Italy, served during the war. Italian mutual-aid societies participated in patriotic demonstrations in the city and purchased Liberty bonds. (Courtesy of Marianne Peri-Sack.)

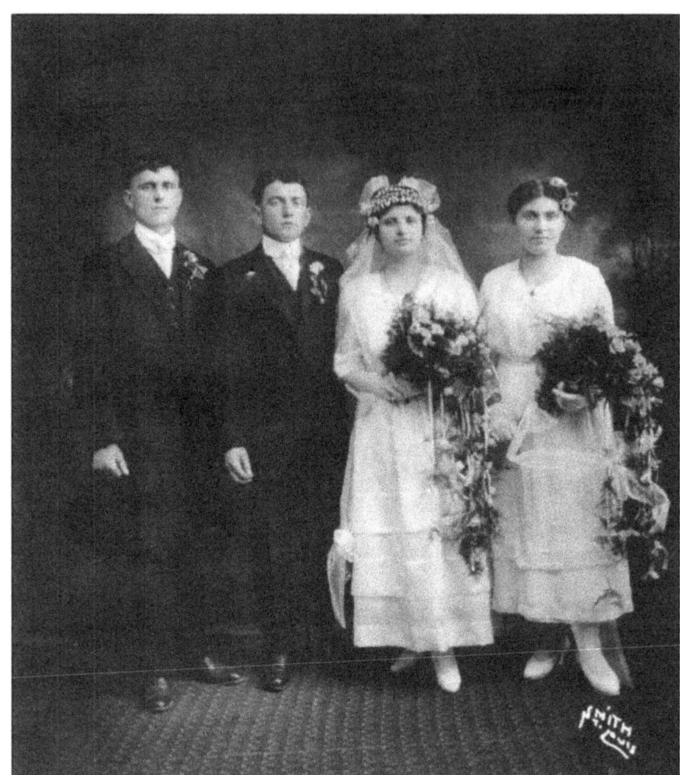

Many immigrants, like Lewis Savio, 32, served in World War I shortly after his arrival in the United States. He also served as a member of the US Citizens Defense Corps in World War II. Shown here are, from left to right, Lewis Savio, his brother Carlo Savio (groom), Pierina Vismara (bride), and Rachael Savio. (Courtesy of Johanna Savio Gramoldi.)

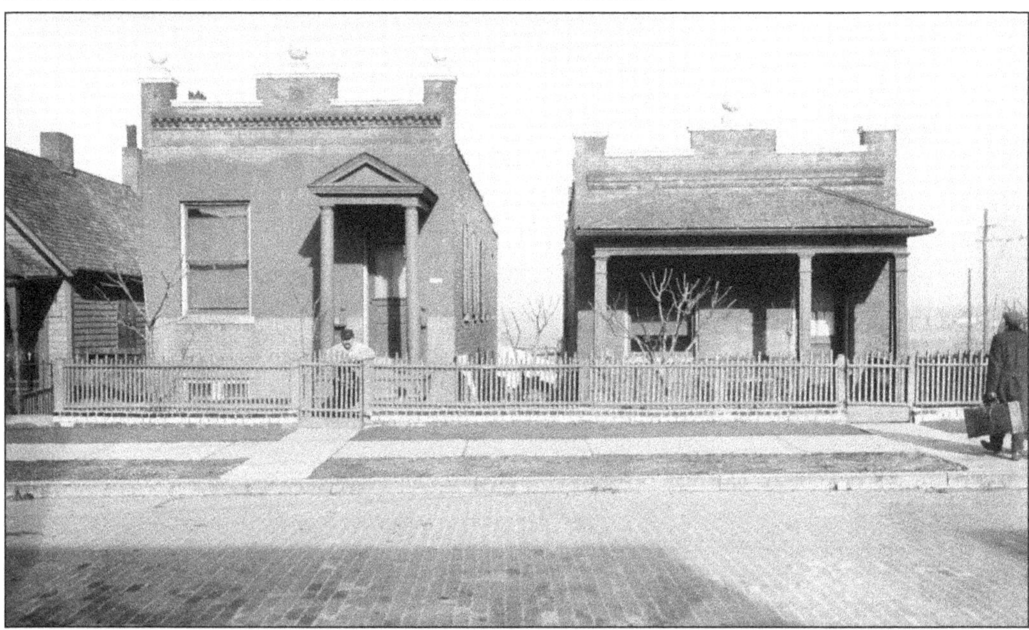

Working-class residential homes are seen on Pattison Avenue on the Hill in the 1920s. Note the suitcase in the man's hand with the single strap across it. On voyages to America, only one suitcase was allowed on the ship. After the 1920s, most of the streets were paved with brick, a sewer system was installed, and utilities became available for home installation. (Courtesy of Missouri History Museum, St. Louis.)

Immigrants had to work in difficult conditions in order to make a better life for their families. Despite the obstacles, Italian immigrants still found time to socialize and enjoy themselves, with events sponsored by churches and various clubs and societies. (Courtesy of Toni Mugavero McArthur.)

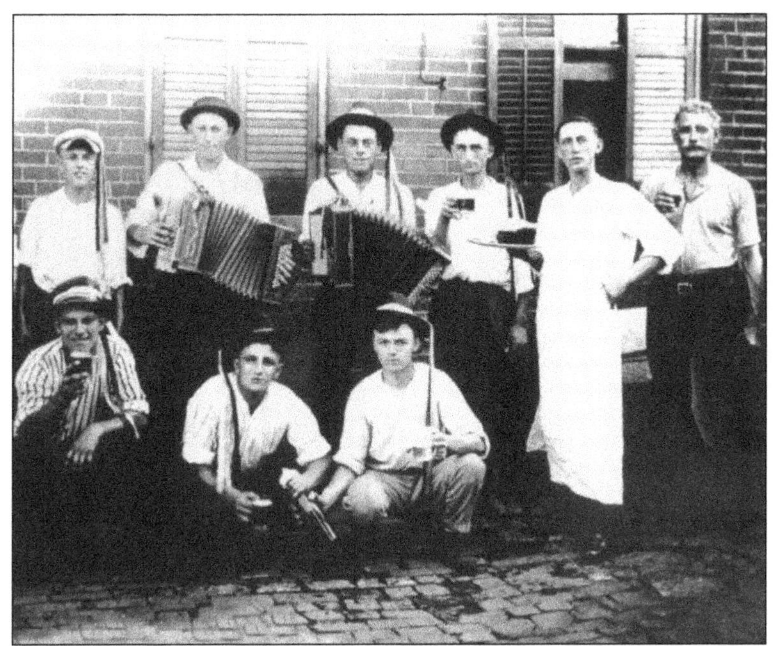

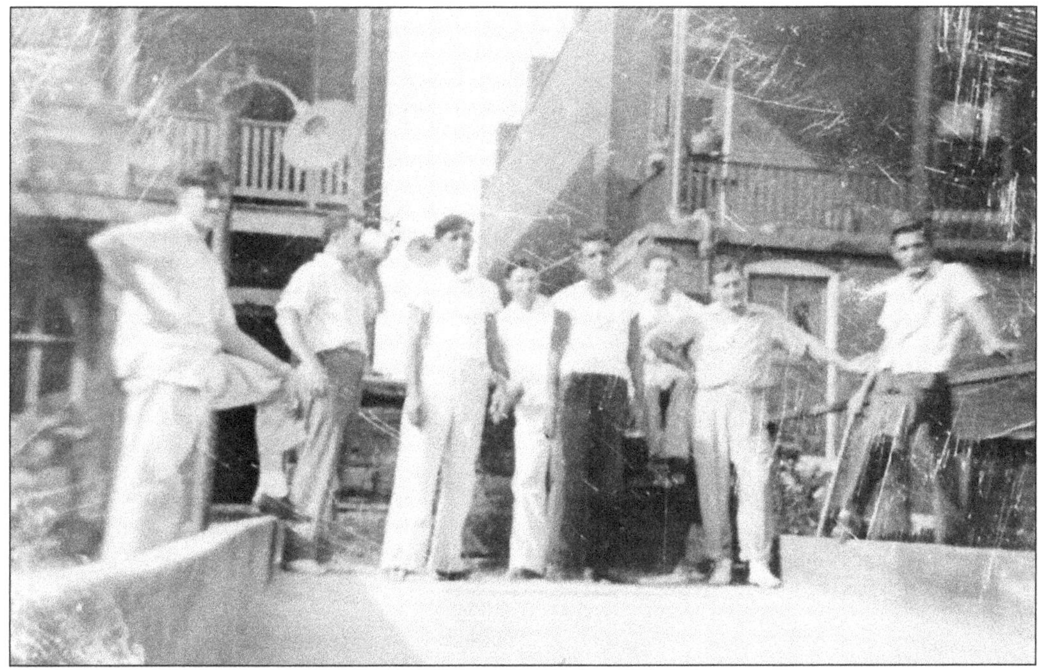

These young men, most likely boarders, enjoy a game of bocce. It was common for residents to gather after work or on weekends for a drink of wine or beer and to play musical instruments, card games, or bocce. (Courtesy of Anthony Garavaglia.)

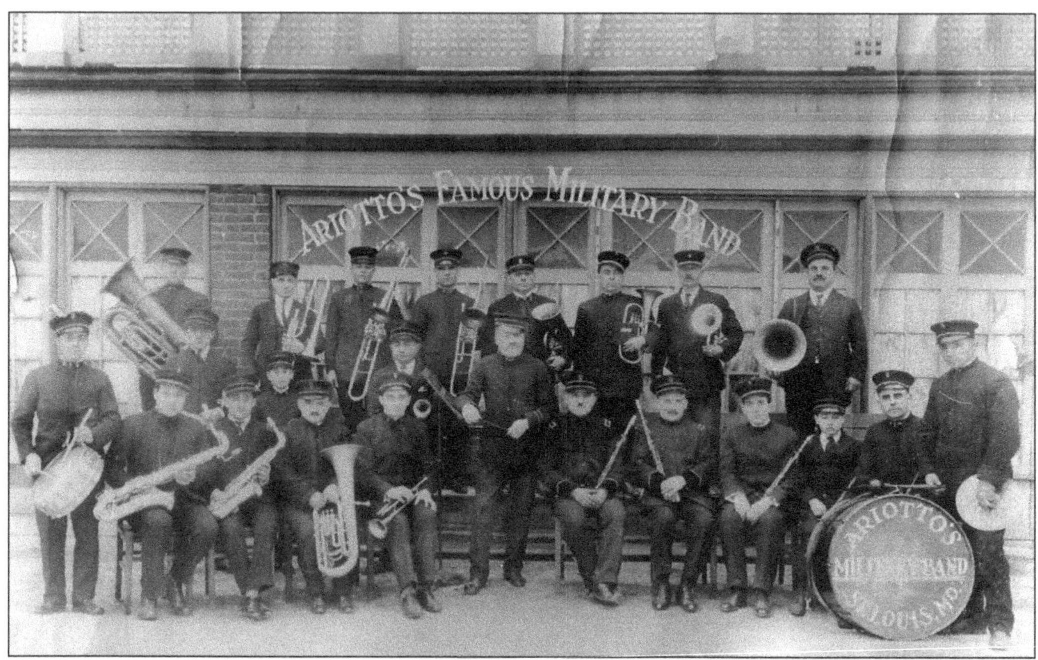

Joe Ariotto was an excellent musician who also owned a saloon on Marconi Avenue. He formed Joe Ariotto's Famous Military Brass Band, which entertained at the saloon, parades, weddings, and processions. Many children from The Hill would take their lessons from Joe Ariotto. (Courtesy of James Merlo.)

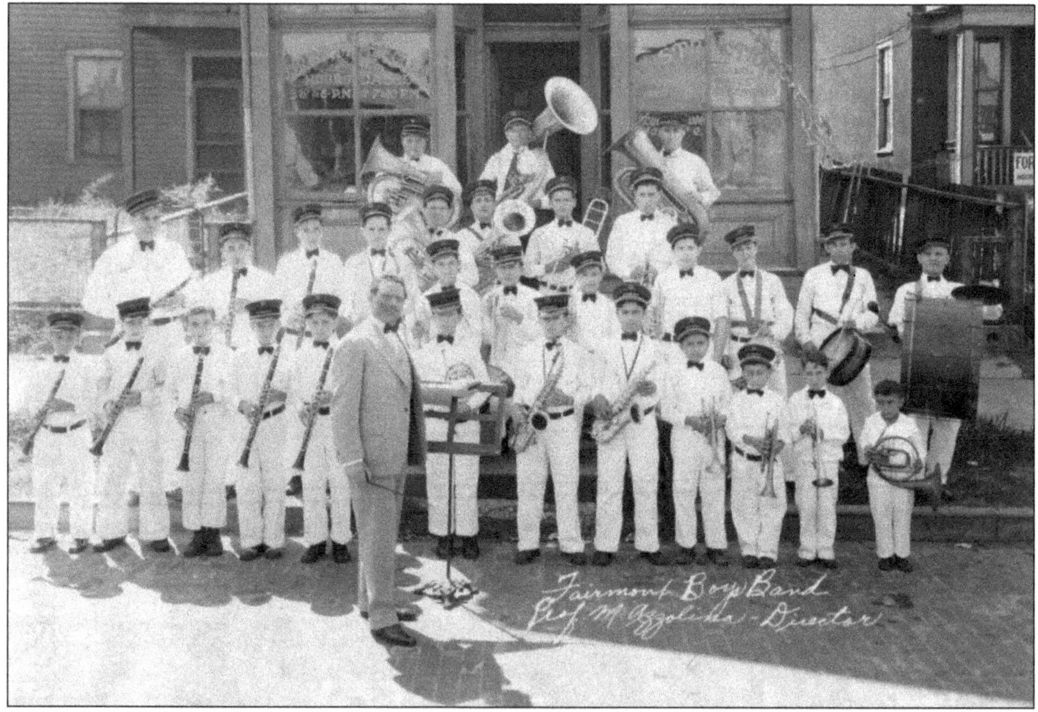

Another popular band was the Fairmount Heights Italian Boy's Band, directed by maestro M. Azzolina. It was organized and sponsored by Luciano Vangardo. (Courtesy of LoRusso's Cucina.)

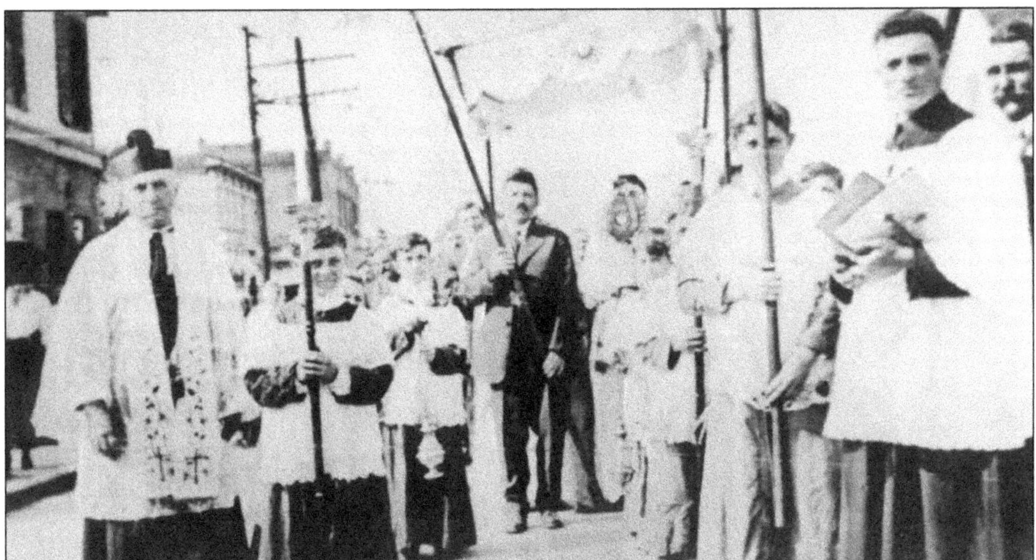

This 1918 Corpus Christi Procession was one of many processions on the Hill beginning at St. Ambrose Church. Along the procession's route, families would put up their own little altars in their front yards. The priests would stop at these altars and pray, then move on until they came upon another yard altar, repeating the pattern all the way back to the church. (Courtesy of Evelyn Colombo Nettemeyer.)

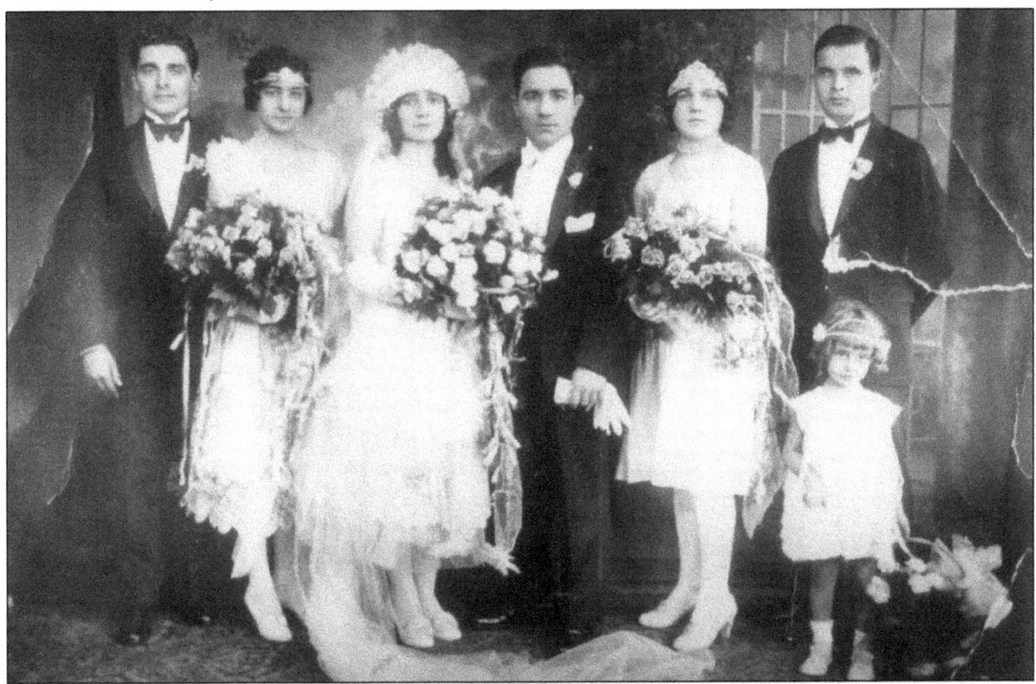

Mr. Lamantia was born in Monreale, Sicily, and worked as a shoemaker. He met his wife in St. Louis on the Hill, and they were married for over 60 years at the time of his death. Lamantia loved gardening and was known as one of the best gardeners on the Hill. The community's gardens, unlike typical American ones, had plum tomatoes, squash, grapes, fig trees, and eggplants. (Courtesy of Diana Maria Powell Lamantia.)

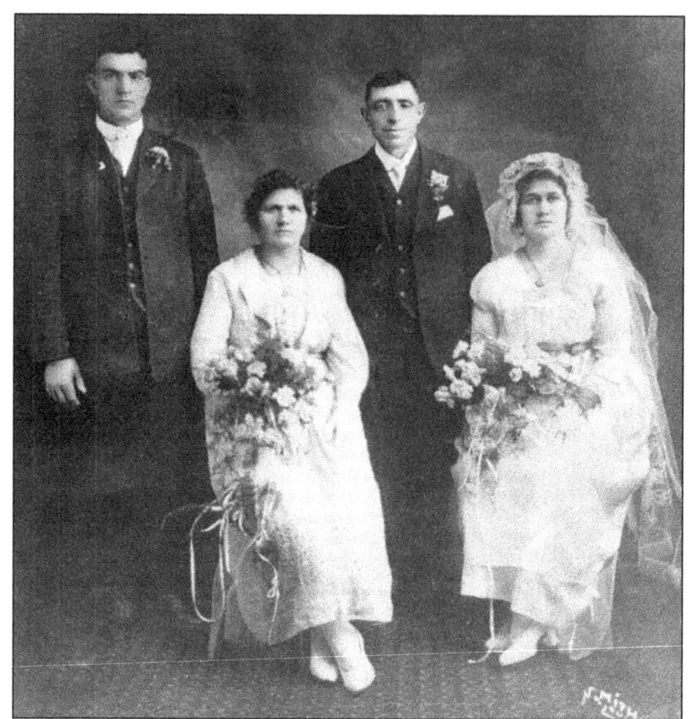

Pasquale Riva (second from right) and Francesca Gualdoni (far right) were married on September 21, 1919. The 1930 census lists their children as Adele, Robert, Antone, Mary, Charlie, and Rosie Riva. The attendants at their wedding were Luigi and Angela Crespi. It was customary for a young man, if interested in a young lady, to ask a mutual friend for an introduction to the girl's family. (Courtesy of Martina Garagiola Bettlach.)

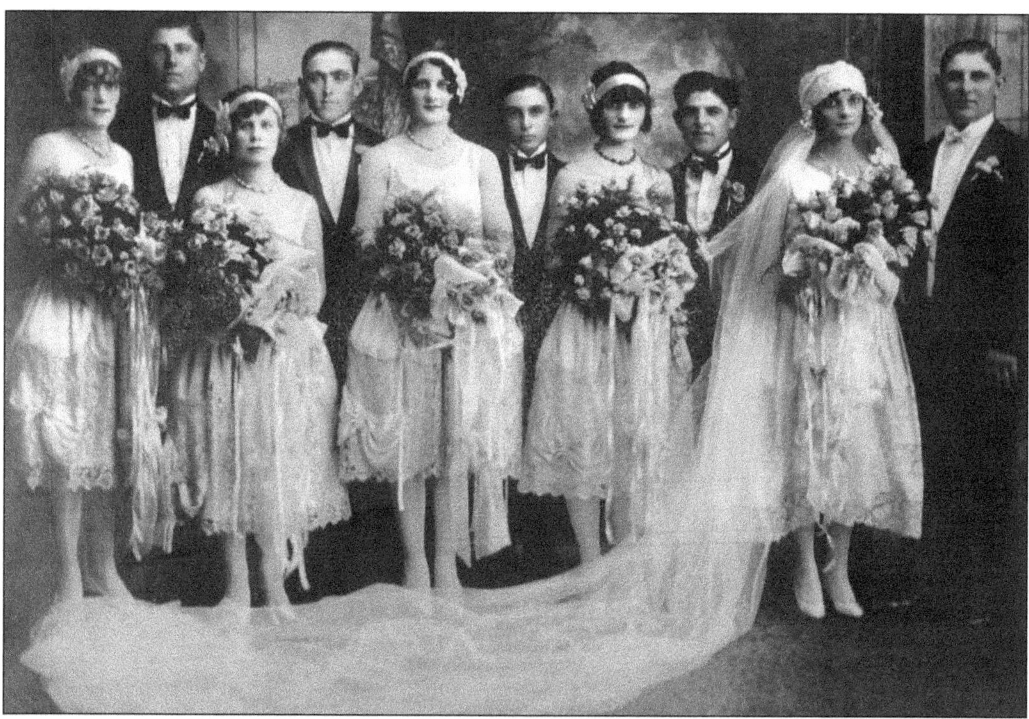

Parents urged their children to be loyal to the traditional Italian way of life. When a young man met the approval of a young lady's family, all meetings would be chaperoned until the marriage. Louisa and Mike Pisani, on the far right, were married in the late 1920s. He is listed as a painter in the census. (Courtesy of Barbara Torretti.)

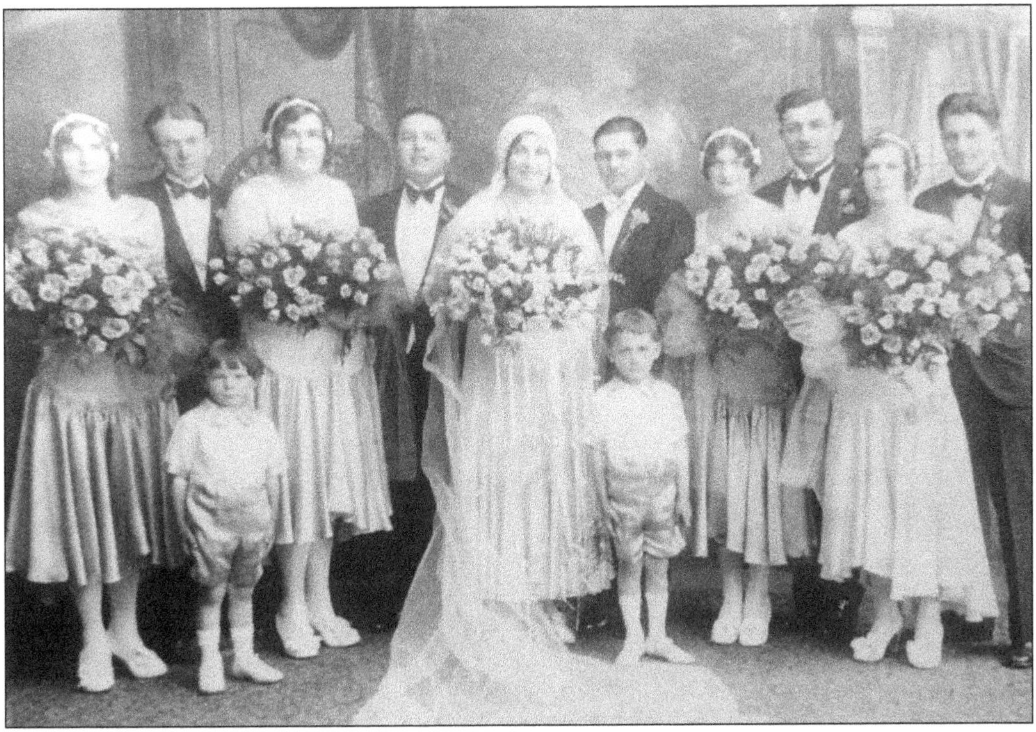

Married couples would purchase their own narrow homes, which often had front porches and enough property for a garden in the back. These homes were well taken care of, with manicured lawns. Shown here in the center are Tony Merlo and Victoria Crespi on their wedding day. The boy in the middle is Richard Crespi, the brother of St. Louis Cardinals baseball player Frank Crespi. The man third from right is the groom's brother, Lewis Merlo. The man on the far right is Angelo Crespi, who was killed in Italy during World War II. (Courtesy of Julie Crespi Tiejens.)

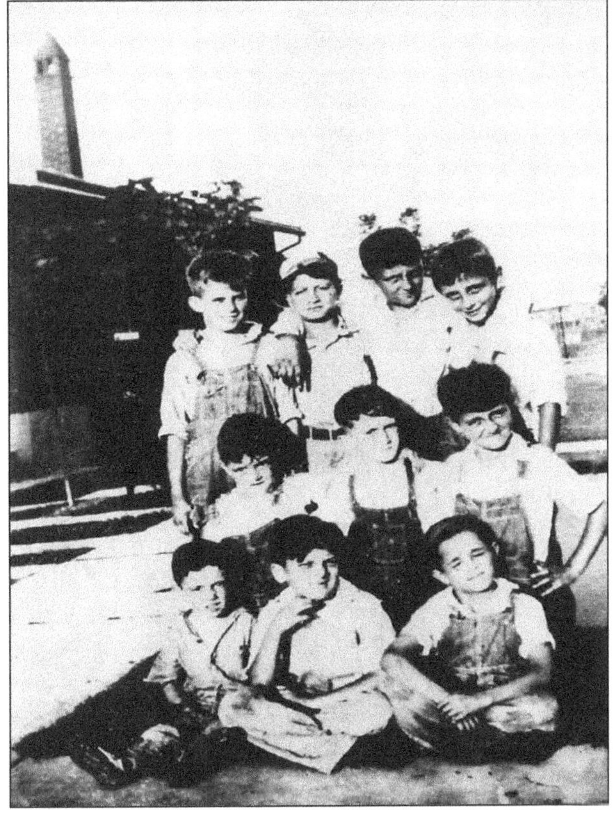

The 1920s and 1930s were times of residential development on the Hill, as it moved southward toward Bischoff Avenue. According to the 1930 census, there were few boarders living on the Hill. (Courtesy of Barbara Torretti.)

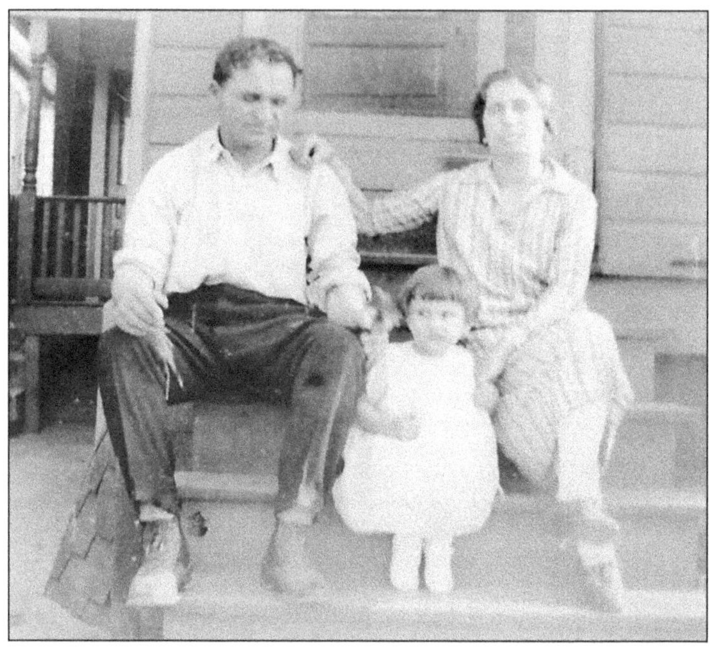

Vittorio Pera, from Piozzano, Piacenza, arrived at Ellis Island in 1909. Paolina Passaglia, from Gragnano, Piacenza, arrived in 1922. Vittorio was a laborer; Paolina, a trained seamstress/tailor, worked at Famous-Barr. They met in St. Louis. Here they are pictured with their daughter Angeline, enjoying some time in front of their home on Northrup Avenue. (Courtesy of Barbara Torretti.)

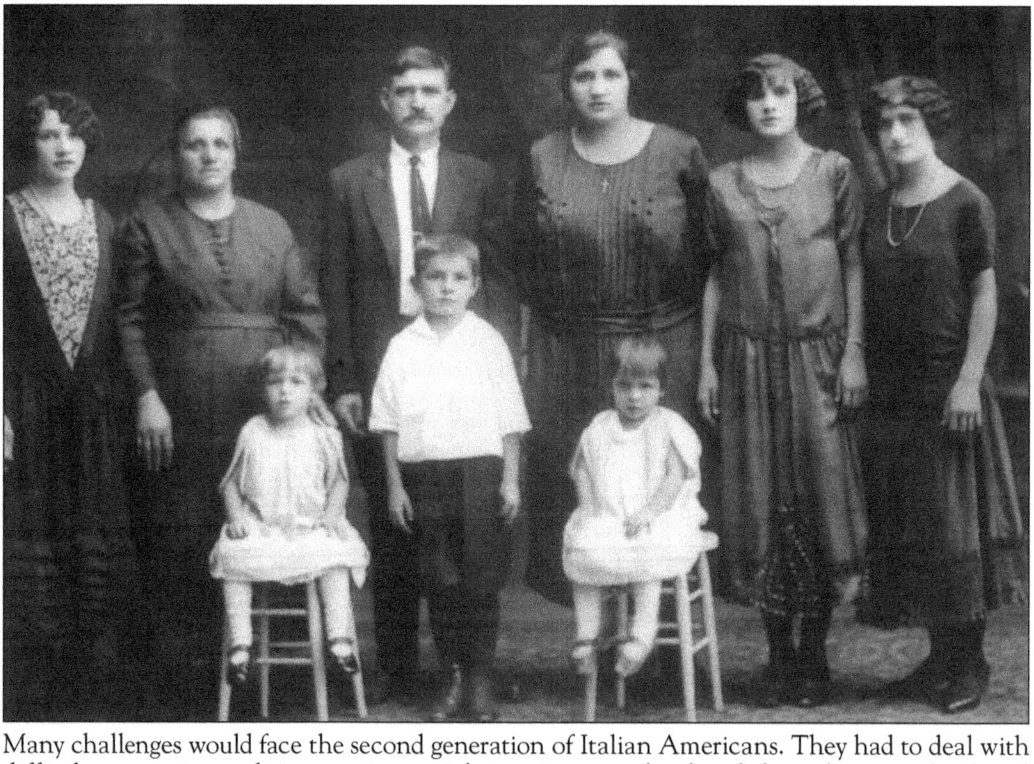

Many challenges would face the second generation of Italian Americans. They had to deal with difficult economic conditions, trying social situations in school and the military, and cultural changes. The Carlo Colombo family is pictured here in 1924. The 1910 census listed Carlo's occupation as brickyard laborer. (Courtesy of Evelyn Colombo Nettemeyer.)

Three

BUILDING A NEW CHURCH

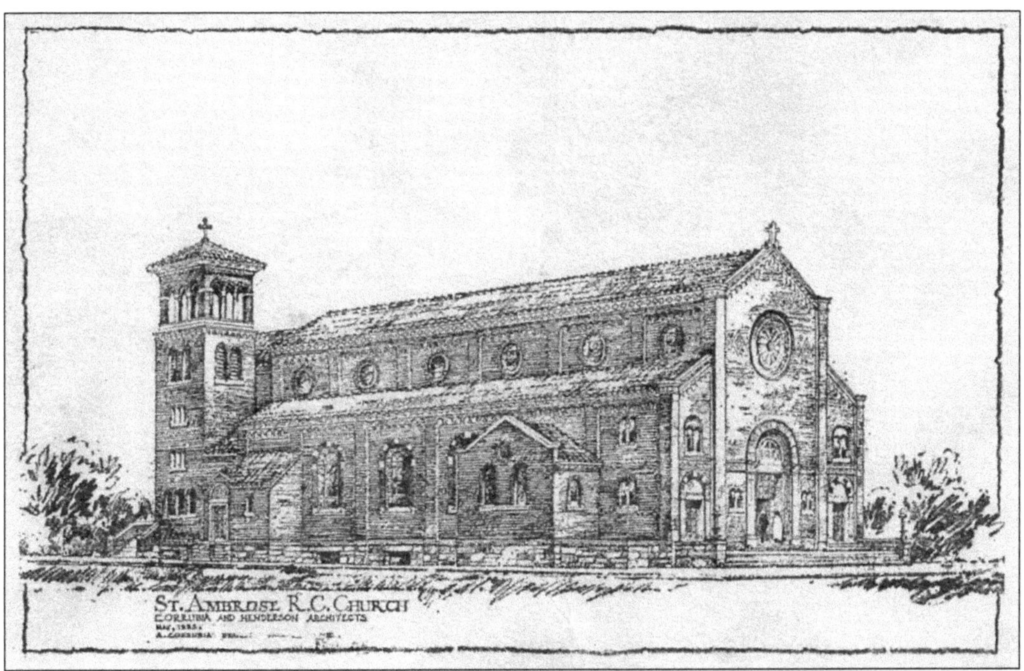

On January 20, 1921, at 9:00 in the morning, the first St. Ambrose Church was destroyed by fire. Rev. Luciano Carroti requested that all of the residents, regardless of status, come to the Big Club at 5200 Shaw Avenue to discuss building a new church. A special committee was established and assigned the duty of making a plan of action. On February 18, at the Big Club Hall, a sketch of a new brick church was displayed, and the architect, Angelo Corrubia, was there to make the presentation. This was one of the most critical times for St. Ambrose Parish, with the grave illness of Father Carotti and a debt of $30,000. To show their continued support, 600 Italian families pledged to pay $60 each to discharge the debt that was still on the old church. (Courtesy of Barbara Torretti.)

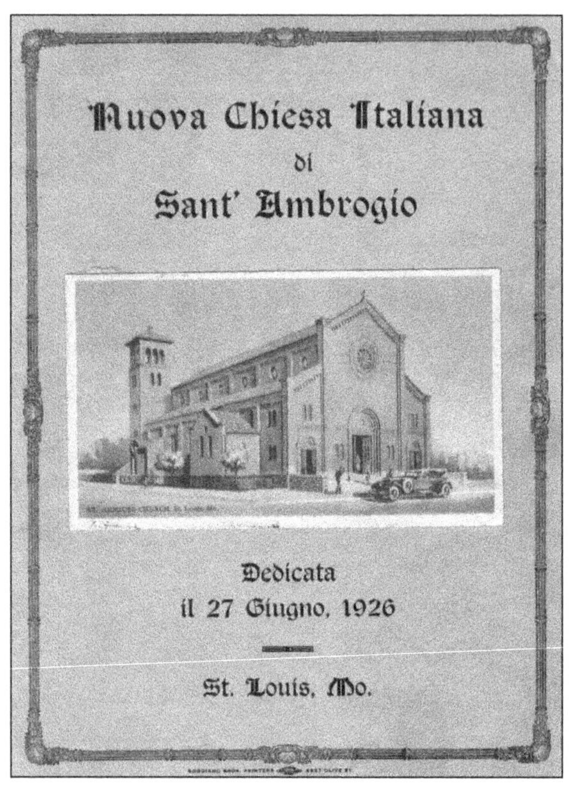

The parishioners nominated the following persons for the committee charged with the construction of a new church: Isidoro Oldani, president; Calogero Mugavero, vice president; Giovanni Gioia, secretary; Emilio Maganza, vice secretary; Ignazio Riggio, treasurer; Emilio Ponciroli, vice treasurer; and Luigi Galli, trustee. This church would become the center of the community. Rev. Julius Giovannini united the parishioners and welcomed any contributions. (Courtesy of Faye Berra Venegoni.)

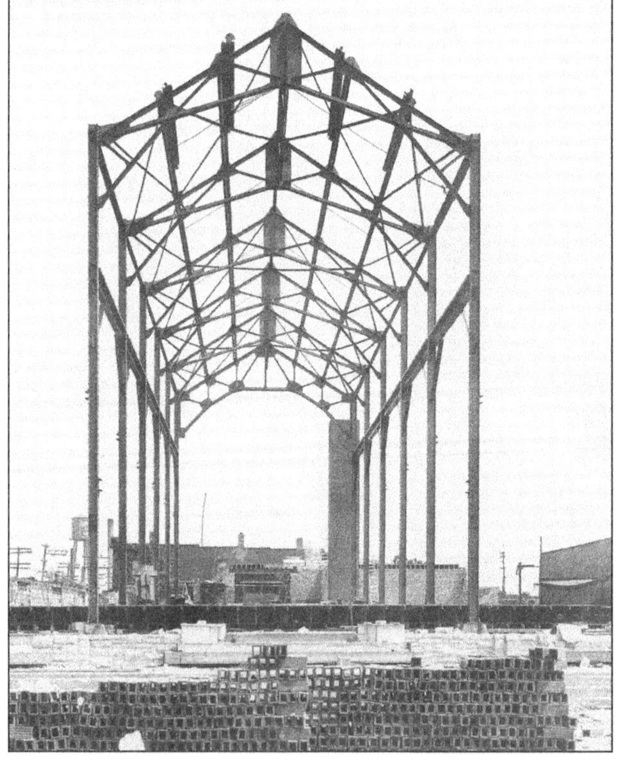

The church basement was completed in March 1922, and on March 26 of the same year, the archbishop blessed the new church and Mass was celebrated. With Reverend Carotti's health failing, Rev. Julius Giovannini was appointed pastor of St. Ambrose on April 23, 1923. He overcame all difficulties and, with the cooperation of his parishioners, paid $7,000 on the debt in three months. By May 1, 1924, the parish had paid off all its debt. (Courtesy of James Merlo.)

Rev. Peter Barabino, "The Flying Priest," arrived at St. Ambrose one month after the fire that destroyed the first church. He was an assistant to Reverend Carotti and Reverend Giovannini until November 1929, when he became the pastor. He remained in that role until his death in 1934. He directed the various dramatic organizations that helped provide funds for the new church. (Courtesy of James Merlo.)

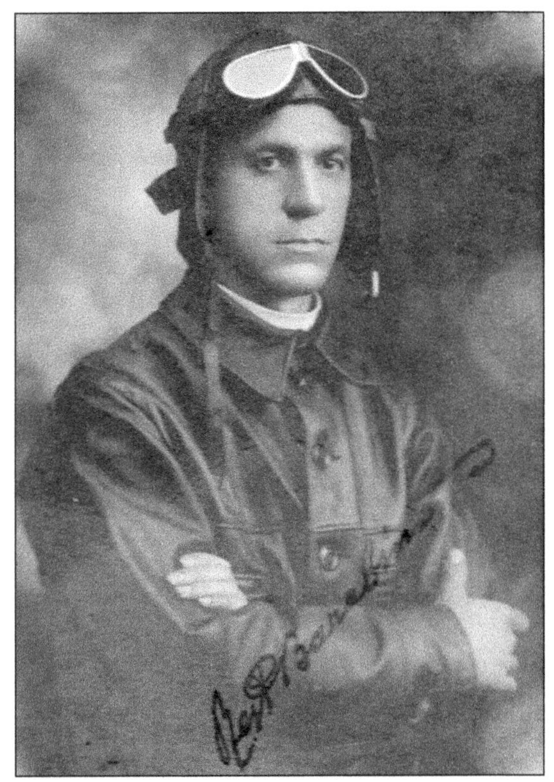

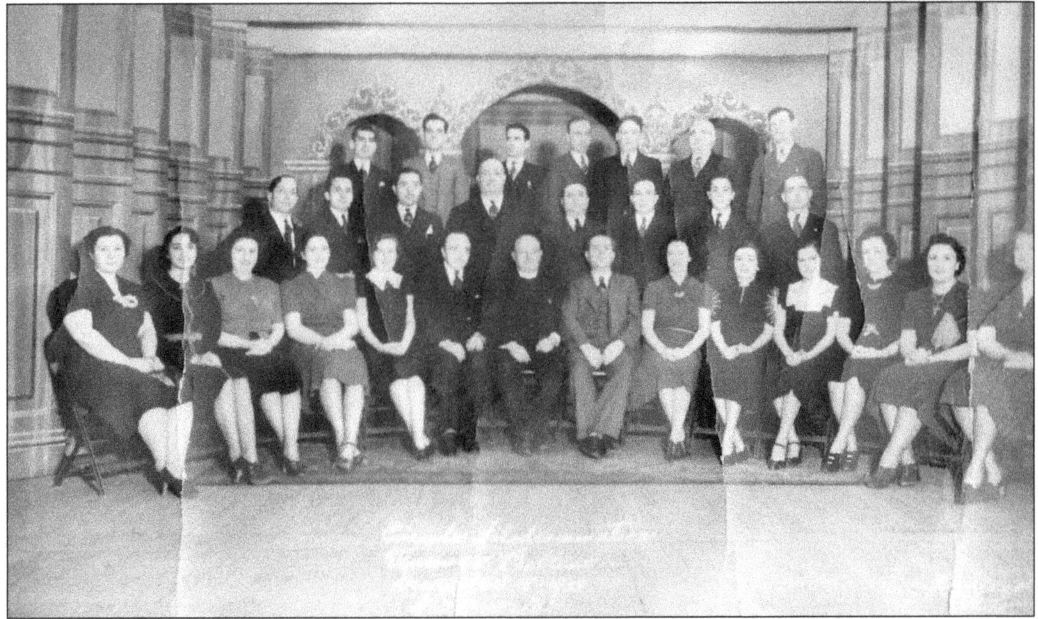

The Vincenzo Bellini Dramatic Club was one that Reverend Barabino directed. Its male members, recently returned from World War I, resumed their work and donated proceeds toward the new church. The purpose of the Circolo Filodrammatico Vincenzo Belli organization was the diffusion of Italian culture by means of recitations in the Italian language. Vincenzo Bellini was a 19th-century Italian opera composer. (Courtesy of Marianne Peri-Sack.)

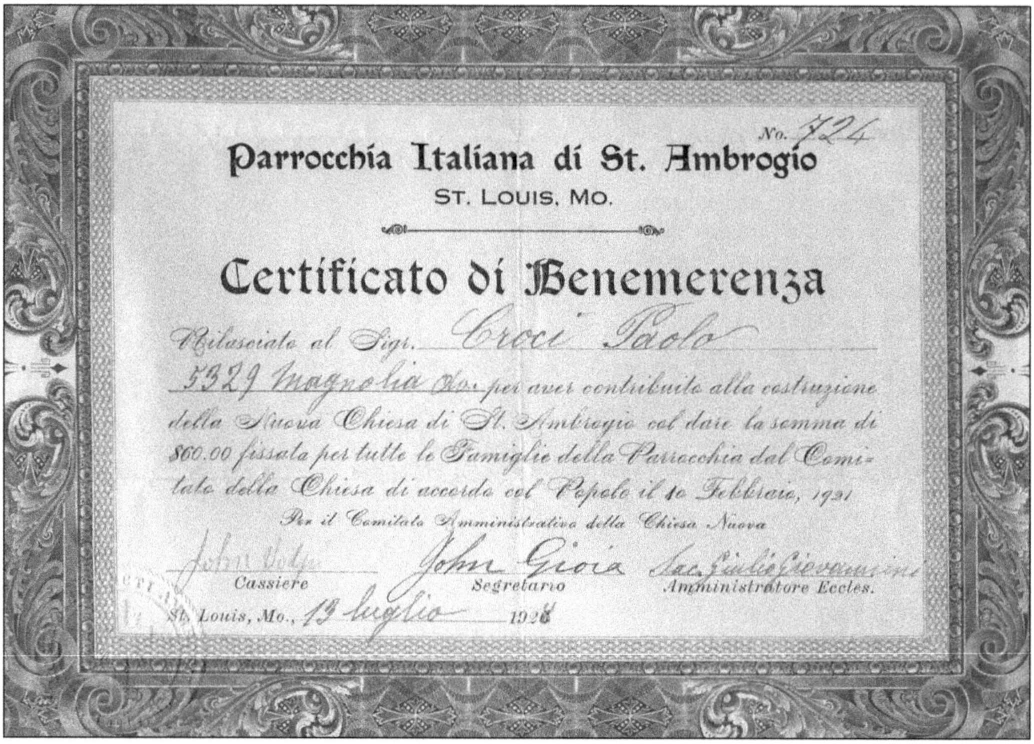

No. 724

Parrocchia Italiana di St. Ambrogio

St. Louis, Mo.

Certificato di Benemerenza

Rilasciato al Sigr. Croci Paolo 5329 Magnolia Ave. per aver contribuito alla costruzione della Nuova Chiesa di St. Ambrogio col dare la somma di $60.00 fissata per tutte le Famiglie della Parrocchia dal Comitato della Chiesa di accordo col Popolo il 10 Febbraio, 1921

Per il Comitato Amministrativo della Chiesa Nuova

Cassiere — John Gioia, Segretario — Sac. Giulio Giovannini, Amministratore Eccles.

St. Louis, Mo., 19 luglio 192[illegible]

The parishioners' support continued, allowing work on the construction of the new church to begin. The cornerstone was laid on May 30, 1925. The church, the pride of the neighborhood, was built by the men of the Hill with contributions from people of modest means. On May 1, 1926, the new Church of St. Ambrose was built at a cost of $200,000. By 1934, at the time of Reverend Barabino's death, its debt was reduced to $75,000. (Courtesy of Faye Berra Venegoni.)

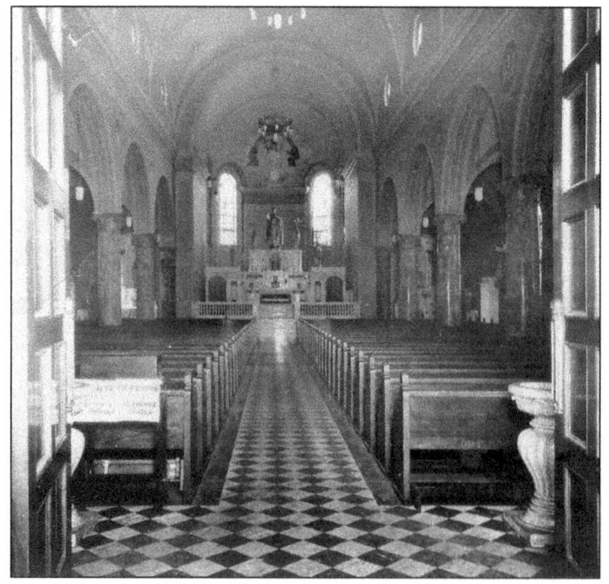

This is the interior of St. Ambrose Church shortly after it was built in 1926. Reverend Giovannini suggested that the faithful from the various towns of Italy unite and donate as many bells as there were Italian towns represented on the Hill. As a result, five bronze bells were ordered with the following inscriptions: "The people of the Parish," "The faithful of Cuggiono," "The faithful of Inveruno," "The faithful of Marcallo," and "The faithful of Casteltermini." It is the spirit of unity and the love of homelands past and present that made the Hill a thriving community and contribute to its existence today. (Courtesy of James Merlo.)

On the afternoon of June 13, 1926, the blessing of the bells took place, officiated by Reverend Tannrath, Rev. Julius Giovannini, and Monsignor Spigardi. The five new bells rang out for the first time, and hundreds of children received their First Holy Communion that morning. The ceremony concluded with a procession, and the Blessed Sacrament was carried through the streets of the Hill while being greeted by the sound of the bells. (Courtesy of James Merlo.)

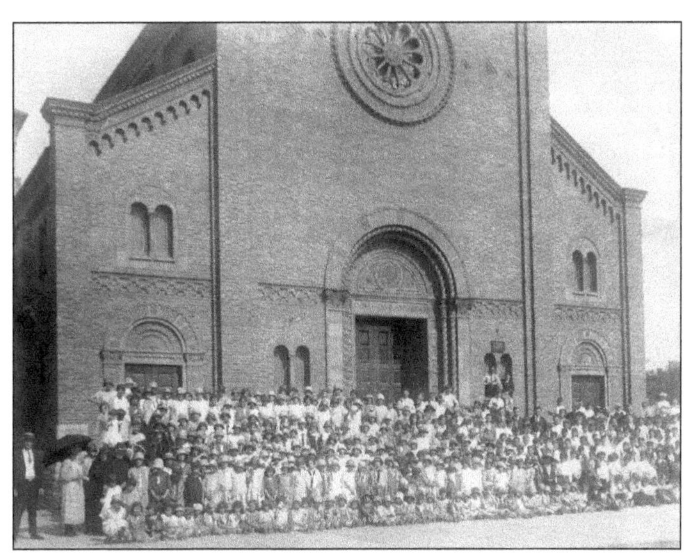

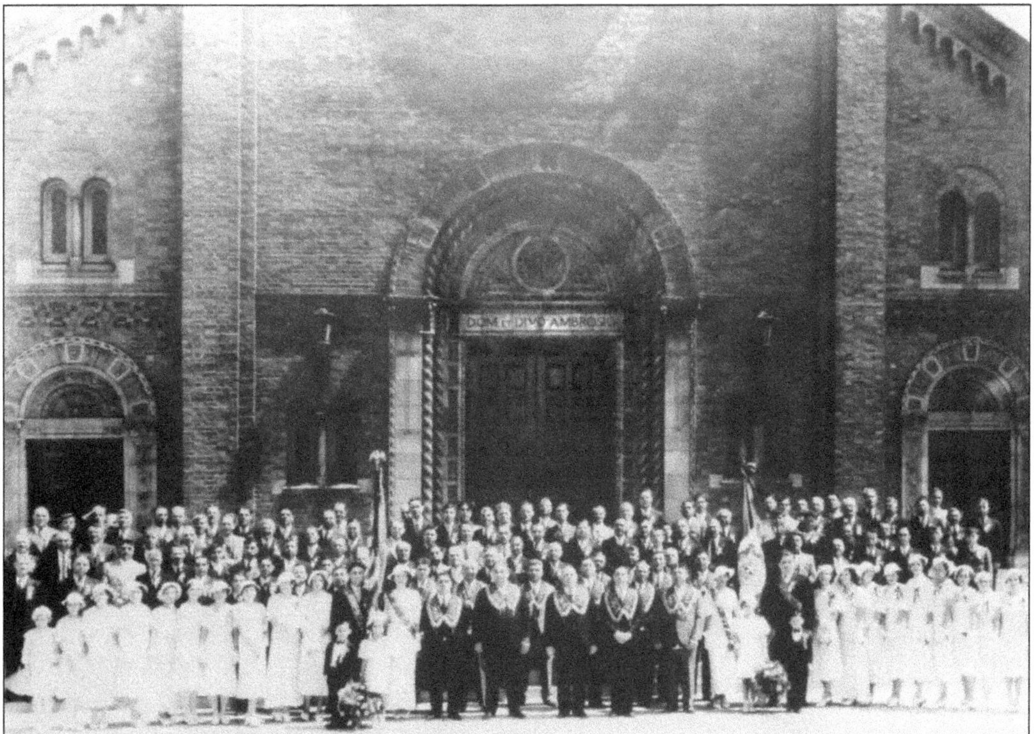

The Hill had a number of thriving mutual-aid societies. These societies helped to keep the Italians together in order to maintain their native culture and create strength in numbers, while promoting the welfare of the group. Many of these societies were formed around a regional Italian province or town based on birth or ancestry, and the organizations had close ties with the church of St. Ambrose. (Courtesy of the Society of Casteltermini.)

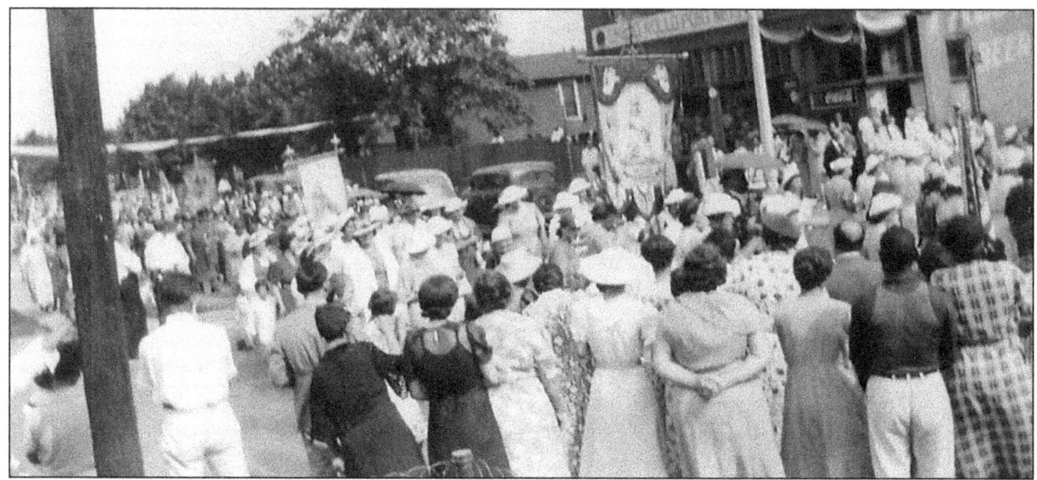

The annual Corpus Christi Procession makes its way from the church to the northern end of the Hill. The procession coincides with the Feast of Corpus Christi (Latin for "body of Christ"). The procession begins and ends at St. Ambrose Church. The route was planned to encourage full participation of the people and to allow those watching to be drawn into the celebration. (Courtesy of Barbara Torretti.)

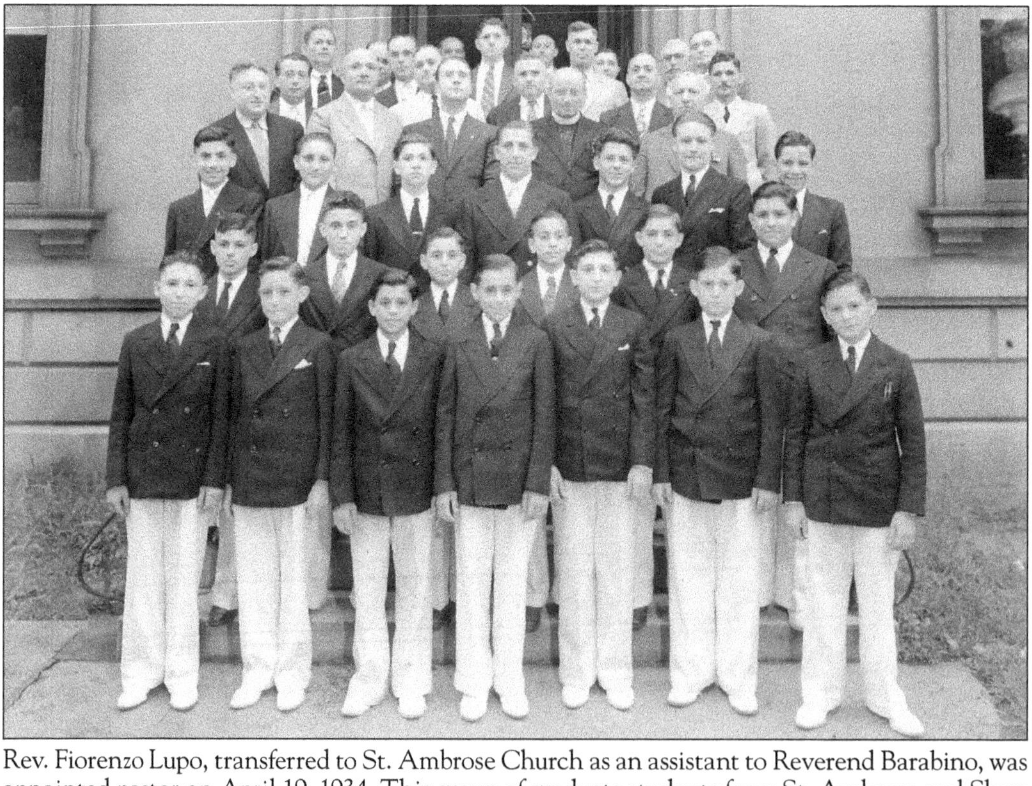

Rev. Fiorenzo Lupo, transferred to St. Ambrose Church as an assistant to Reverend Barabino, was appointed pastor on April 19, 1934. This group of graduate students from St. Ambrose and Shaw School took a trip to Italy in 1936, accompanied by Reverend Lupo. The Italian consul in St. Louis helped make provisions for this trip. The Italian government and the parents of the students were hopeful that these American citizens would continue to be proud of their Italian roots. The Italian government considered them Italians living abroad. (Courtesy of Barbara Torretti.)

Four

POPULATION GROWTH

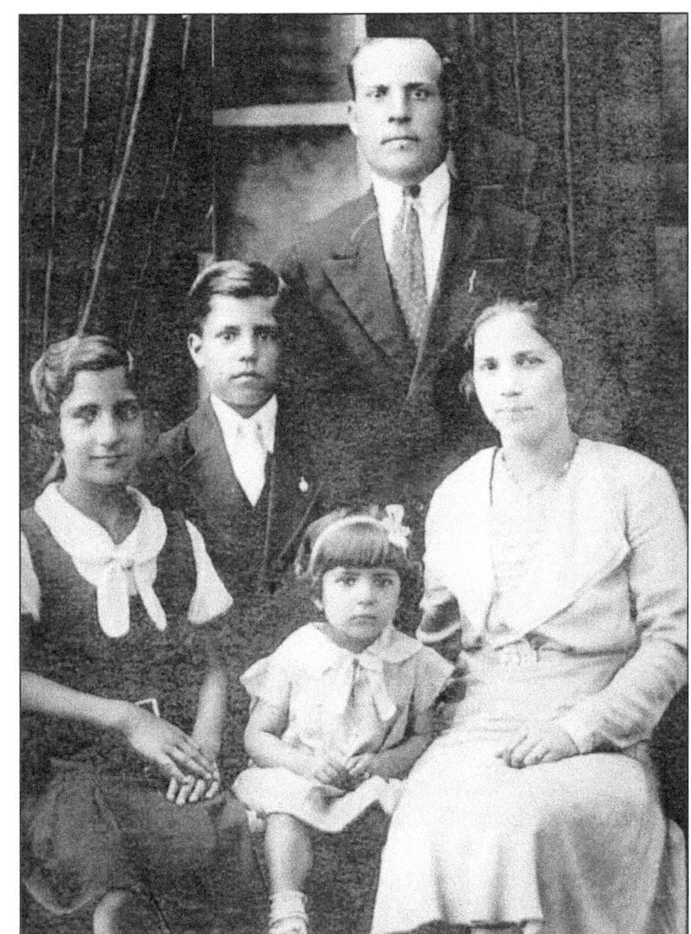

Mario Diliberto and his wife, Carmela Callari, are pictured with their children. They were from Casteltermini, Sicily. Mario and his brother Gaetano Diliberto were the only two of their family who came to America. Gaetano came when he was only 16 and worked at the Laclede Christy Brick Yard. He stayed in a boardinghouse on Shaw Avenue and later sponsored his older brother Mario who was employed at Laclede Christy Brick Yards as well. Charlie Diliberto, the young boy pictured here, would serve in the Army with the 103rd Infantry during World War II and fight in the Battle of the Bulge. (Courtesy of Carmen Diliberto.)

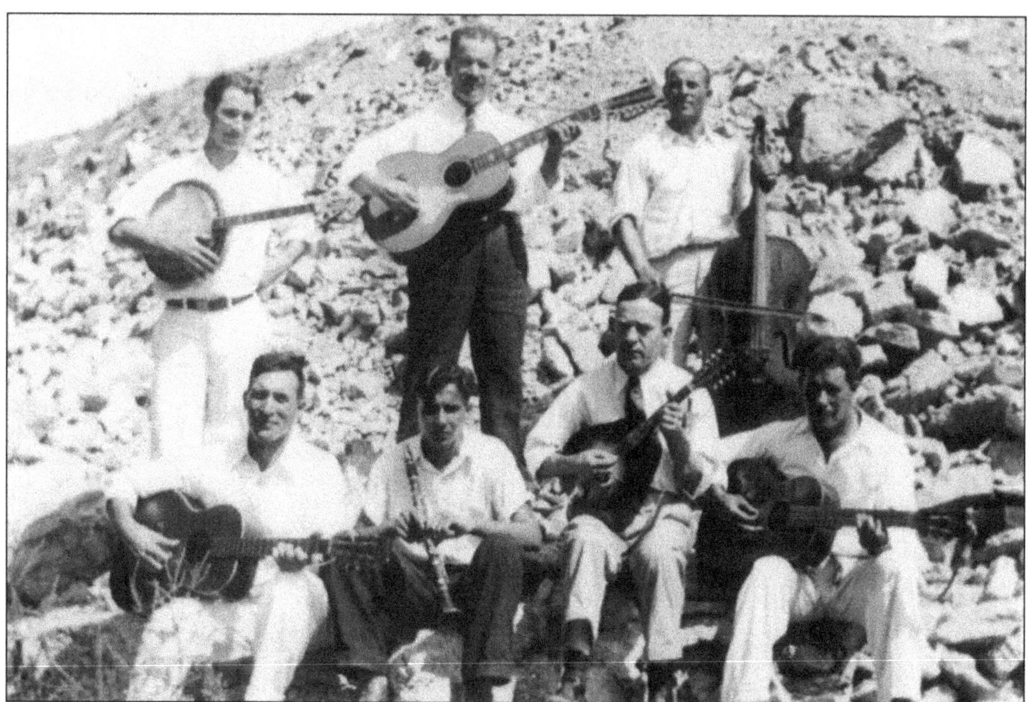

The Society of Casteltermini would have occasional picnics of fun and music at Creve Coeur Park. The Diliberto brothers played together in the band. Nearly 30 percent of the homes built from 1900 to 1950 were erected in the 1920s. Dramatic changes occurred during the 1920s, with small brick bungalows constructed and, later, larger houses on the edge of the community. Residents began to purchase cars and better clothing and furniture. (Courtesy of the Society of Casteltermini.)

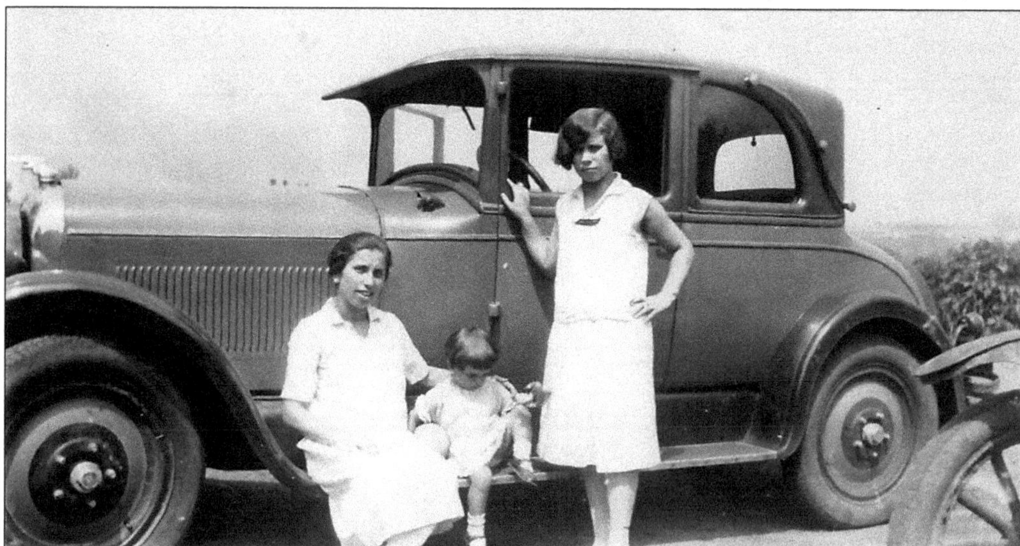

From left to right, Paolina Passaglia Pera, her daughter Angeline, and Concetta Parsaglia are ready for a drive. Weekdays on the Hill, men were out working, and the women spent the day shopping, washing, and preparing dinner. The children would be playing outside or attending school. When the men came home, everyone had dinner. After dinner, music could be heard outside the homes, then the families would retire early for the next day of labor. (Courtesy of Barbara Torretti.)

The backyard parties and barbecues were great escapes from the hard work. Every family in the neighborhood had a backyard garden that provided produce for their meals, including grapevines that would be used to make wine. The most popular musical instruments were the mandolin and the accordion. There would be singing, beer drinking, and card games. Shown here are twins Joe (left) and Frank Pozzoli with their mother. (Courtesy of Barbara Torretti.)

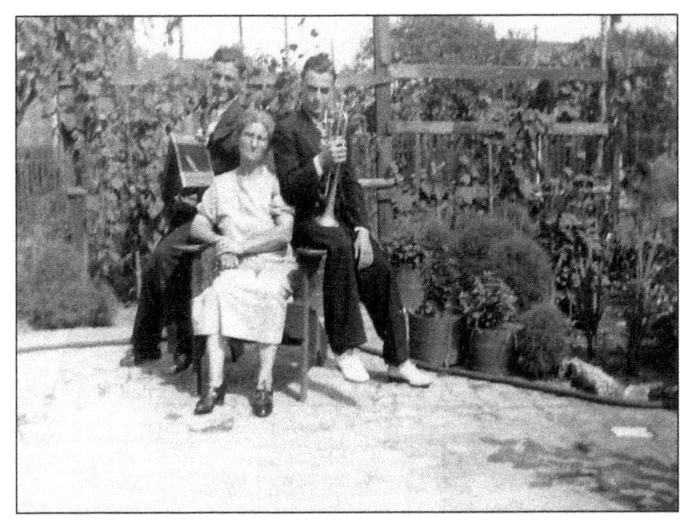

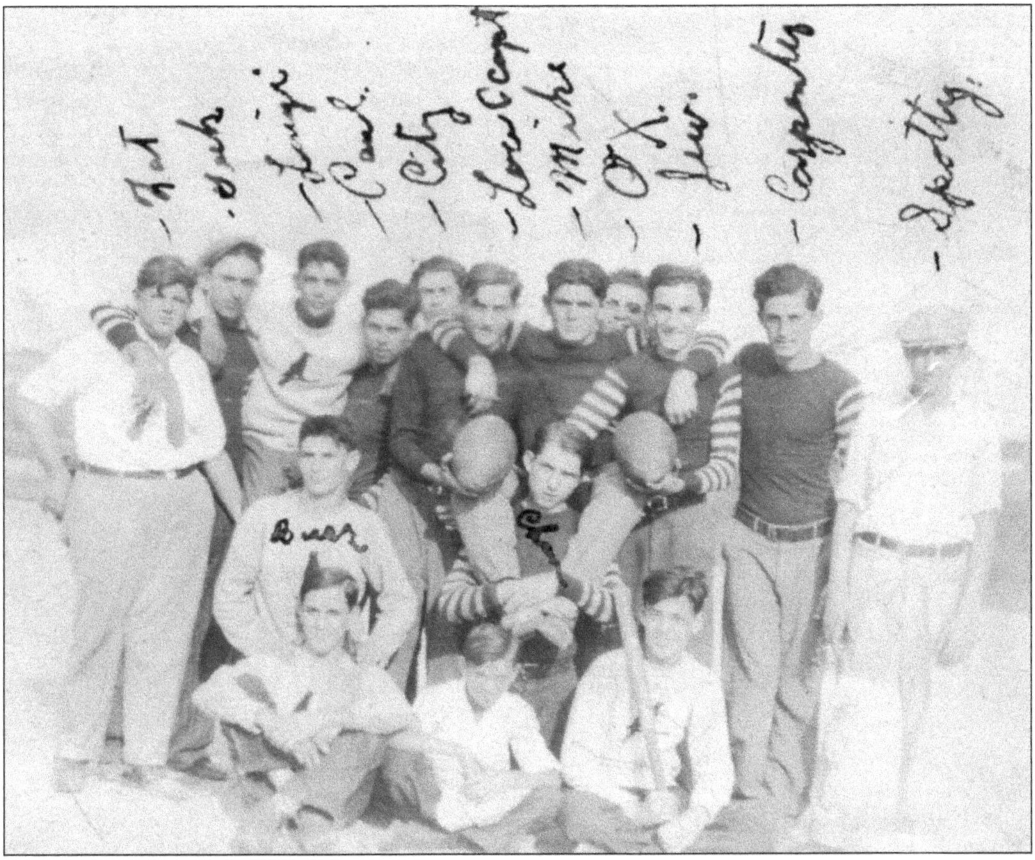

Sports became of interest to the children of immigrants in the 1920s, and several athletic clubs were formed. Athletics provided acceptable competitiveness among parishes and neighborhoods in the St. Louis area. On the Hill, every club member had a nickname (like the ones written on this photograph), as did most residents. *Sopranomi*, Italian for "above the name," refers to dialect nicknames. Though some names may seem harsh or cruel, they were terms of endearment that provided a sense of belonging. (Courtesy of Faye Berra Venegoni.)

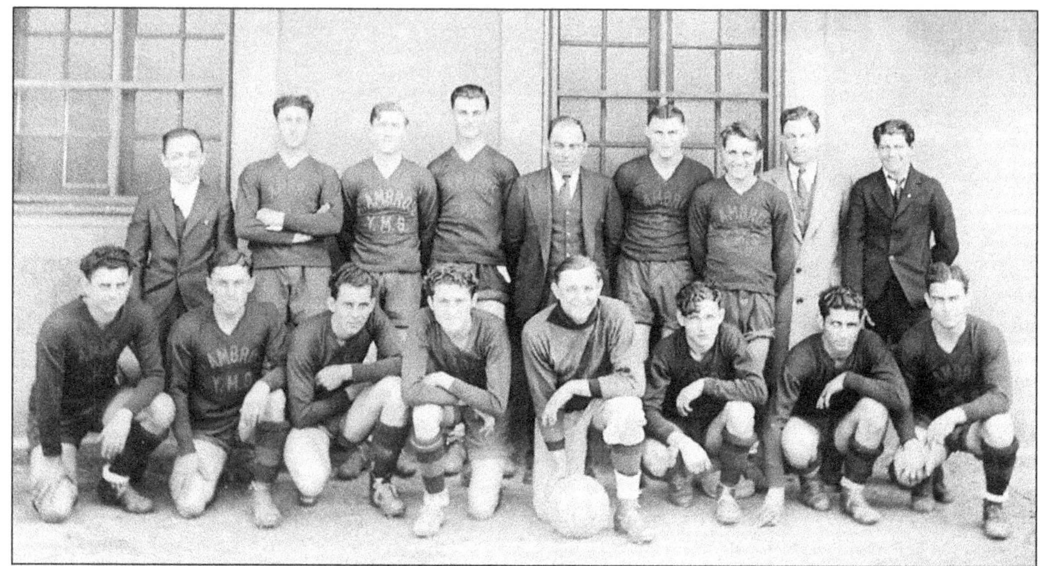

The Fawns Club is a well-known and accomplished club on the Hill. Clubs such as this gave young people the opportunity for a better social life and an identity as a group, keeping the community strong. Energetic and enthusiastic young men and women who had a flair for athletics would become the leaders in the community. During wartime, many of the men fought for the country, and the women worked in the factories. (Courtesy of Scott and Chris Stephens.)

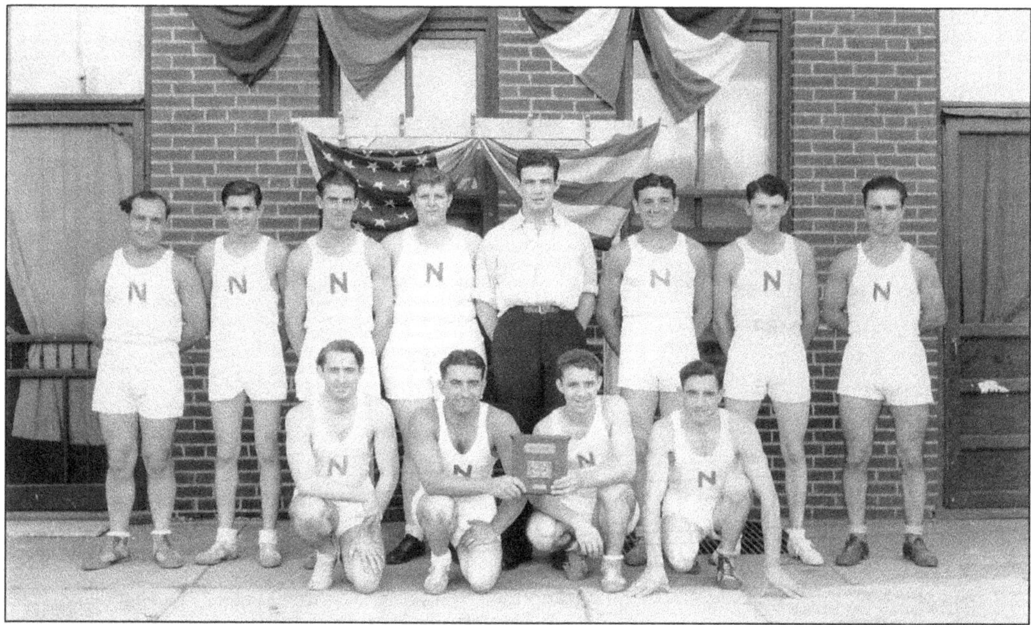

Businesses on the Hill, such as Blue Ridge Bottling Company, Calcaterra Funeral Homes, and McQuay Norris sponsored athletic teams from the neighborhood. In 1902, the Italian American Athletic Club had roughly 50 young men as members. The organization rented a suite of club rooms, where they kept athletic equipment purchased from funds raised at picnics and balls. The Fratellanza initiated 41 men from the Italian American Athletic Club. These men would take over offices in the organization and make improvements, turning big profits at dances and picnics. This routine was followed by other clubs on the Hill. (Courtesy of James Merlo.)

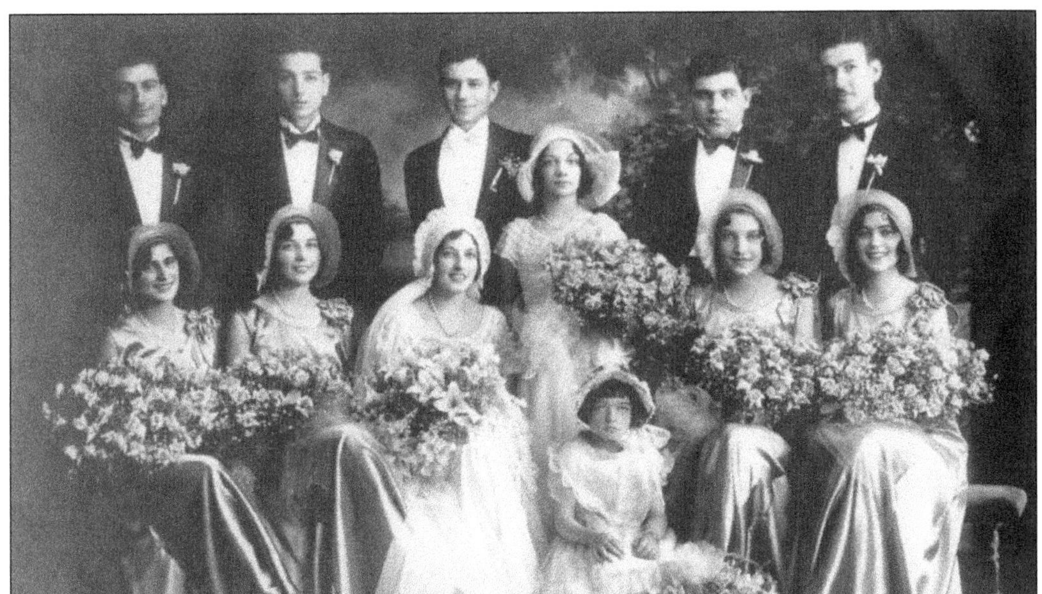

Josephine Matranga (seated, center) and John Tornetto (standing, center), both born on the Hill, were married on June 14, 1931. Josephine was a seamstress, and John worked at Carondelet Foundry and McQuay Norris. It was not unusual for an entire extended family to live and work on the Hill. As the children of these early immigrants were employed on the Hill, marriages occurred between residents, often hailing from the same hometown in Italy. (Courtesy of Paula Tornetto Gusmano.)

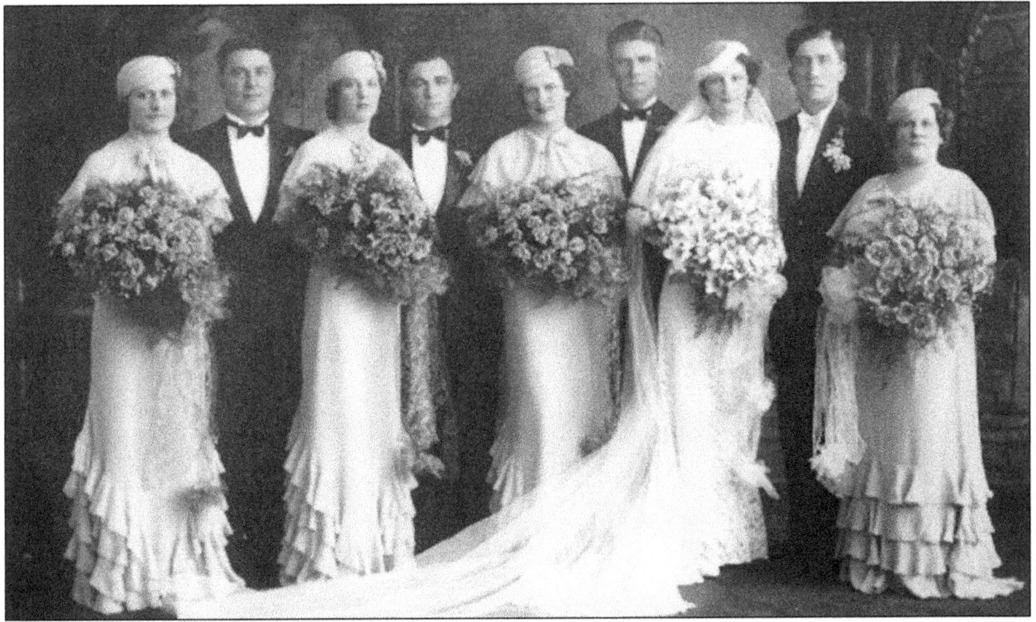

The wedding party are, from left to right, Rose and Paul Cassani, Jenny Barbaglia and Tony Venegoni, Anne and Gino Ruggeri, groom Mario Ruggeri (also known as "Mike" and "Monk"), and bride Maria Colombo. Next to the bride is maid of honor Rose Grassi. The couple were children of Italian immigrants, born on the Hill, and were married in December 1935. (Courtesy of Chris Stephens.)

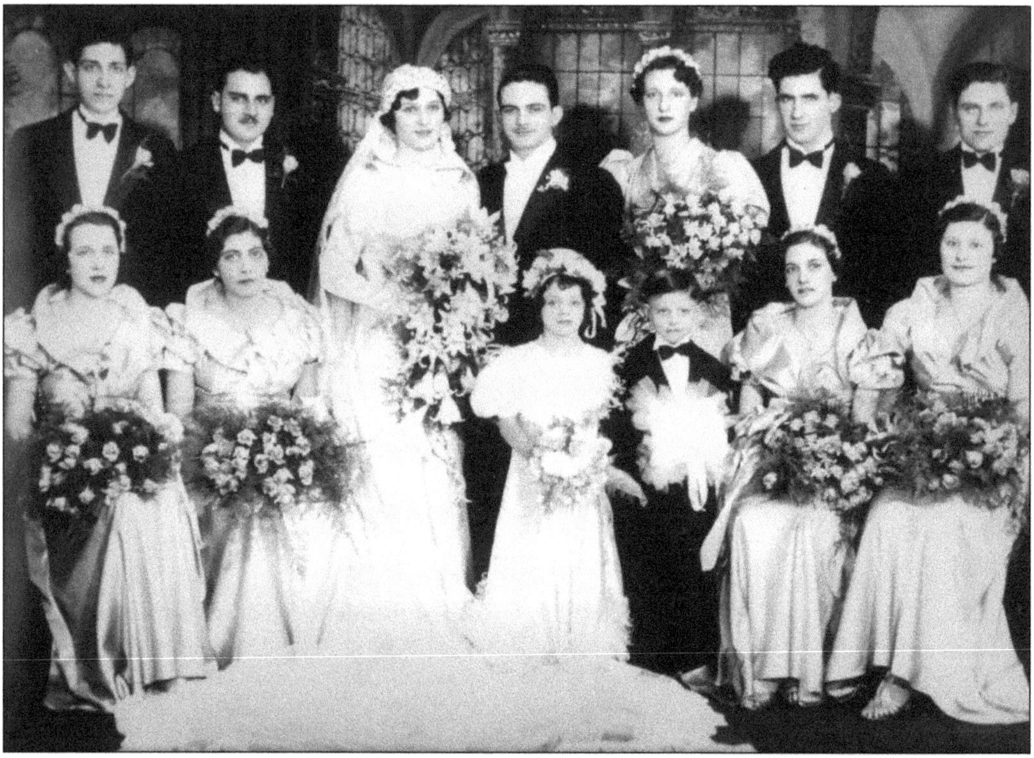

Vincent Vitale and Lena DeLuca were married in 1937. Both were the children of Sicilian immigrants from Little Italy in downtown St. Louis. Many Italian Americans lived and worked downtown, but they would eventually have an impact on the Hill. Many would move out of the tenement homes for a better life on the Hill. As the churches closed in Little Italy, many residents moved north, attending the Italian church; others attended and supported St. Ambrose. The ring bearer in this photograph is the future Msgr. Salvatore Polizzi, who would serve at St. Ambrose for many years. (Author's collection.)

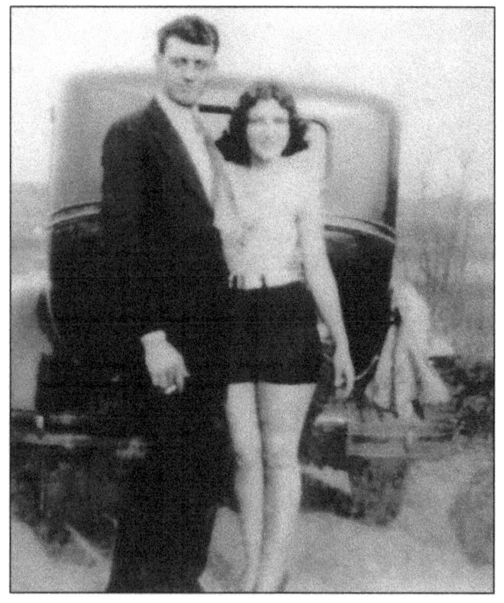

Louis Colombo married Mary Bufetta, who was born in Herrin, Illinois. Louis and his twin brother, Peter, were born on the Hill in 1907. They delivered newspapers to residents of the community and the surrounding neighborhoods for decades. Mary Bufetta is the daughter of Bernardo Bonfiglio and Angelina Merlotti, who emigrated from Bernata Ticino and Malvaglio, Italy. Bernardo Bufetta (the family name was Bonfiglio, but they went by Bufetta) worked in the deep-shaft coal mines in Herrin, eventually dying of black lung disease. (Courtesy of Evelyn Colombo Nettemeyer.)

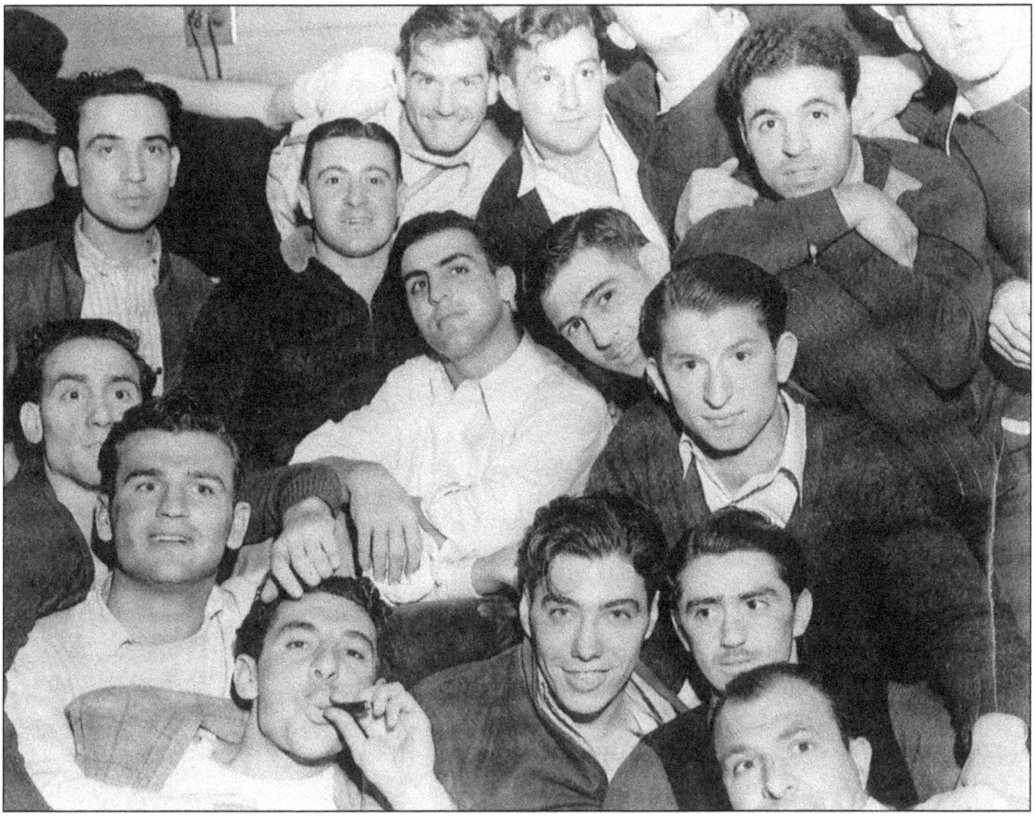

In the 1930s, a larger number of young men developed an interest and talent for athletics, and Rev. Anthony Palumbo made sure these boys had the equipment to play. This interest was fueled by the formation of many athletic clubs, such as the Golden Panthers, pictured here in 1934. During this period, Hill athletes were reaching for supremacy in many sports. The Fairmount Athletic Union promoted tournaments and intramural competition. (Courtesy of James Merlo.)

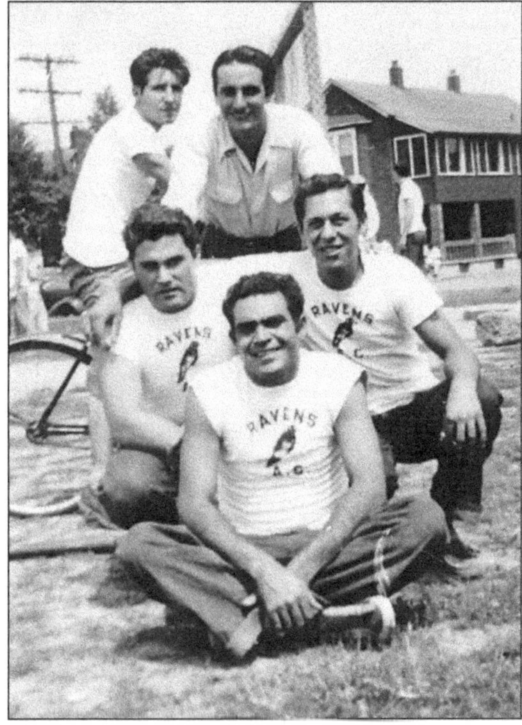

The Ravens and other athletic clubs were serious business in the Hill neighborhood. Sports provided youth with a powerful symbol of ethnic identity while giving the athletes firsthand experience with American culture. The clubs engaged in intra-city competition. Each area of the Hill had its own club and competed in athletic games. However, sports tended to revolve around St. Ambrose, which remained the social center of the community. (Courtesy of Faye Berra Venegoni.)

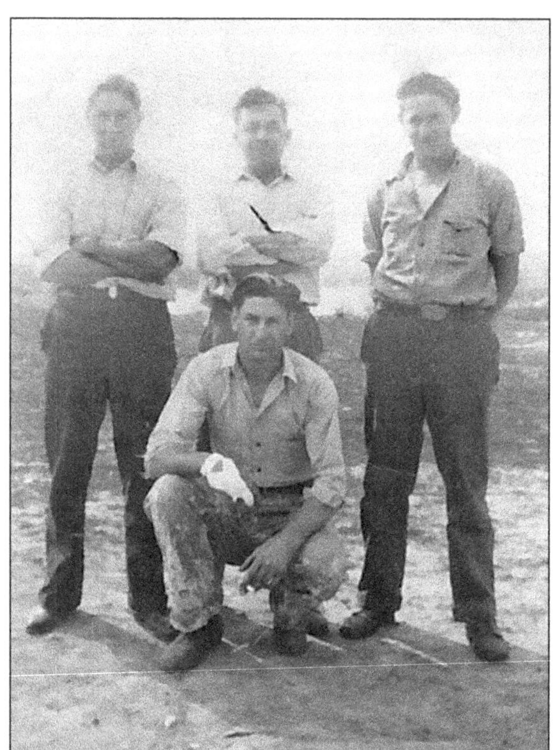

Shown here are a few of the members of the Alley Rats, including Lance Berra (front) and Louis Berra (far right). The Alley Rats were a group of young men who lived close to where Berra Park is located today. Unlike the other Hill clubs, it had no permanent structure to call its own. Its members used their creativity and available materials to create their temporary clubhouse in the Macklind Dump. Like all of the boys' clubs of that time, the Alley Rats had to create their own fun: swimming in River Des Peres, flooding Macklind Avenue in the winter to ice skate, and making bonfires in the dump. (Courtesy of Faye Berra Venegoni.)

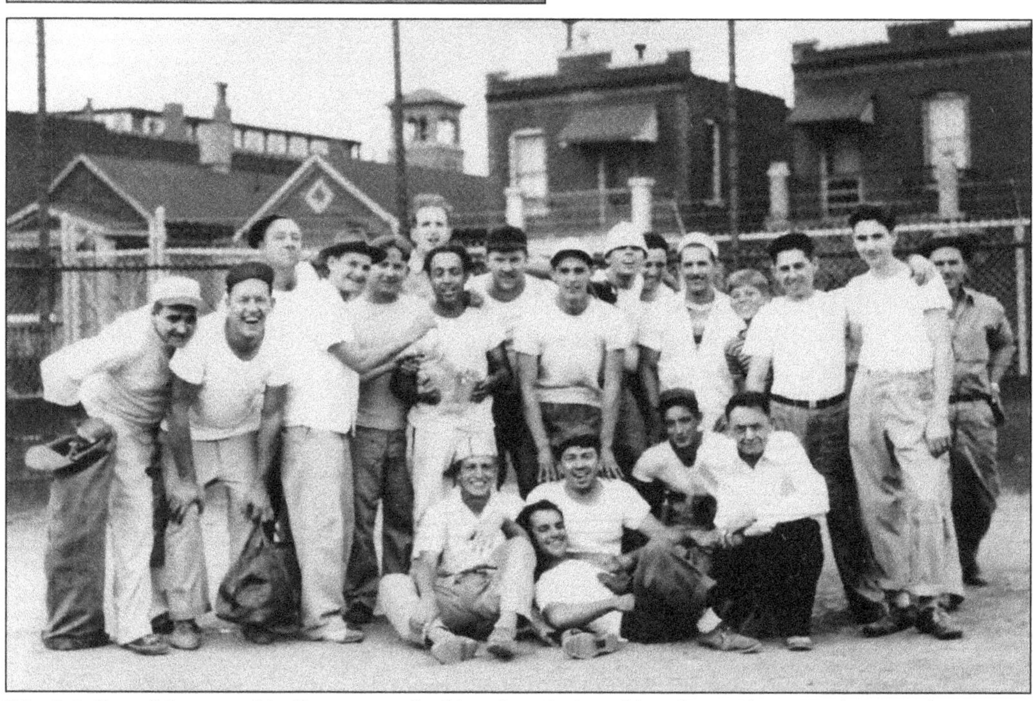

The McQuay Norris softball team worked hard and played hard together on what was known as the Foundry Field, near the corner of Bischoff and Marconi Avenues. Many of the athletes from the neighborhood played on Foundry Field or Macklind Field. They also took responsibility for maintaining the fields. (Courtesy of Barbara Torretti.)

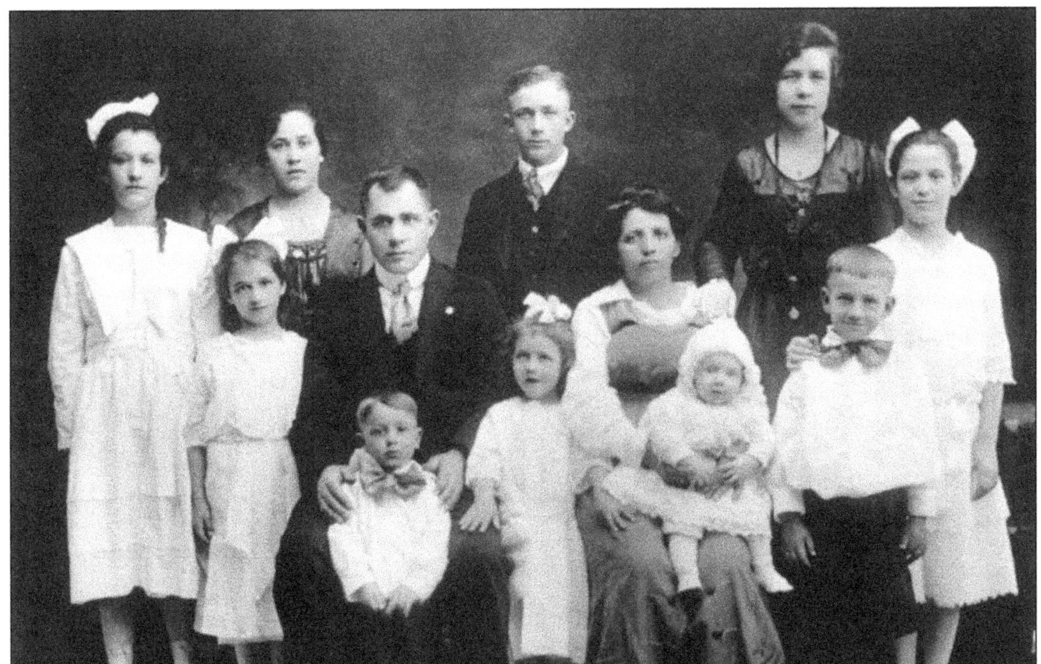

The Angelo Colombo family and the Angelo Torno family lived next to one another on Edwards Street. Angelo Colombo's son John married Angelo Torno's daughter Mary. The Tornos were from Nosate, and the Colombos were from Inveruno. (Courtesy of Martha VanLeuven.)

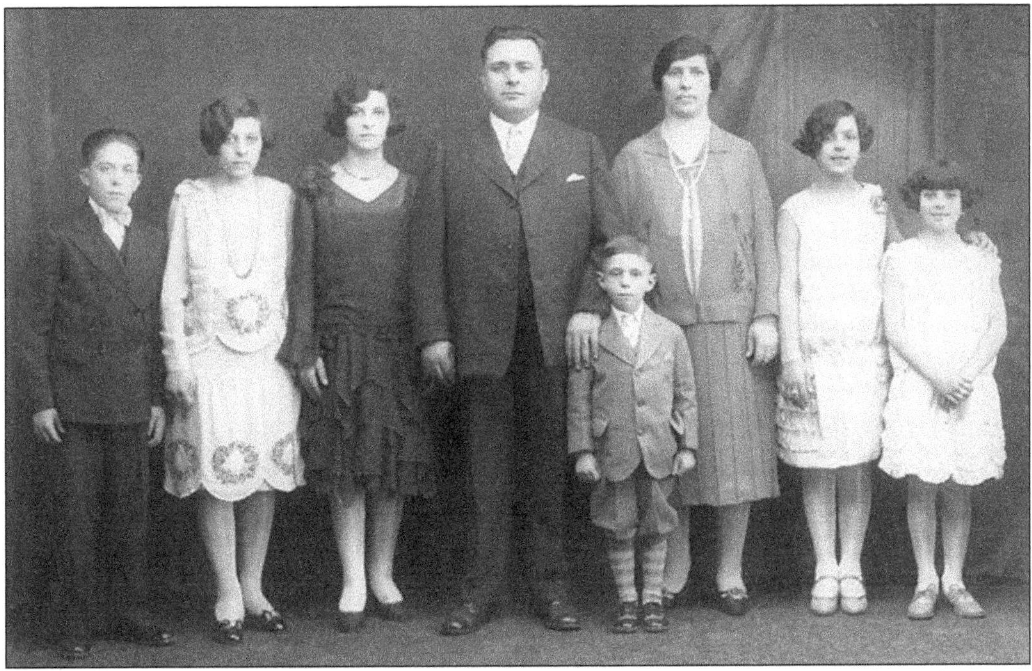

The Vincenzo Minnella family emigrated from Casteltermini, Sicily, in 1923. Shown here are, from left to right, Giusseppe, Anna V., Maria Giuseppina, Vincenzo, Thomas, Vincenza (Buttice), Filomena, and Maria Rosemarie. Vincenzo was a sulfur miner in Casteltermini. The 1920 census lists his occupation as a clay miner. (Courtesy of Tommy Lorentz.)

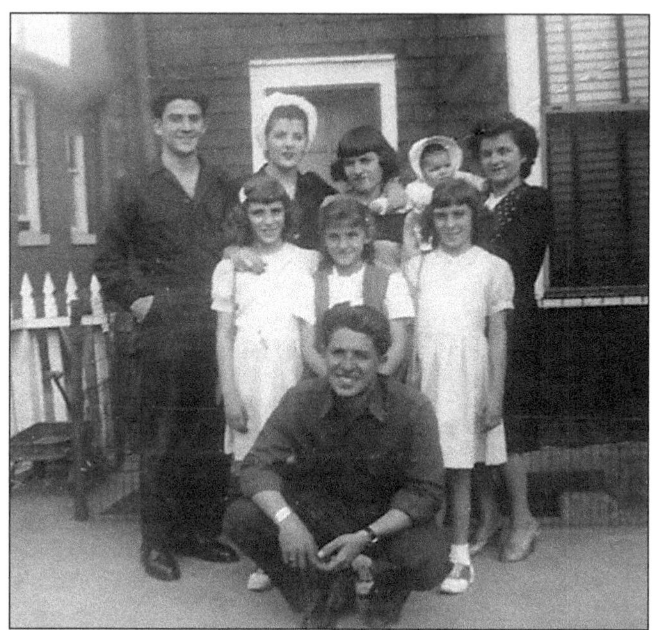

The Torrisi family lived at 2315 Marconi Avenue, according to the 1940 census. James Torrisi (front) is only one example of the many from this generation who would contribute countless hours of service to the Hill community, working on stages, with Boy Scouts, with the Italia America Bocce club, and on functions too numerous to mention. (Courtesy of Michelle Casey.)

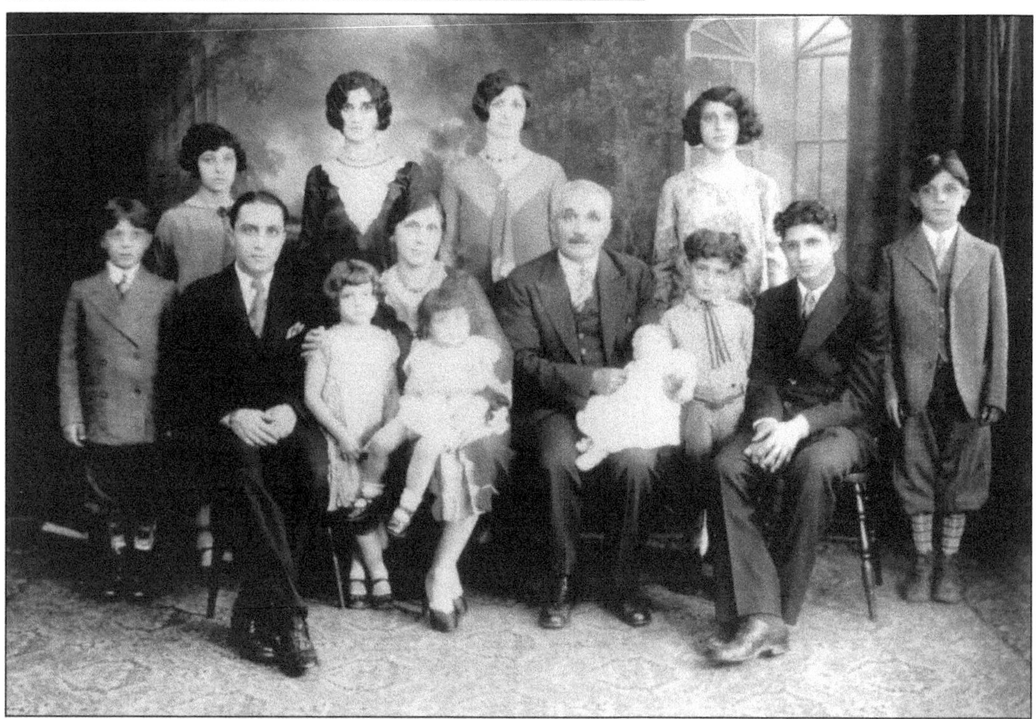

Mario Calogero "Charles" Mugavero (center) was born in Caltavuturo, Sicily, and immigrated to America on April 22, 1893, at the age of 17. He married Anna Catanzaro (left of center), who was born in Termini Imerese, Sicily. She immigrated in 1895. Mario was an insurance salesman. Together, the couple raised 12 children. Annie was brought here by her parents, Lorenzo and Concetta (Lombardo) Catanzaro, who lived with the family until their deaths. Family units remained close after marriage, and many elderly parents lived with one of their children. (Courtesy of Tonette Mugavero McArthur.)

Five

Industrial Growth

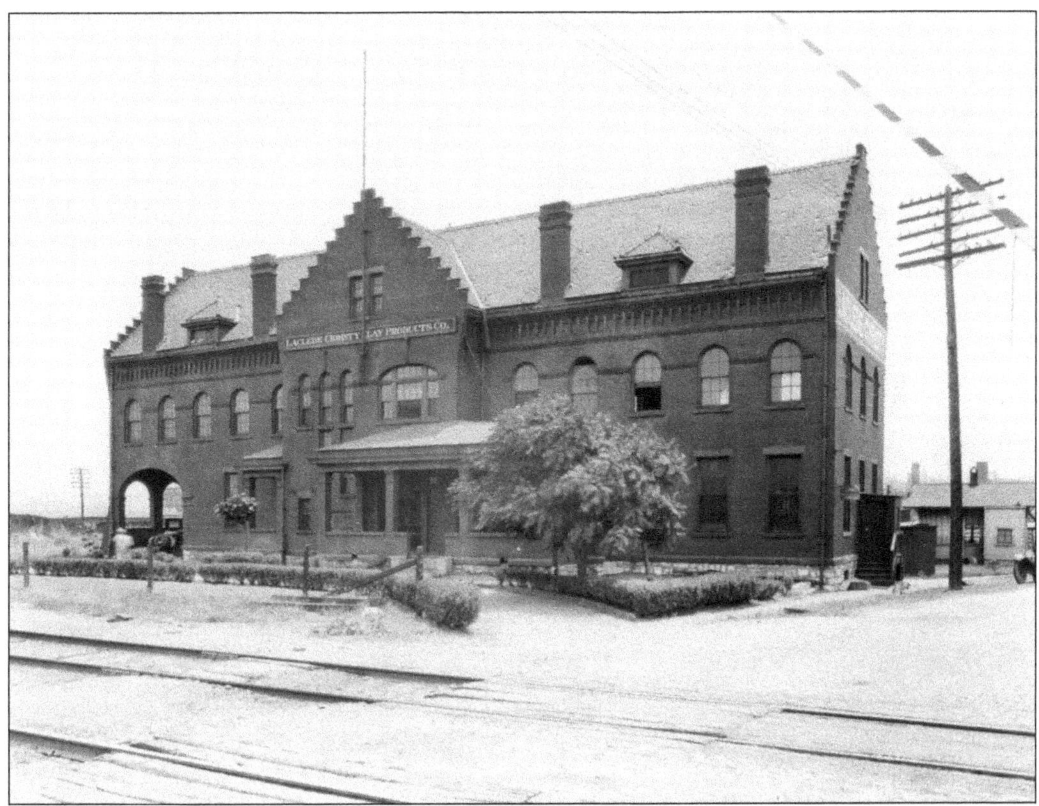

This is the building of the Laclede Christy Clay Products Company, located at 5900 Manchester Avenue. Shortly after 1910, a number of factories began to grow and move to the Hill. These industries provided the residents with more employment opportunities and allowed them to remain in the neighborhood, where all their needs were met. Italians began opening small businesses to provide needed services. Taverns, cafés, butcher shops, pharmacies, and grocers sprang up within a few blocks of each other. (Photograph by W.C. Persons; courtesy of Missouri History Museum, St. Louis.)

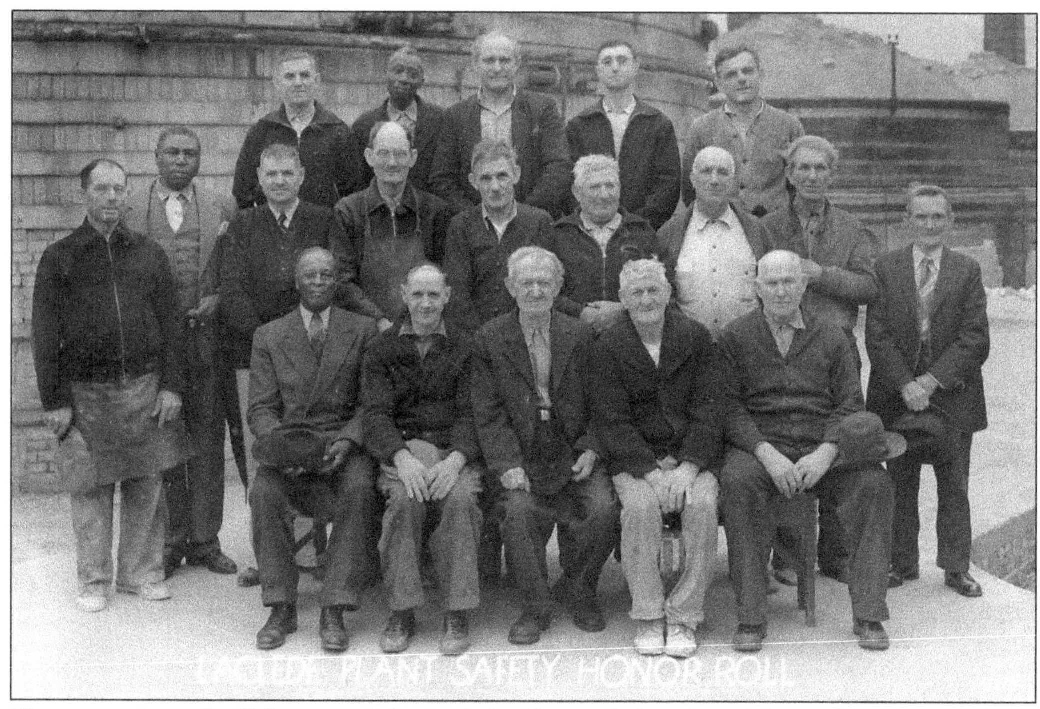

These men from the Hill received the Laclede Christy Safety Award for working years without an accident. While the clay mines, glass works, stone mines, and brickyards continued to be the major sources of employment, other industries came to the Hill due to its reputation for hard-working, reliable residents. (Courtesy of James Merlo.)

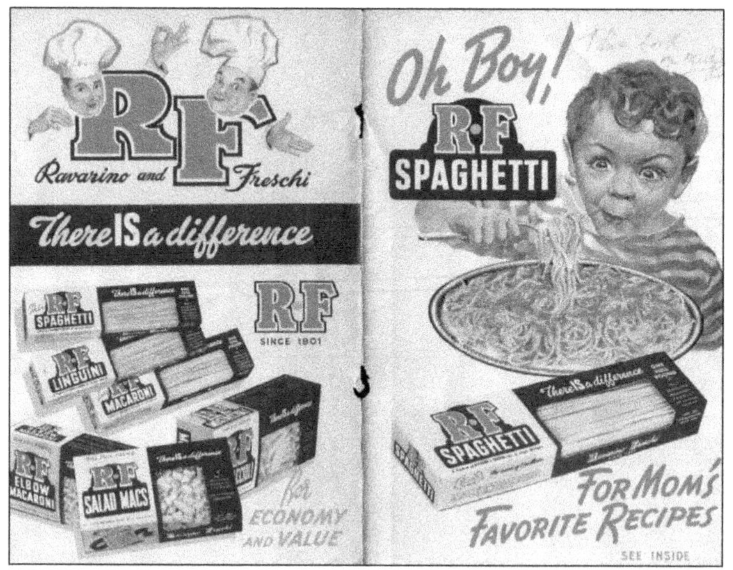

The Ravarino & Freschi spaghetti plant moved to the Hill in 1916. Its brand La Terminiese won a gold medal at the 1922 Milan Exposition. Giuseppe Freschi, one of the original owners, was a senior officer of Southwest Bank, which opened in October 1920 and employed many local people. With its bilingual communication, as well as loyal customers and employees, the bank survived the Great Depression without losing any deposits. (Author's collection.)

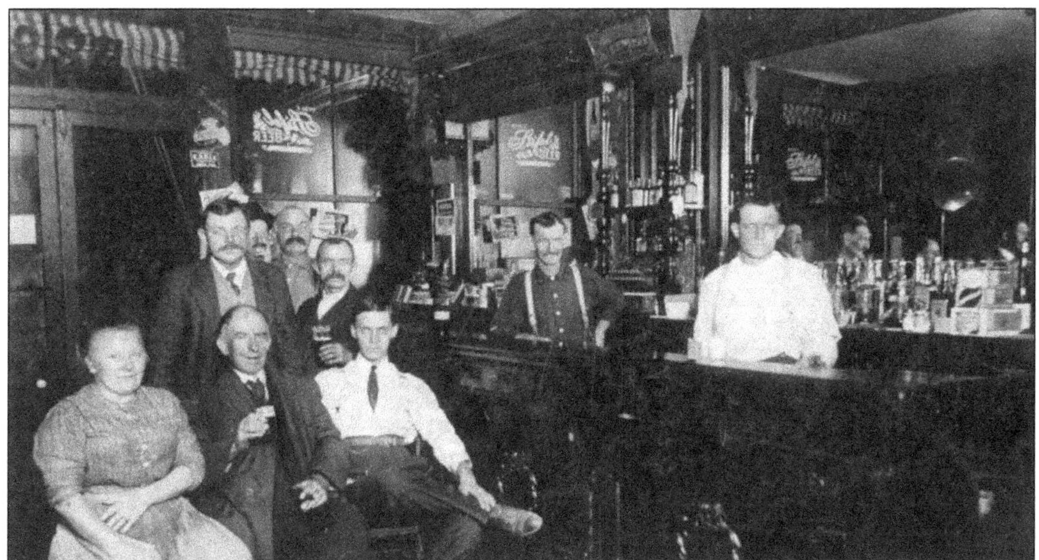

O'Connell's Tavern was one of the many taverns around the Hill. Laborers stopped in for a pail of beer after a long day's work. Another pasta manufacturer on the Hill was the St. Louis Macaroni Manufacturing Company, at the corner of Bischoff Avenue and Hereford Street, which hired a majority of Italian Americans. The company provided cultural entertainment throughout the years to help preserve the Italian heritage in the neighborhood. (Courtesy of Faye Berra Venegoni.)

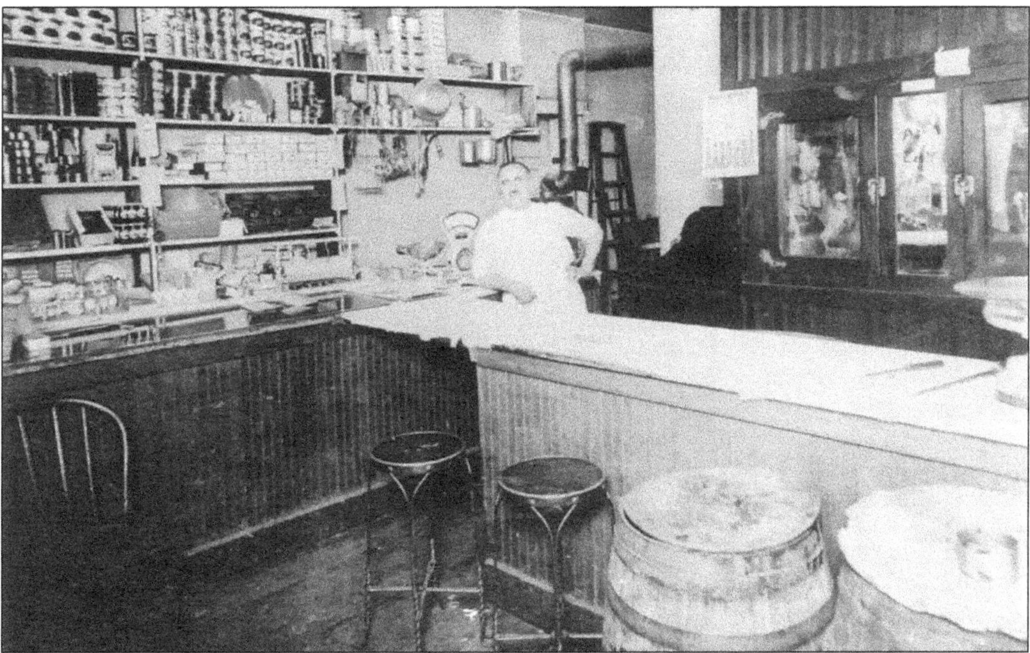

The DiMartino Grocery store at Shaw and Marconi Avenues was established in the early 1900s. Giovanni DiMartino, the owner, gave credit to many Hill residents and sponsored many immigrants coming over from Sicily. Most small businesses on the Hill between 1900 and 1920 were started by Italian immigrants who had worked in the mines or brickyards. These individuals saved enough money to open a business that would help meet the community's needs. (Courtesy of James Wohlert.)

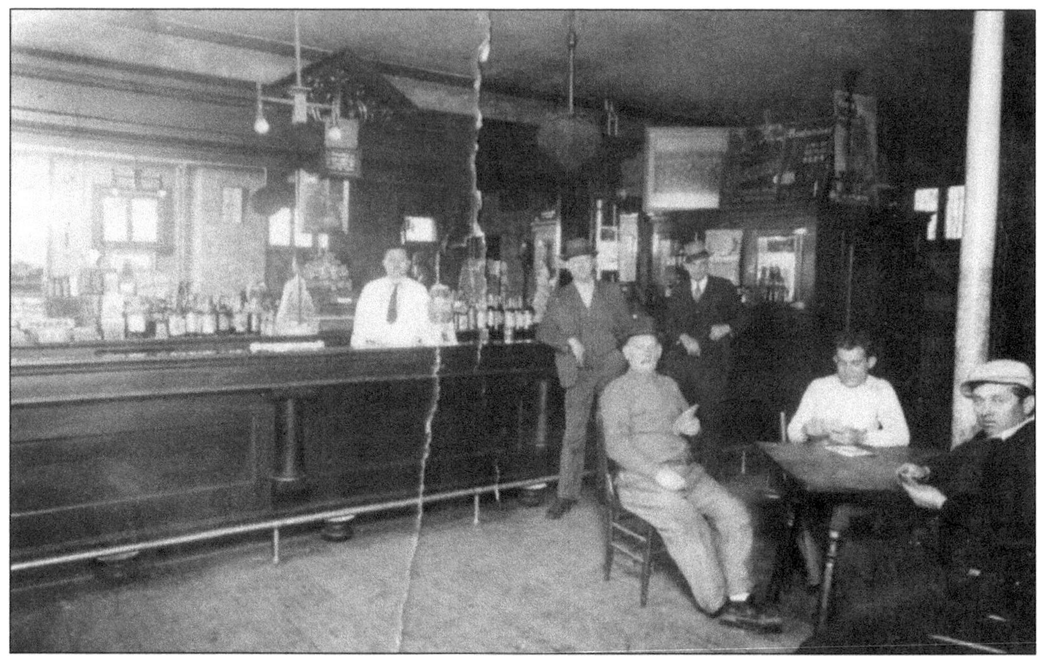

This tavern, at Marconi and Wilson Avenues, was located across from St. Ambrose Church. Owned by the Merlo family, the tavern's name was Merlo's, but it was known by locals as Forchett's. Mr. Merlo, a farmer in Italy, worked with a pitchfork, so the family named the tavern Forchett (*forchetta* is Italian for "fork"). No drinks were served during the ringing of the church bells. Mr. Melo used that time as an opportunity for prayer and reflection, and he expected his customers to do the same. (Courtesy of Angelo Marnati.)

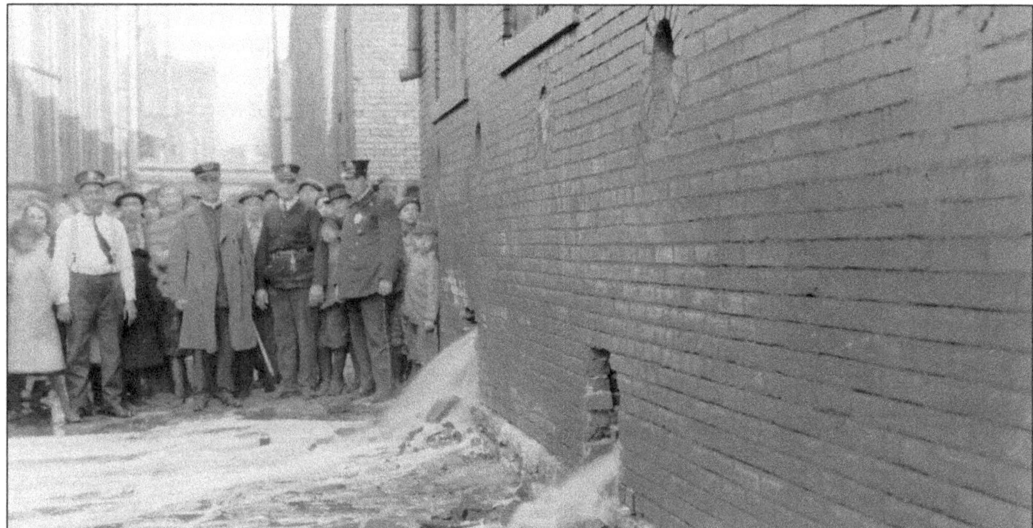

Police officers supervise the draining of a mash vat on Franklin Avenue in downtown's Little Italy district. During Prohibition, there was a cooperative nature among the residents, who turned a blind eye to the moonshine being manufactured. When raids did occur, the residue would flow into the streets and gutters. The Hill was well known for its supply of sugar and drink-making ingredients, which would be moved in advance of a raid. (Courtesy Missouri History Museum, St. Louis.)

The Quick Meal Stove Company, founded in 1881, was relocated to the Hill in 1910, at 2001 South Kingshighway Boulevard. The gas-burning Magic Chef oven was introduced in 1929 as the Quick Meal Magic Chef stove. By 1943, the building comprised approximately four city blocks of the Hill. (Courtesy of Julie Giannino.)

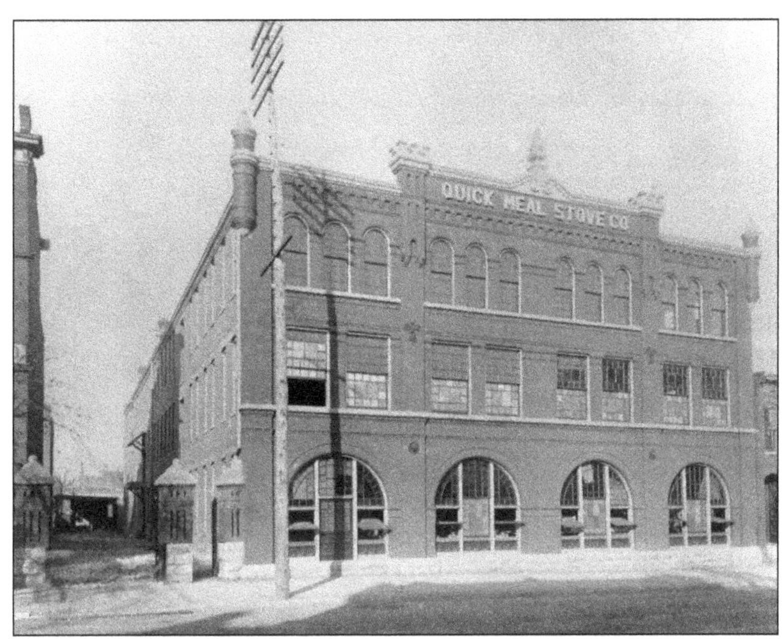

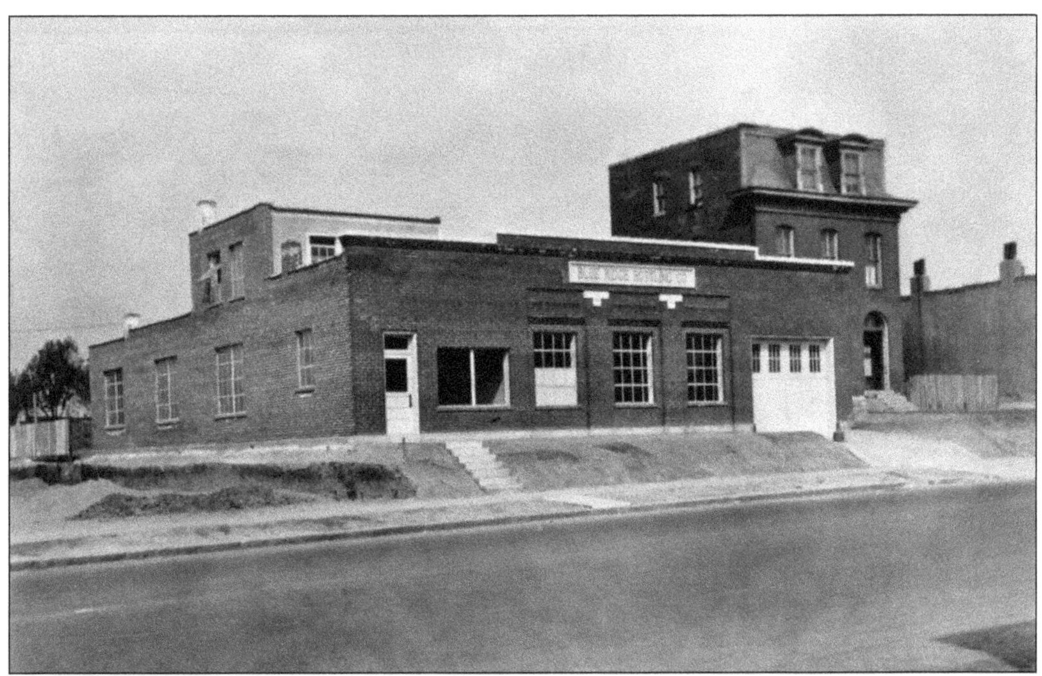

Blue Ridge Bottling Company, originally located at 827 South Kingshighway Boulevard, manufactured carbonated beverages and distilled waters. It produced major brands with names like Smile, Roman Club Ginger Ale, Lemon, and Hires Root Beer. The company also sponsored many sports teams. (Courtesy of Faye Berra Venegoni.)

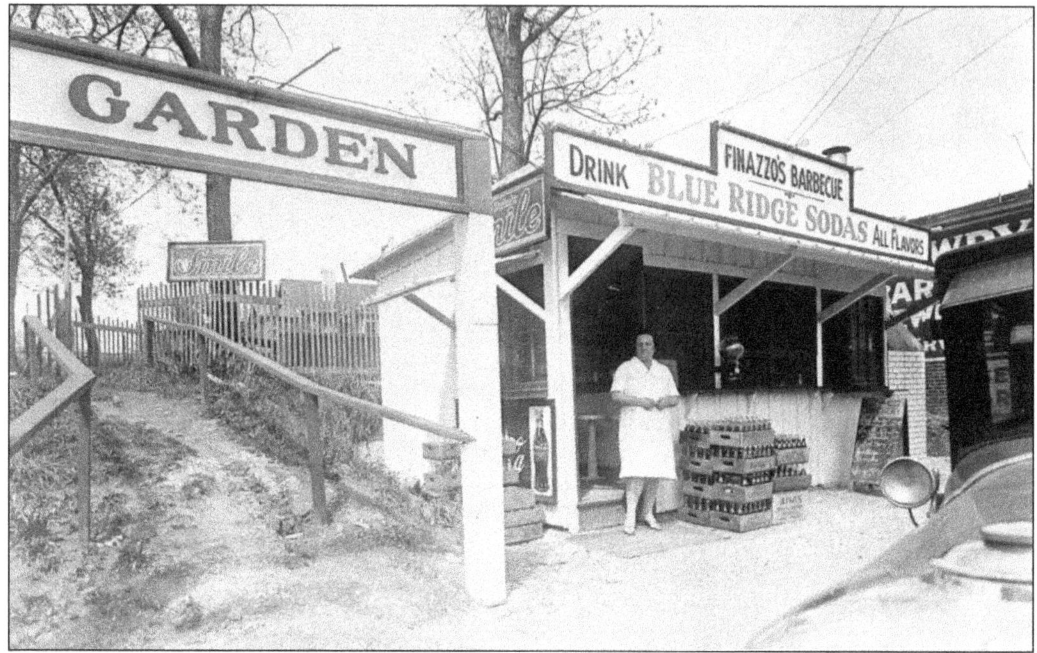

Barbecue was one of the residents' favorite meals. Many restaurants and bars set up tables in garden areas, allowing customers to enjoy the outdoors while eating. This was especially popular among the younger crowd. Blue Ridge soda was served at this establishment. (Courtesy of Faye Berra Venegoni.)

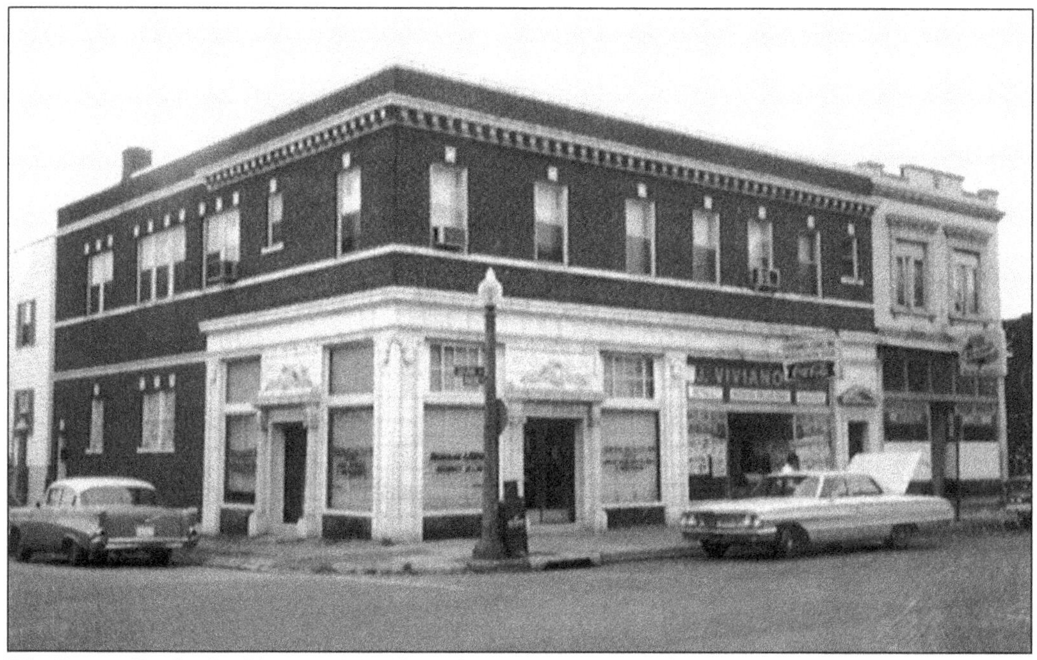

The Riggio Realty Building at 5149 Shaw Avenue was one of the nicest structures on the Hill in the 1920s. Ignazio Riggio, president, and his brother Joseph Riggio, vice president, were trusted individuals who helped people in need and gave assistance to Italians who wanted to become American citizens. (Courtesy of Shaw's Coffee.)

Angelo Sala was born in Cuggiono and came to America in 1904. Within four years, he opened a café at Franklin Avenue and Levee Street, near Little Italy in downtown St. Louis. In 1912, the Sala Café opened at Kingshighway Boulevard and Daggett Avenue on the Hill. (Courtesy of Gino Mariani.)

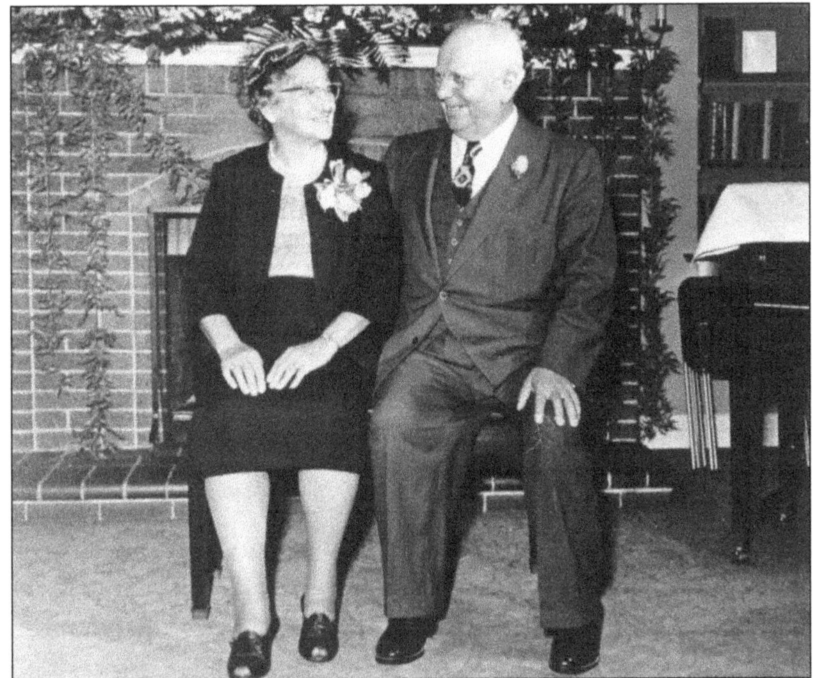

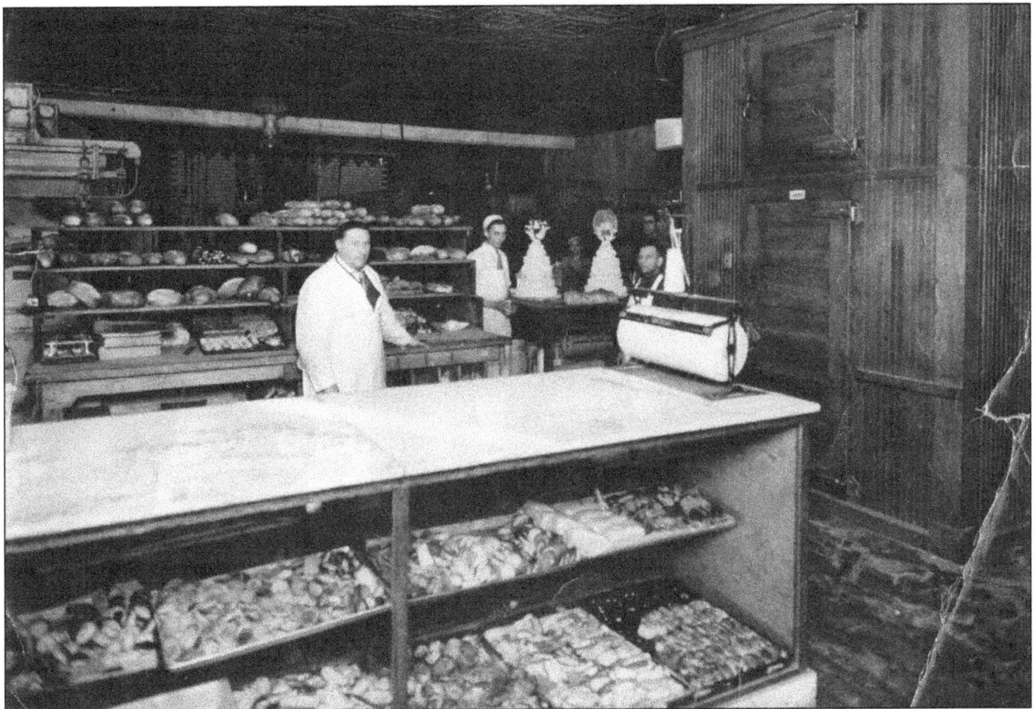

Missouri Bakery Company was established in 1909 by two brothers, Eugenio and Francesco Arpiani, and their brother-in-law Steve Gambaro. Francesco Arpiani had been in charge of the pastry department at the Hotel Belvedere of Baltimore before coming to St. Louis. Eugenio Arpiani worked at the Knickerbocker Hotel in New York. Missouri Bakery, still in operation on the Hill, is run by the descendants of the family. (Courtesy of Missouri Bakery.)

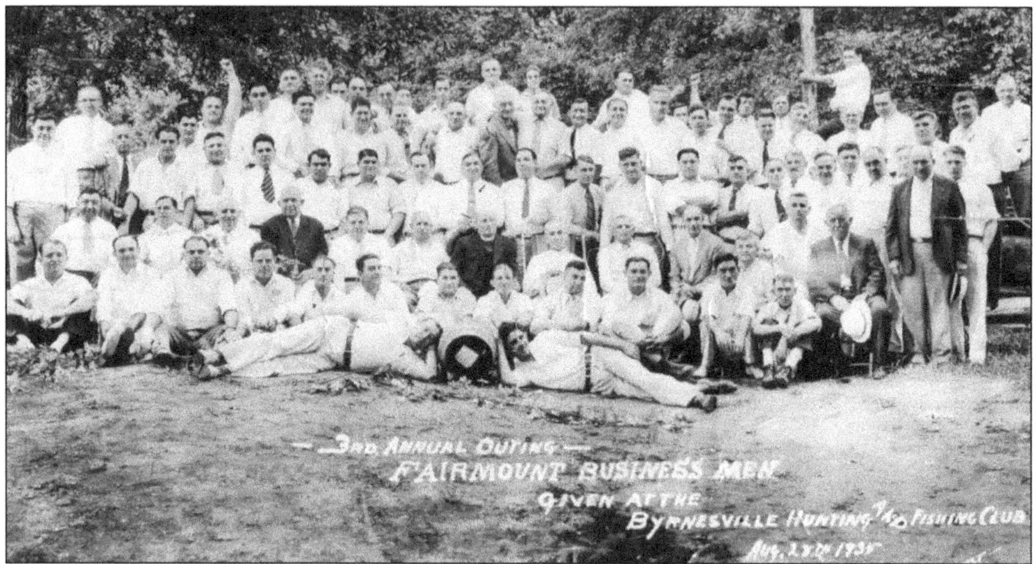

These men are attending the third annual Fairmount Business Men's picnic. Silvio Pucci was a longtime president of the Fratellanza, the oldest Italian society in St. Louis. He also was the president of the Italian American Republican Club on the Hill and the president of the Fairmount Heights Improvement and Business Men's Association. (Courtesy of Barbara Torretti.)

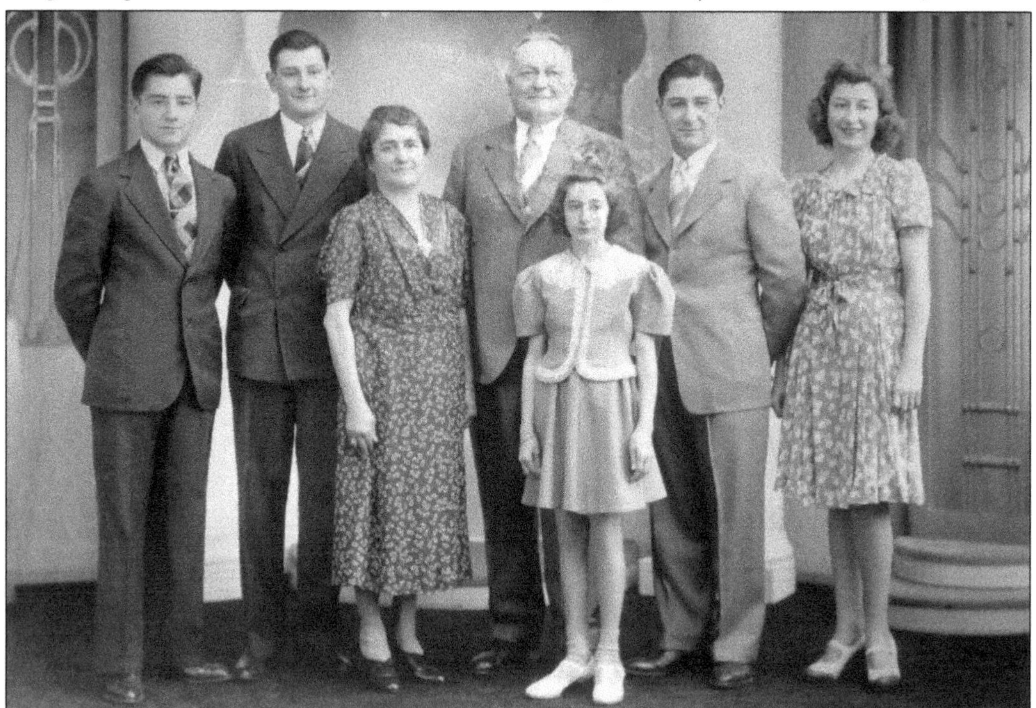

Charlie Gioia (center), a native of Marcallo, Italy, began his life in the grocery business by opening Gioia's Deli in 1918. The deli's building was constructed of wood and brick from the 1904 St. Louis World's Fair. The Gioia family conducted business on the Hill as a grocery store and as purveyors of their homemade sausage, Salam De Testa. The recipe is known today as Hot Salami. (Courtesy of Gioia's Deli.)

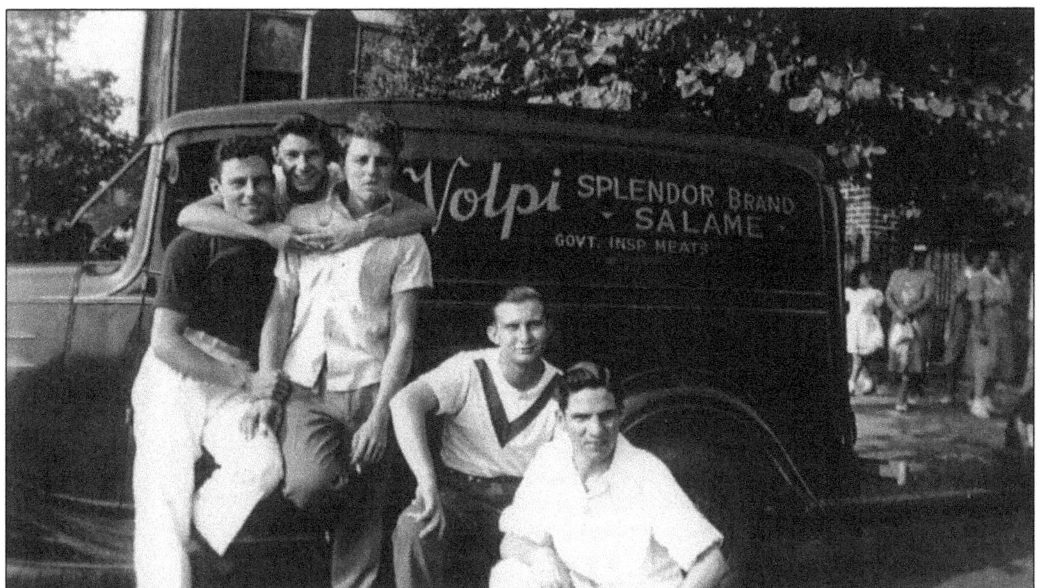

In 1907, John Volpi established a business at Edwards Street and Daggett Avenue. It continues to operate and manufacture Italian salami and sausage today. John Volpi was assisted for many years by Gino Pasetti. In 1922, their products were awarded a gold medal at the Cremona Exhibition in Italy. Armando Passetti (far left) is the nephew of John Volpi. When he was 14, Armando was asked by his uncle to come from Italy to learn the trade. In 1957, Armando Passetti became the president of Volpi Foods Inc. Since then, he has implemented improvements in technology and equipment without sacrificing quality or compromising the founder's standards of excellence. (Courtesy of Angela Passetti Holland.)

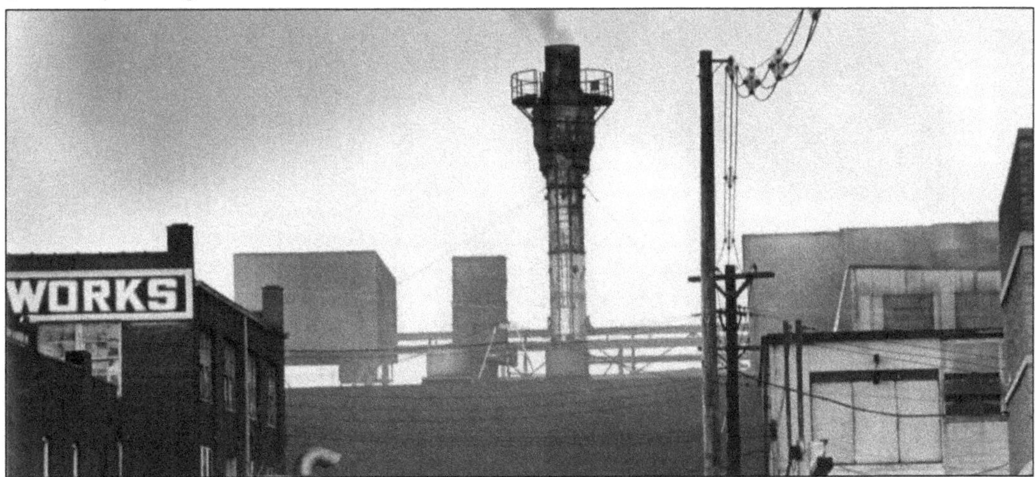

Banner Iron Works was another company located near the Hill. The increase in jobs called for more workers, and by 1940, there were large numbers of Italians and Italian Americans living and working on the Hill. A great many women worked for the Liggett and Meyer Tobacco Company. The Hill now had beautiful edifices and buildings of commerce. Among the community's well-known buildings are Calcaterra's Mortuary, Henry Ruggeri's Restaurant, John Volpi salami factory, Club Casino, Colombo Café, Berra Tavern, Berra's Dry Goods, Serra's Drug Store, Oldani Groceries, Correnti Cleaners, and the White Way Super Service Station. (Courtesy of Marianne Peri-Sack.)

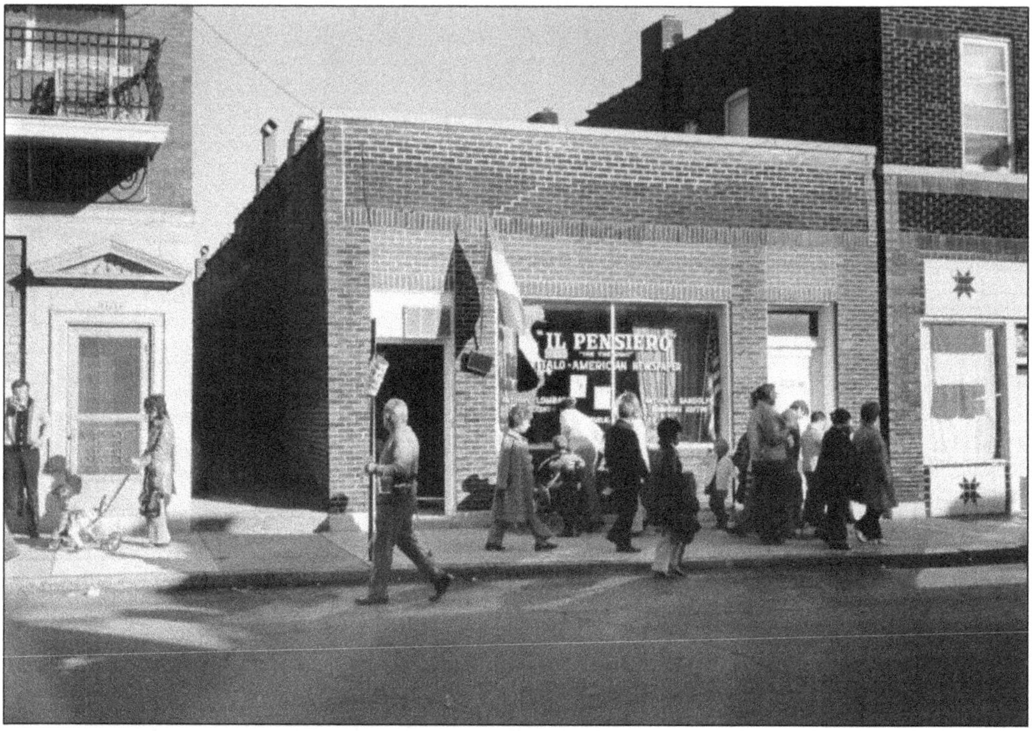

The Italian American newspaper *Il Pensiero* was established in 1904 by Luigi Carnovale. He was succeeded by Cavaliere Giovanni Cottone until his death in 1917. It was then edited by Dr. Cesare Avigni, who increased the size and appearance of the paper. Many Italian newspapers have started publication in St. Louis, but *Il Pensiero* is the only one remaining. A biweekly paper with Italian and English pages, it is published by Cavaliere Antonio Lombardo. (Courtesy of Gino Mariani.)

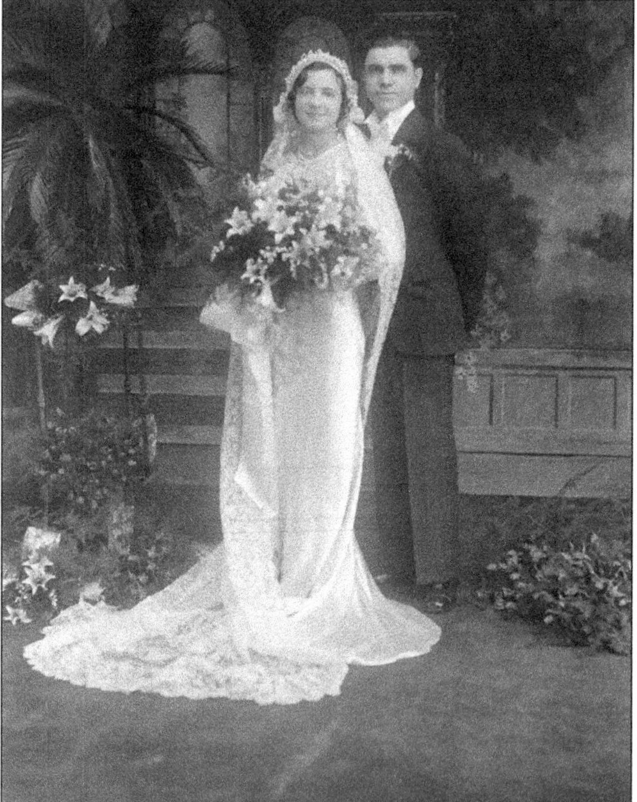

Fred Urzi and his wife, Millie, operated Urzi's Market on the Hill for many years. The family-owned market had its beginnings in 1926, and it is still in operation by the Urzi family. The 1940 census lists their home address as 5342 Bischoff Avenue. (Courtesy of Jim Urzi.)

Some small businesses, though not operated by Italian Americans, were well patronized by them. Rau's Department Store (pictured), on the Hill since 1905, was the place for school uniforms and other clothing. The Spielberg Furniture Company, on Marconi Avenue, was established in 1921. The store's owner began the business by selling door-to-door on the Hill. There were two other furniture stores on the Hill, Fair Mercantile on Shaw in 1920 and Berra Furniture in 1926 on Marconi. (Courtesy of Gino Mariani.)

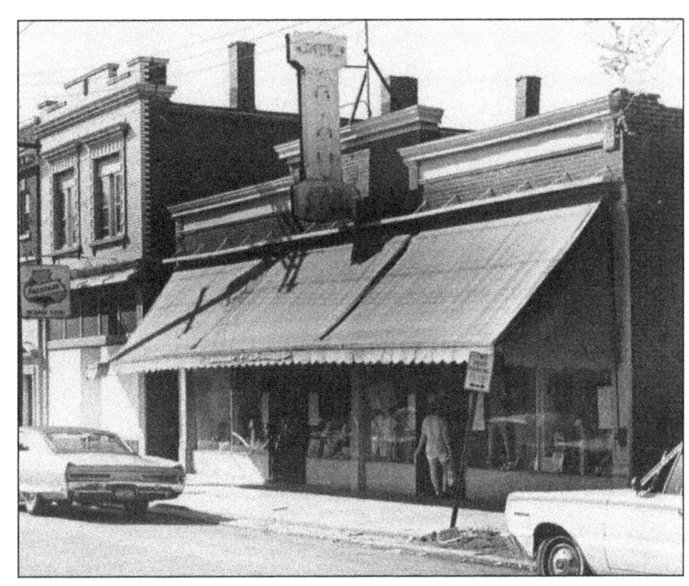

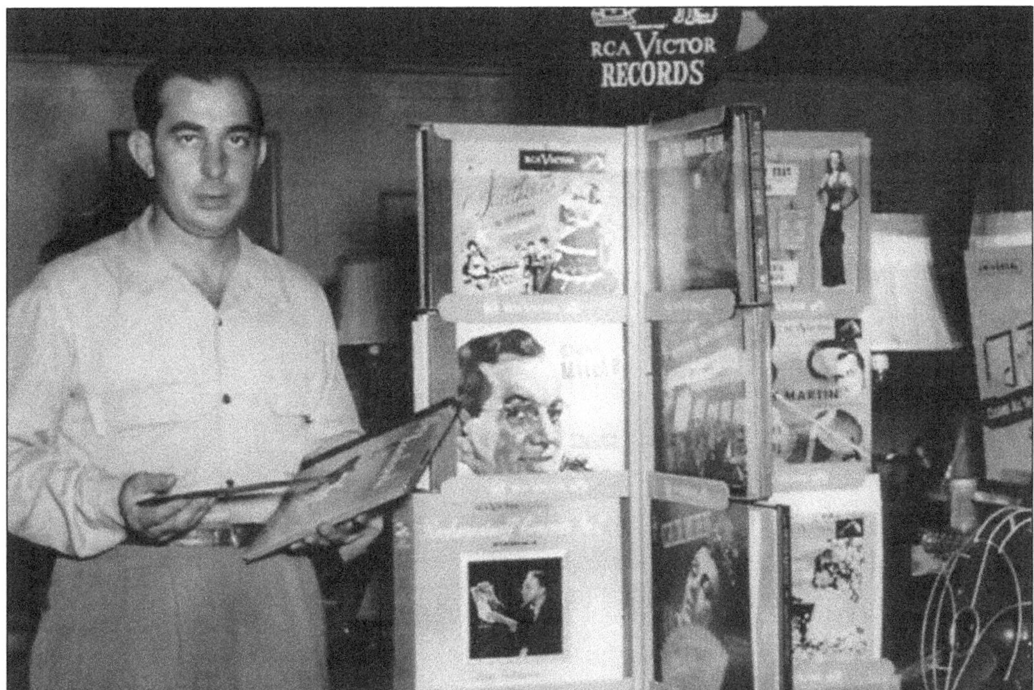

Lou Cerrutti was the manager at Berra Furniture on Marconi Avenue. It was one of the family-owned Italian American furniture stores on the Hill that were located among residential homes. St. Ambrose students often stopped to browse in the store on their way home from school. (Courtesy of Mary Agusti Thompson.)

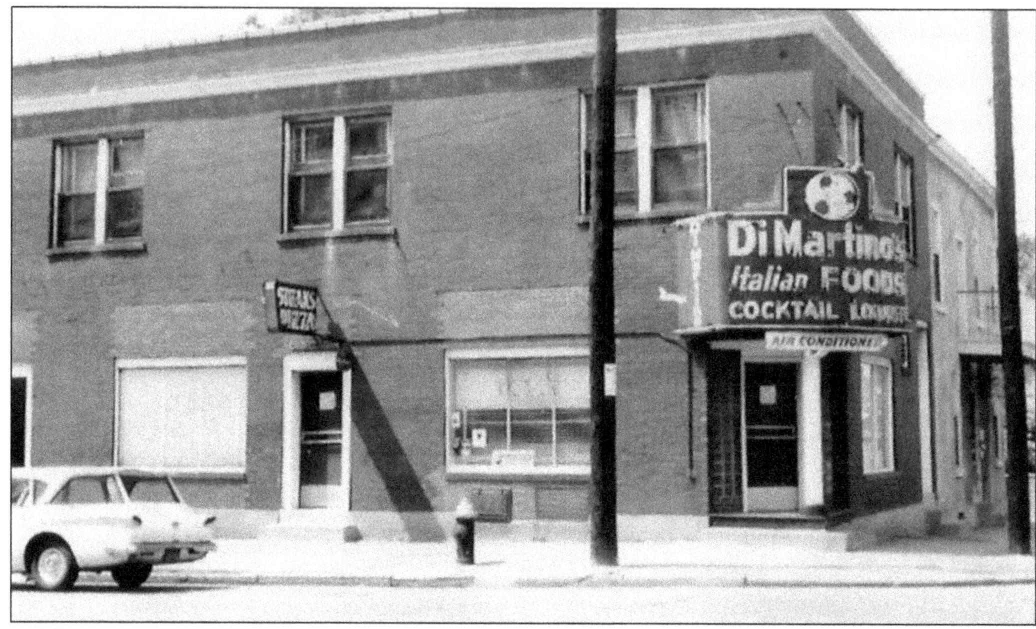

DiMartino's restaurant, owned by Charles John DiMartino, was located at the corner of Shaw and Marconi Avenues. Fazio Bakery is another successful family business. It grew substantially in the 1940s, when Ben Fazio opened his bakery on Elizabeth Avenue. The bakery has relocated on the Hill and remains a family-owned business. (Courtesy of James Wohlert.)

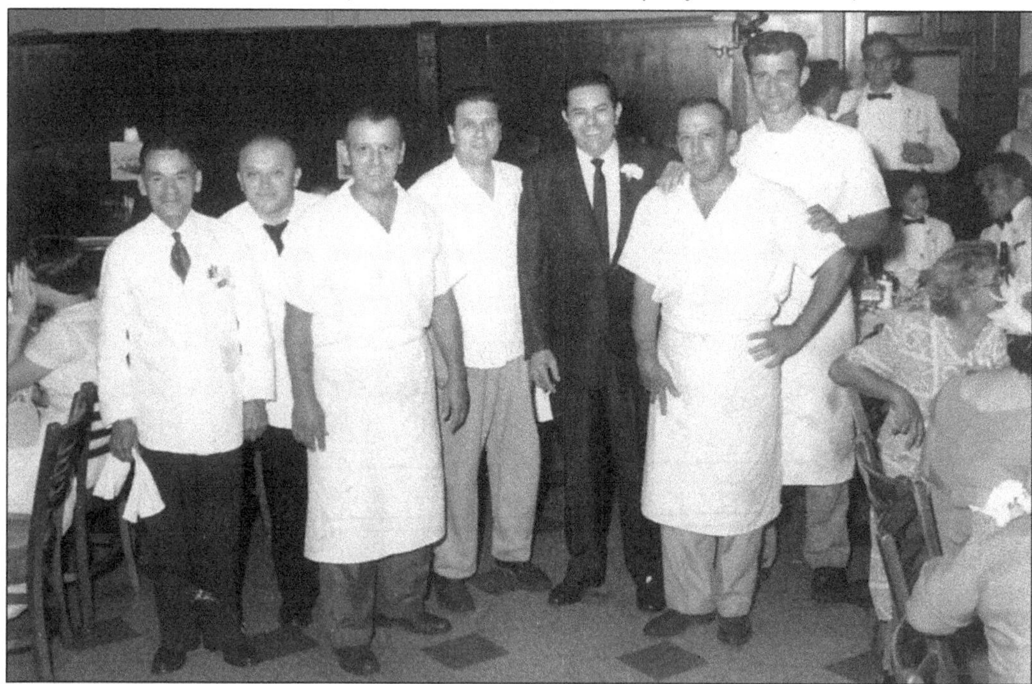

Sala's was owned by Angelo and Emma Sala. Angelo "Jock" Puricelli (dark suit), was the son of Angelo's sister Maria. Angelo Puricelli began working there at 14, becoming the head chef. He continued to work there for over 50 years, but never owned a driver's license. For Hill residents, everything they needed was within a walk. (Courtesy of Firmin Puricelli.)

Frank Gianella was the first owner of Papa Prost Tavern on Pattison Avenue, one of the oldest taverns licensed in St. Louis. Frank's son Paul served as a medical corpsman during World War II and was involved in liberating Nazi death camps. Paul took over the tavern upon his father's death. It was like a second home for families living on the Hill. Children bought ice cream, and adults enjoyed a beverage and played bocce. Holidays were celebrated with rabbit stew on Valentine's Day and roast beef on New Year's Eve. (Courtesy of Gino Mariani.)

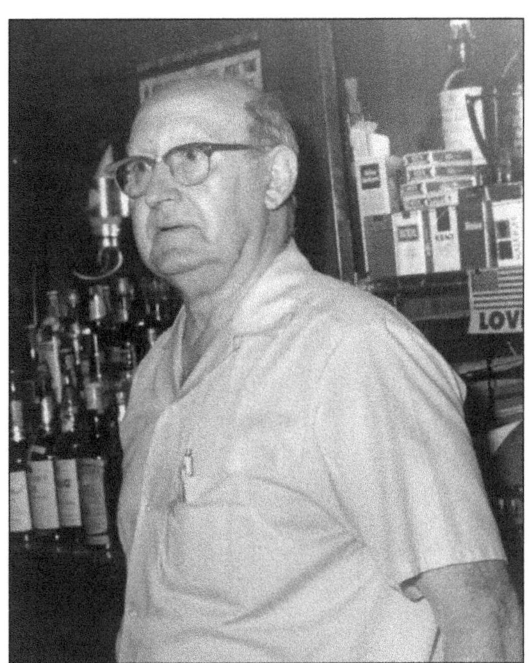

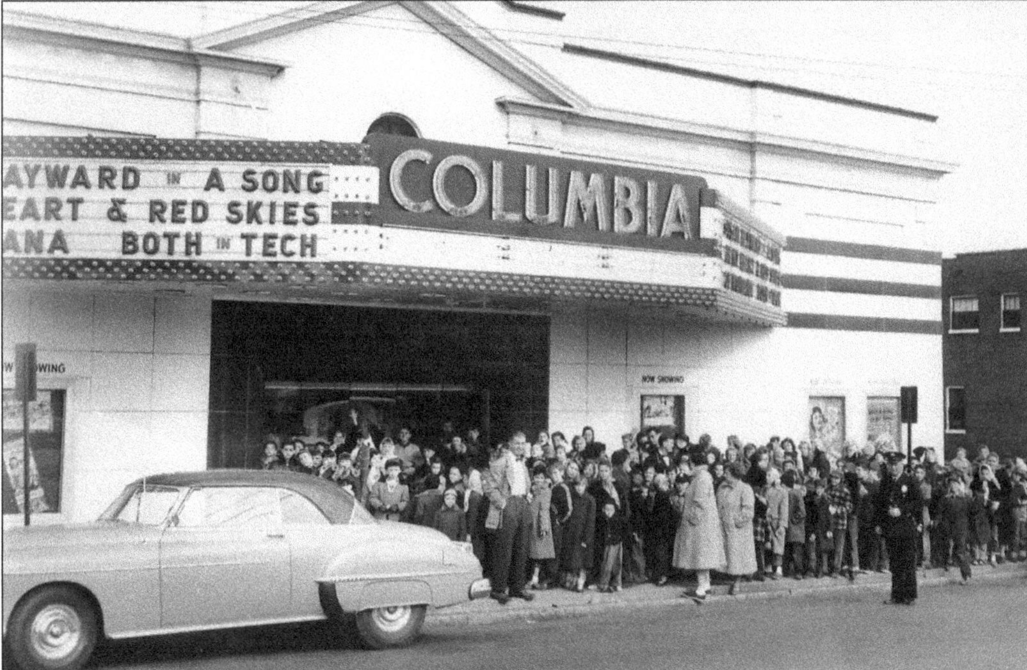

The Columbia Theater opened at the corner of Southwest Avenue and Edwards Street in 1925. Evelyn Colombo Nettemeyer says, "My earliest memories are of living in our home on Macklind Avenue between the homes of my grandmother and my father's twin brother and his family. My aunts' families lived within walking distance. Friends went to the Shaw School playgrounds in the summer and walked to Columbia Show together. These residents remind me who I am and we celebrate the bond that ties each Italian family and their ancestors who came before us to their lives and their sacrifices." (Courtesy of James Merlo.)

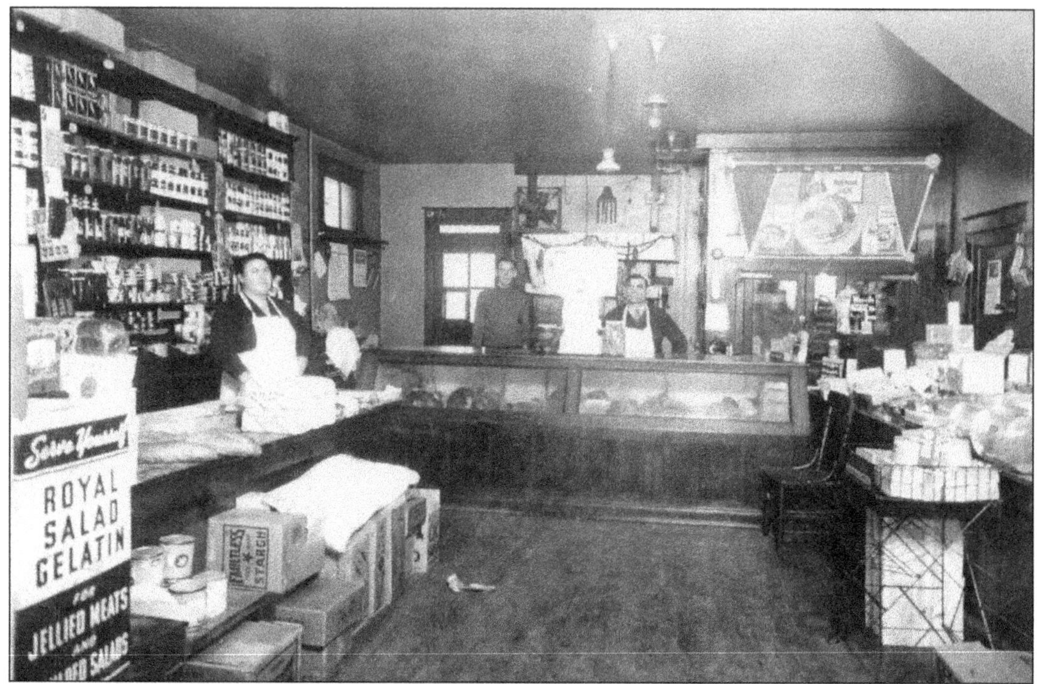

The Italian heritage of the residents has helped the Hill to retain its identity. Along the way, businesses have opened that are now known not only in the St. Louis metropolitan area, but in many cases throughout the United States. The Italian specialty shops attract customers seeking to purchase unique food items. (Courtesy of Vince LoRusso.)

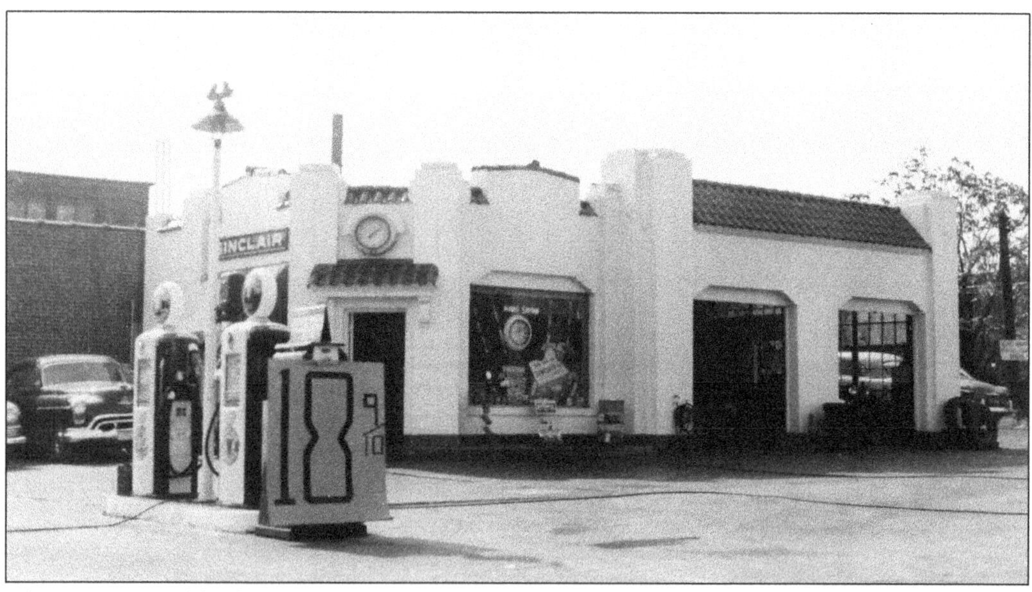

There was a neighborhood gas station at the corner of Shaw Avenue and South Kingshighway Boulevard owned by the Venegoni family. This station was a place for the younger crowd to meet and to buy one of the fine sodas produced by Blue Ridge Bottling. (Courtesy of Faye Berra Venegoni.)

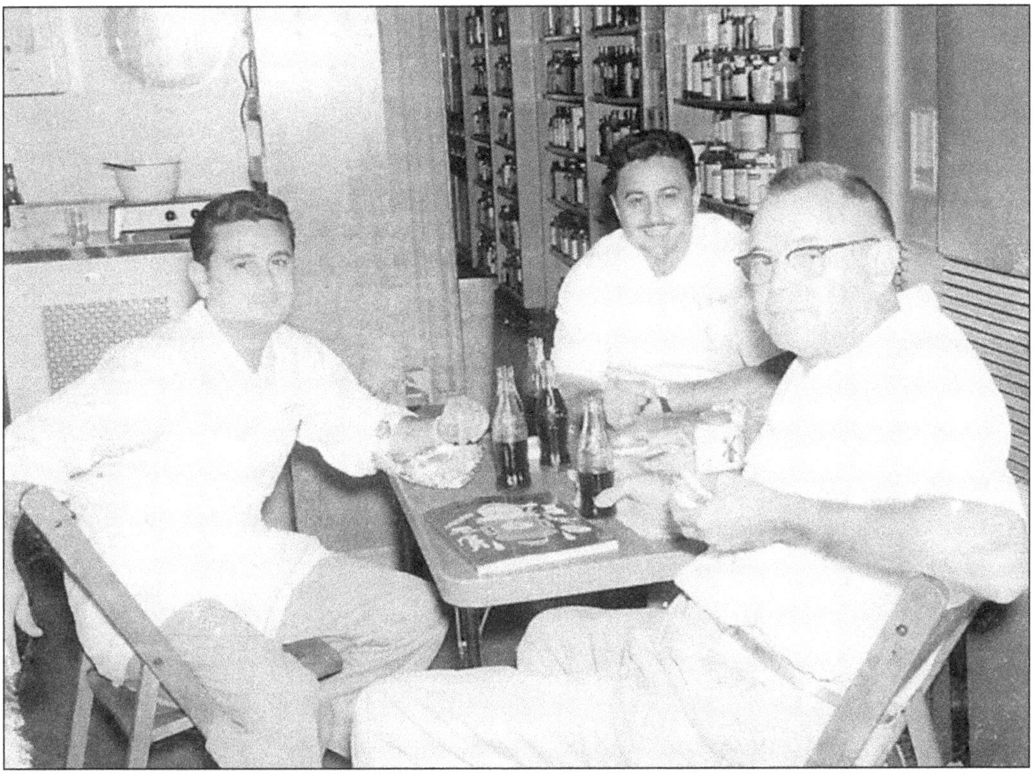

The Cunetto family owned a neighborhood pharmacy. Vince (left) and Joe Cunetto (center) were always cooking in the back room. Friends, doctors, and pharmaceutical salesmen would gather in the small back office for a delicious meal. (Courtesy of Frank Cunetto.)

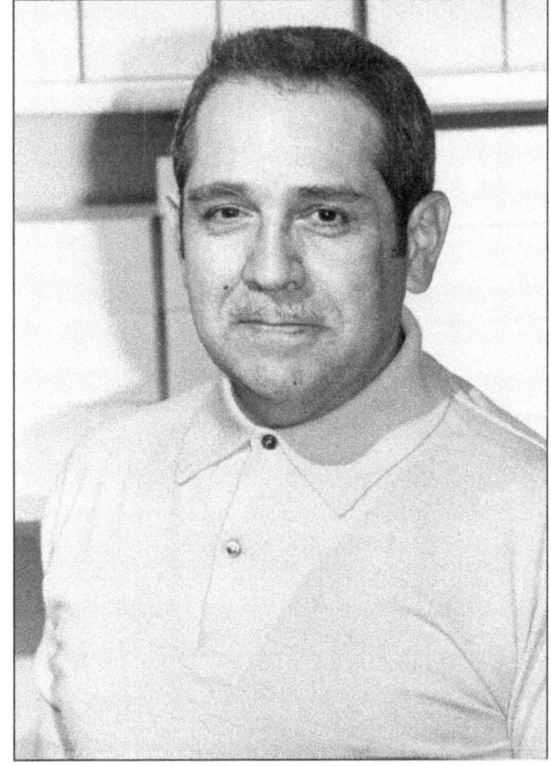

Amighetti's Bakery was founded in 1921 by Louis Amighetti, an Italian immigrant. It was later run by his son Louis Amighetti Jr. (pictured). Called "Junior" by all who knew him, Louis Jr. grew the business to the point that, in the late 1960s, it expanded from a small, traditional bakery into a sit-down sandwich shop. Amighetti's special is a gourmet sandwich overloaded with meats, cheese, and peppers with a secret sauce. The bakery continues to operate in its original location, at the northeast corner of Wilson and Marconi Avenues. (Courtesy of Gino Mariani.)

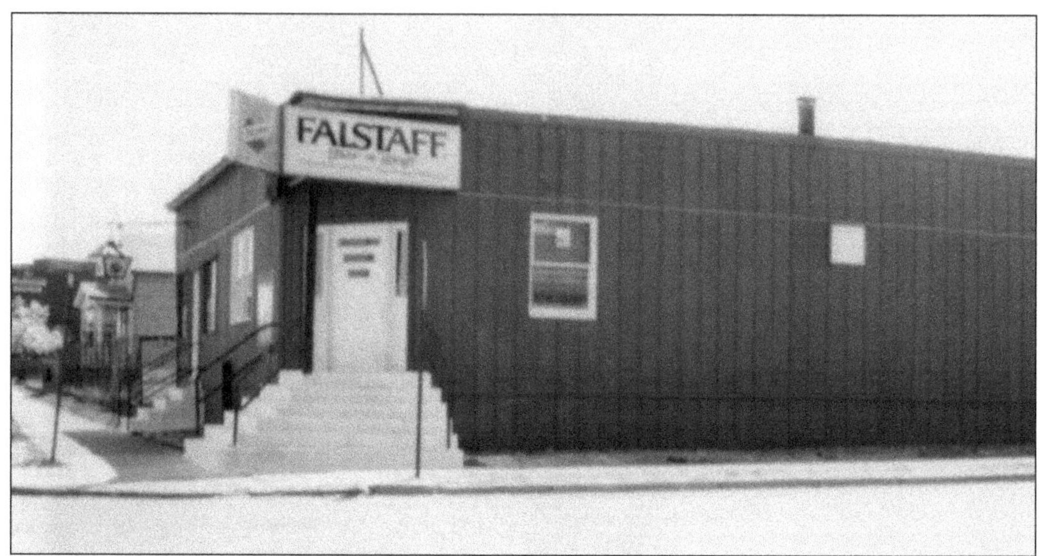

Seven Steps Tavern was named for the number of steps one had to take to enter the tavern, built in 1888. It was also named Pozza's and, later, Regina's. It was operated by Regina and Albino Pozza and located at the corner of Shaw Avenue and Edwards Street. The building is gone, and the lot is now used for parking. For years, the 24th Ward Democratic Club had its headquarters in this building. (Courtesy of Gino Mariani.)

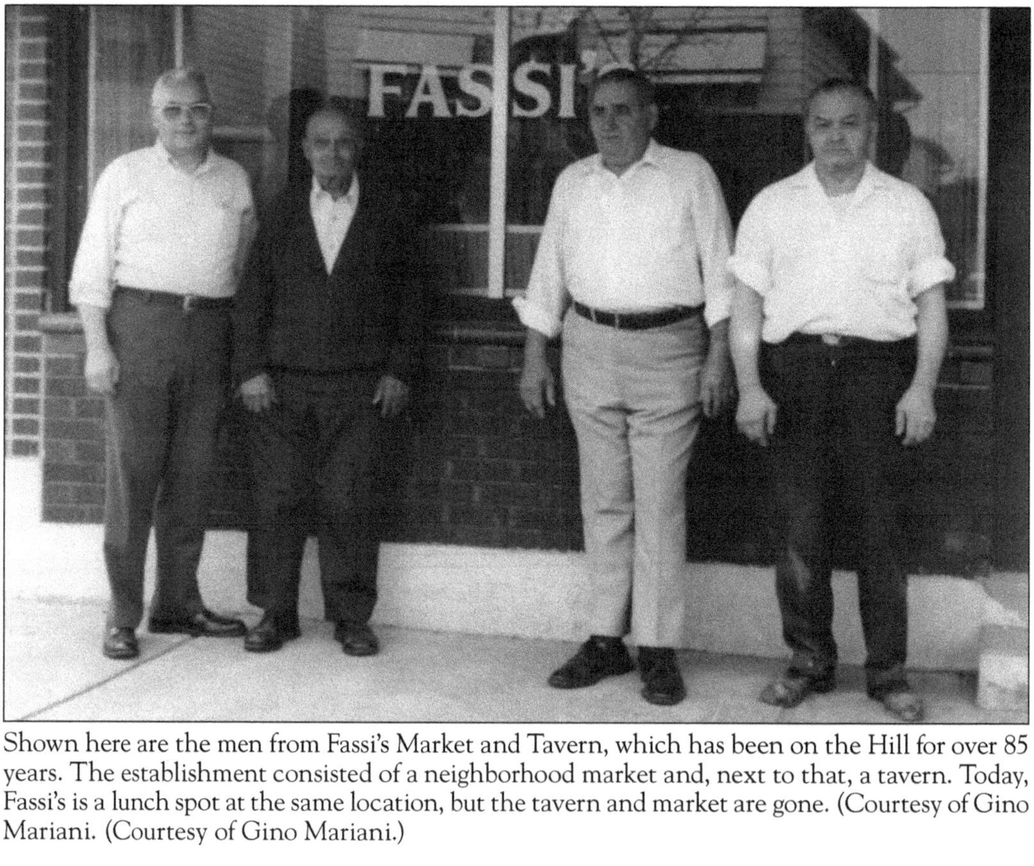

Shown here are the men from Fassi's Market and Tavern, which has been on the Hill for over 85 years. The establishment consisted of a neighborhood market and, next to that, a tavern. Today, Fassi's is a lunch spot at the same location, but the tavern and market are gone. (Courtesy of Gino Mariani. (Courtesy of Gino Mariani.)

Six

EDUCATION

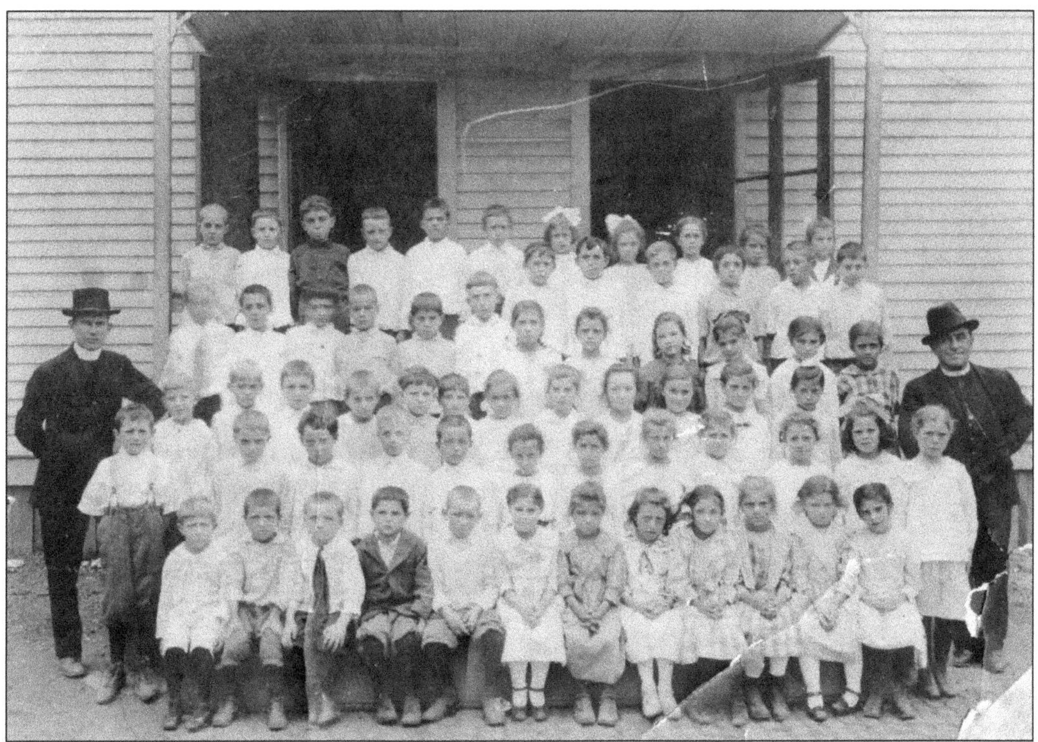

The St. Ambrose School opened in 1906 and was located at 2110 Cooper Street (Marconi Avenue). It was a frame building with two rooms. The school's first registration consisted of about 50 boys and 50 girls who attended the lower grades. Older children attended the public school. By 1908, the school taught up to the fifth grade, with about 100 students. The first formal graduation, in June 1915, took place at the St. Louis Cathedral. All grammar-school graduates from the St. Louis parochial schools were in attendance. Before St. Ambrose School was expanded, the majority of children in the neighborhood received their first years of education at the public school. (Courtesy of Faye Berra Venegoni.)

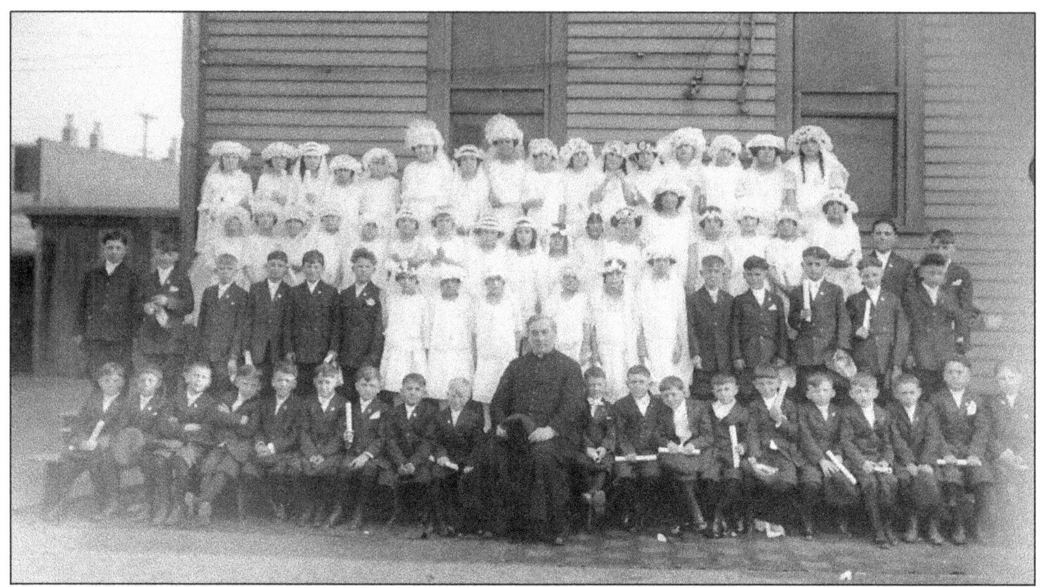

Rev. Julius Giovannini (first row, center) came to St. Louis on October 18, 1914, from Castellino Tamaro, in Cuneo, Italy. He is pictured here with children receiving their First Communion. Children who attended public school were required to receive catechetical instruction once a week. (Courtesy of James Merlo.)

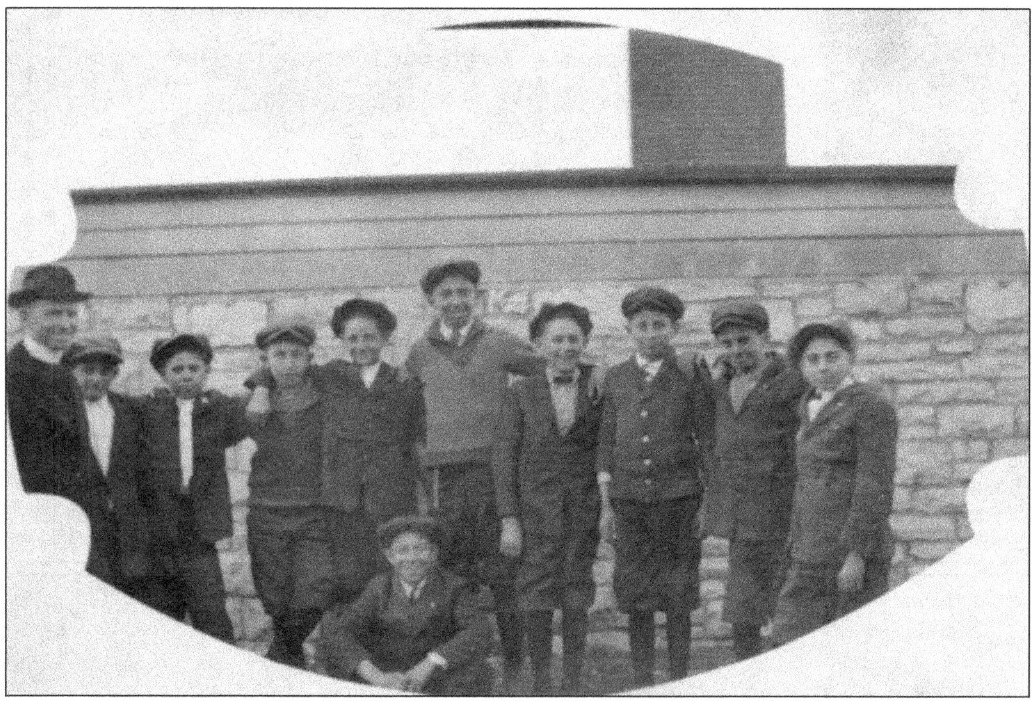

There were two public schools covering the area of the Hill. The children living at the extreme northern end of the Hill attended Wade Elementary. Children living south of Pattison attended Shaw Elementary. Children attending public schools were required to take religion class. The language barrier caused many to leave school, as did financial needs. Many children received a Missouri Employment Certificate at the age of 14 to begin working. (Courtesy of Faye Berra Venegoni.)

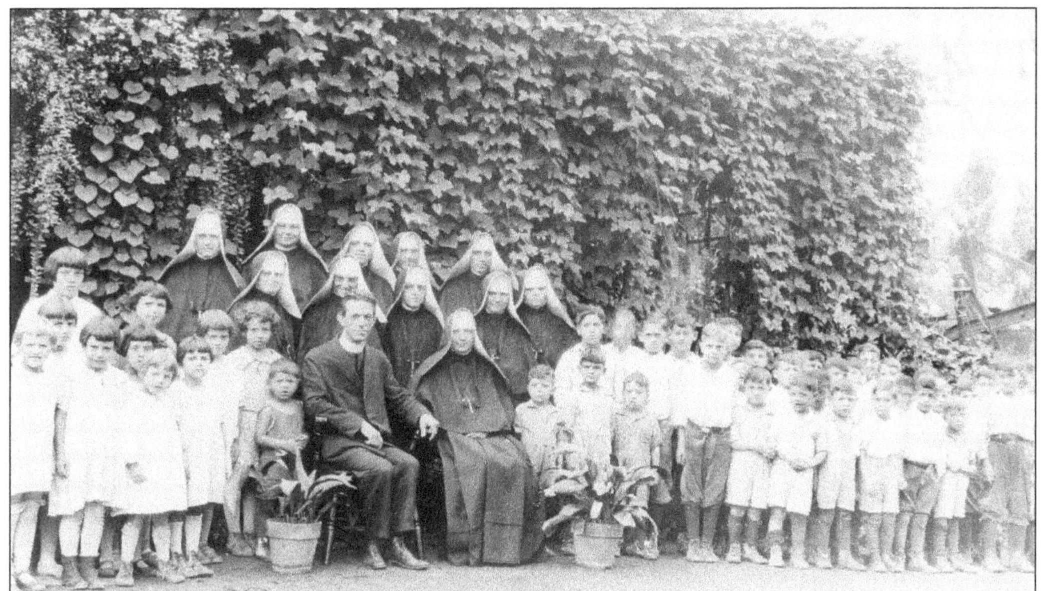

Shown here in the 1930s are St. Ambrose Catholic School students, Rev. Peter Barabino, and the Sisters of Loretto. Reverend Barabino continued to give catechetical instructions to the children while serving as pastor from 1929 until 1934. In the 1930s, he created an extensive youth program for athletics. He had great appeal with the young people of St. Ambrose. (Courtesy of Missouri History Museum, St. Louis.)

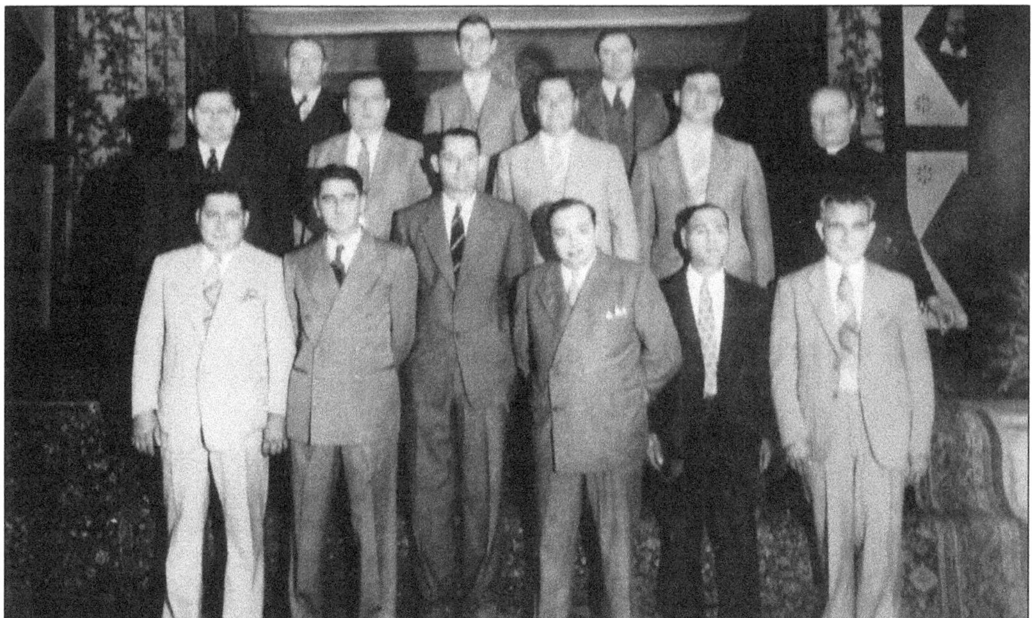

The St. Ambrose School Board was formed in 1935 to plan and construct a new school that could accommodate the majority of children from the parish. The members of the board chosen to lead the project are, from left to right, (first row) Louis J. "Midge" Berra, Paul Calcaterra, David Fantana, Charles Garavaglia, John Barrale, and John Russo; (second row) Louis J. Gualdoni, Paul Berra, Henry Ruggeri, Caesar Gioia, and Msgr. Fiorenzo Lupo; (third row) Charles Clavenna, Louis Visconti, and John Clavenna. (Courtesy of Victor John Clavenna.)

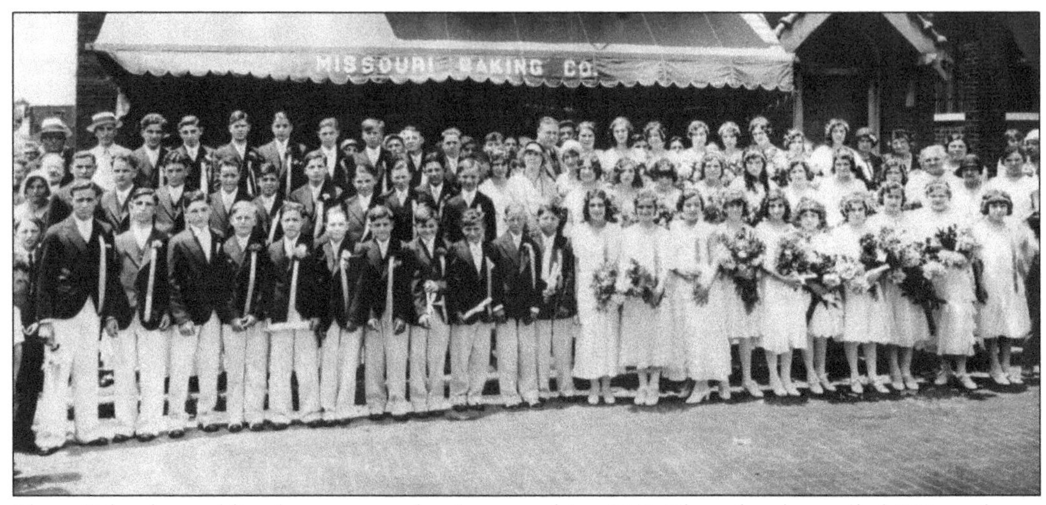

Shaw School, a public elementary school, opened in 1907. The school enrolled 928 students, roughly one-tenth of whom were born in Italy. By 1914, over one-fourth of the students were born in Italy. Shown here are the Shaw School graduates of 1932. (Courtesy of Missouri Bakery.)

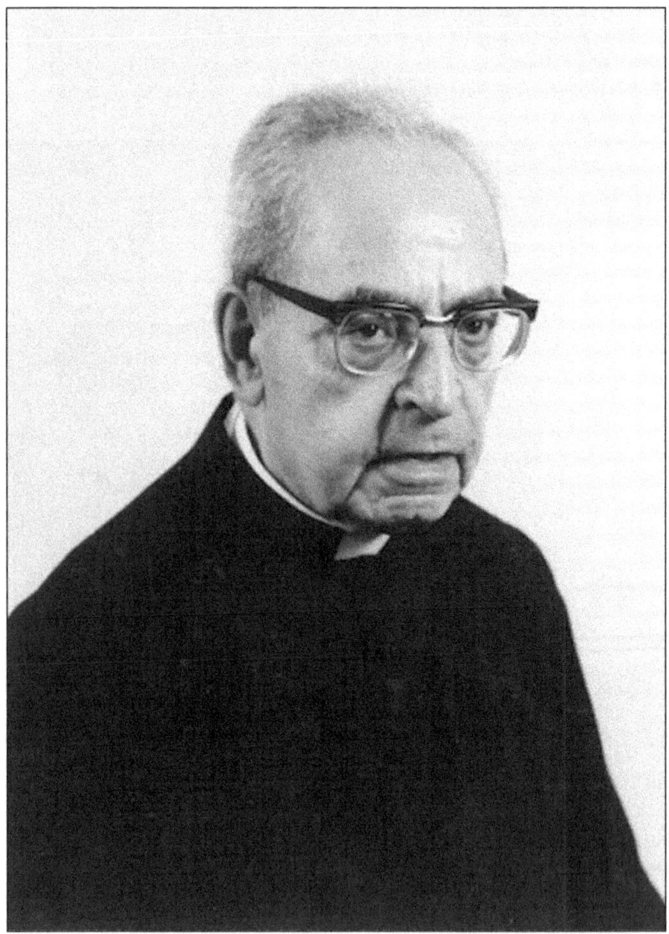

Rev. Anthony Palumbo was very important to many of the boys on the Hill. He was the assistant pastor at St. Ambrose from 1932 to 1948. His athletic skills in soccer, baseball, and handball appealed to young people, and he was instrumental in promoting athletics. He worked with Joe Causino, an employee at the local YMCA, in promoting sports and athletic completion between other city clubs. Reverend Palumbo understood that capturing the attention of the parish's young and providing a structured environment for them to grow would keep the community strong for years to come. (Courtesy of Marianne Peri-Sack.)

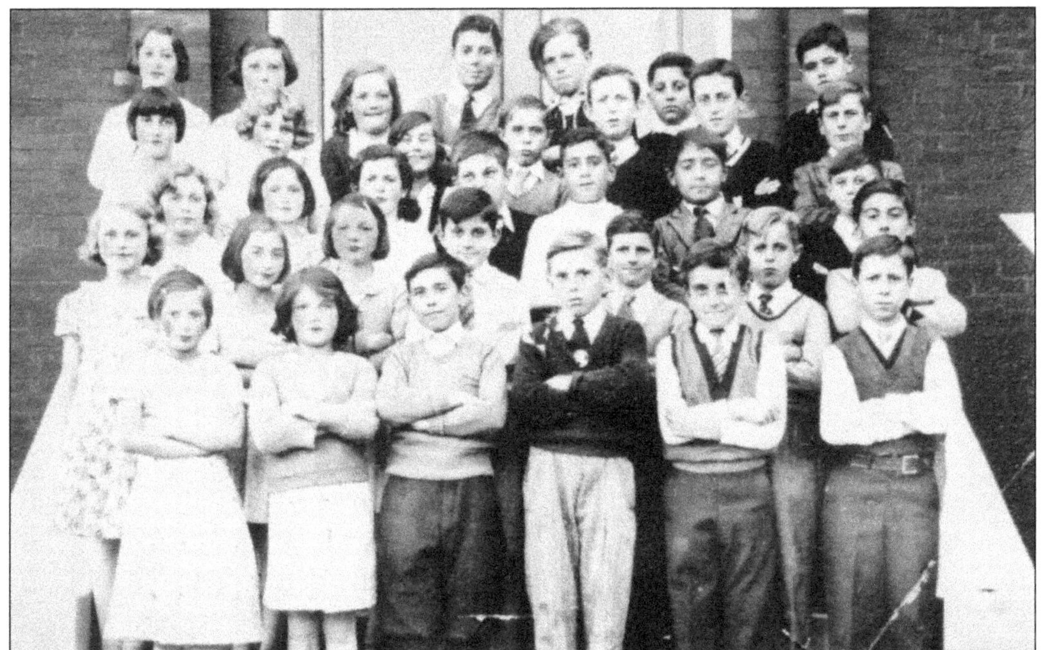

From 1920 to 1929, St. Ambrose Parish experienced a remarkable development, with hundreds of families coming to the Hill. By 1935, the current school with 300 students was aging and not meeting the needs of the parish. It was agreed that a modern school would be built that would be large enough to welcome the greater number of children so that the majority might receive basic Catholic training. (Courtesy of Dave Tidoni.)

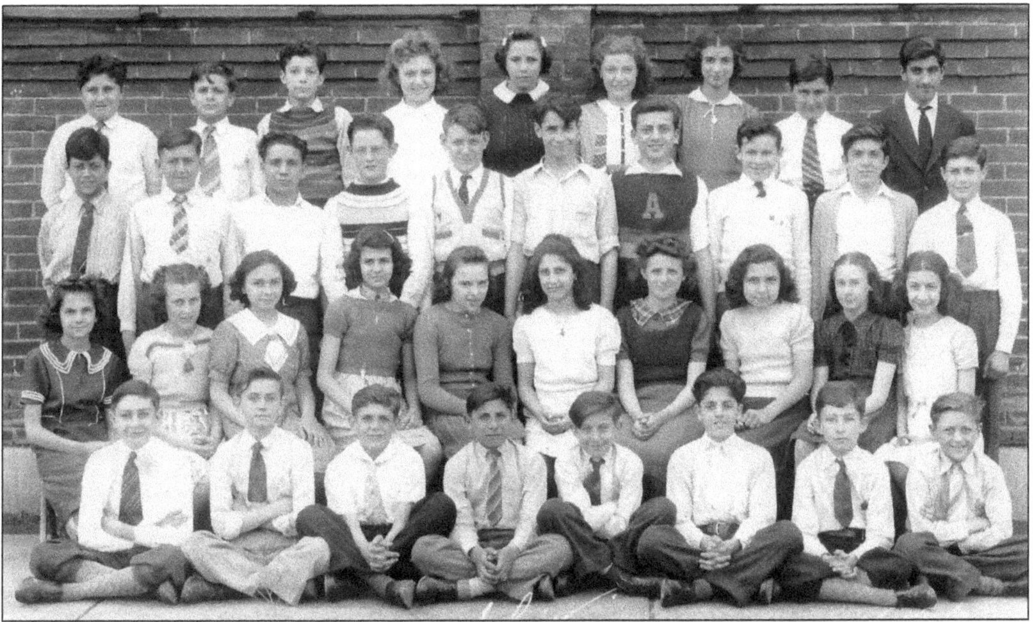

The first nuns to teach at St. Ambrose, from 1916 to 1919, were the order of St. Theresa. The climate in St. Louis was not agreeable with the health of these sisters and they had to leave the United States. The Sisters of Loretto began teaching in 1919 and continued until 1941, when they were replaced by the Missionary Zelatrices of the Sacred Heart. (Courtesy of Tom Cissi.)

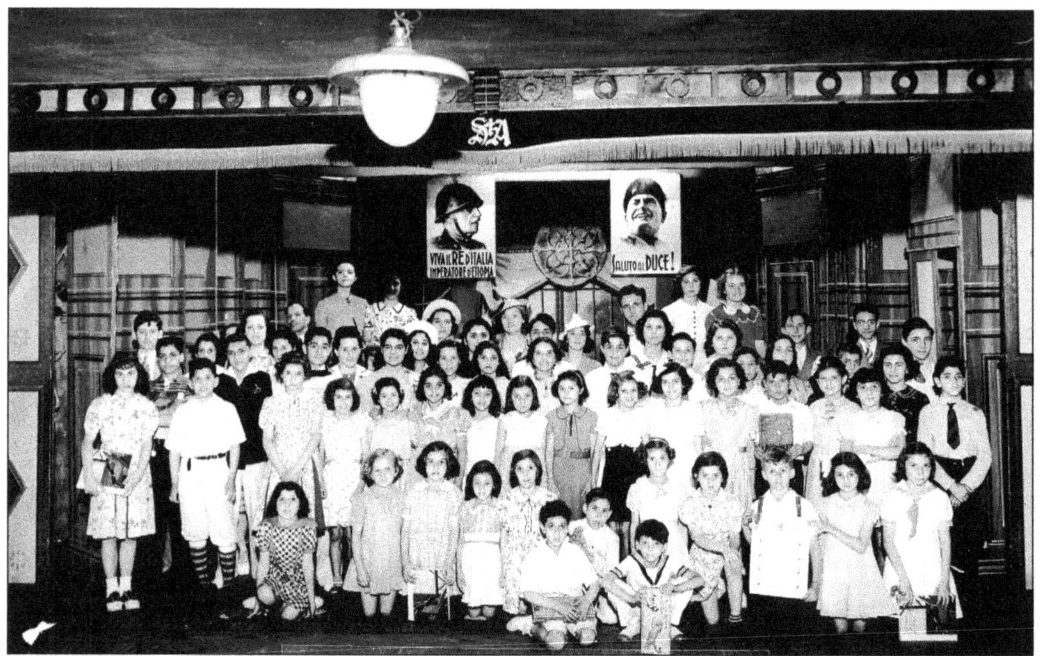

This photograph was taken in the St. Ambrose auditorium. The occasion was the handing out of certificates for success in learning the Italian language. This was an after-school Italian language program sponsored by the Italian Fascist government. Benito Mussolini, a past college professor, promoted a single national language to replace the multitude of dialects, and extended this program to the United States. (Courtesy of Pete Puleo Sr.)

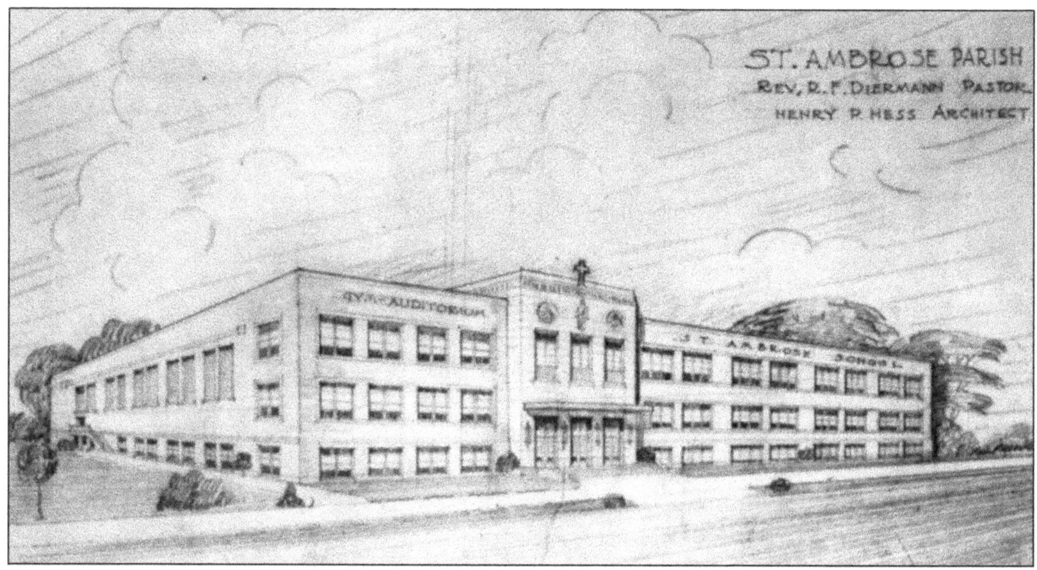

The St. Ambrose School was limited to 300 students; thousands of children in the neighborhood had to attend public school. This is a drawing of the new school, designed by architect Henry P. Hess. The school was built at the corner of Hereford Street and Wilson Avenue. (Courtesy of Faye Berra Venegoni.)

In addition to the new school, a nursery and kindergarten were built. Mother provincial of the Missionary Zelatrices of the Sacred Heart, Sister Hildegarde Campodonico, accepted this construction project. The sisters' order bought the land at the corner of Macklind and Wilson Avenues, and construction began in March 1939. (Courtesy of James Merlo.)

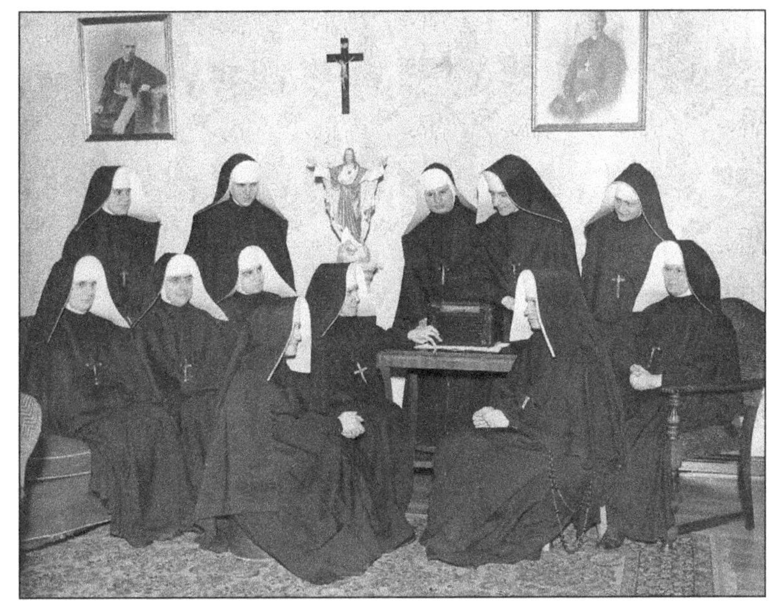

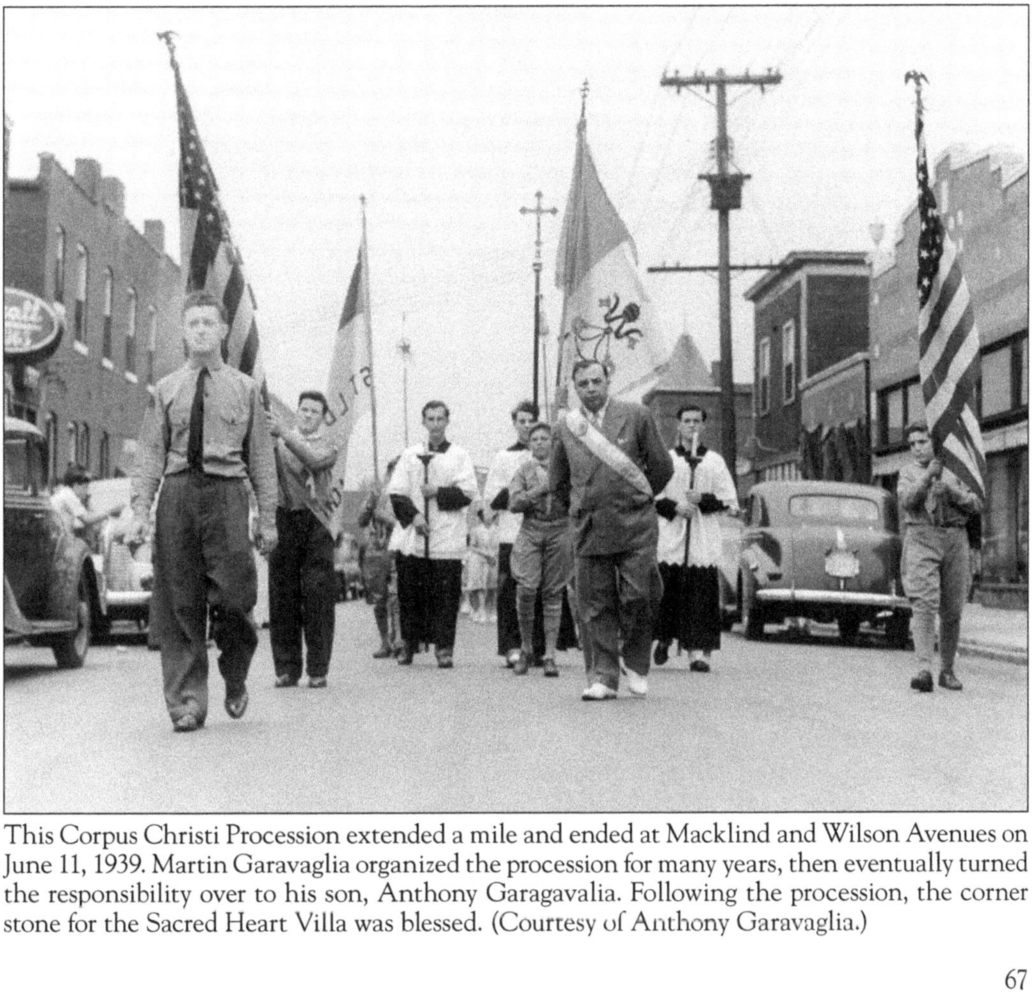

This Corpus Christi Procession extended a mile and ended at Macklind and Wilson Avenues on June 11, 1939. Martin Garavaglia organized the procession for many years, then eventually turned the responsibility over to his son, Anthony Garagavalia. Following the procession, the corner stone for the Sacred Heart Villa was blessed. (Courtesy of Anthony Garavaglia.)

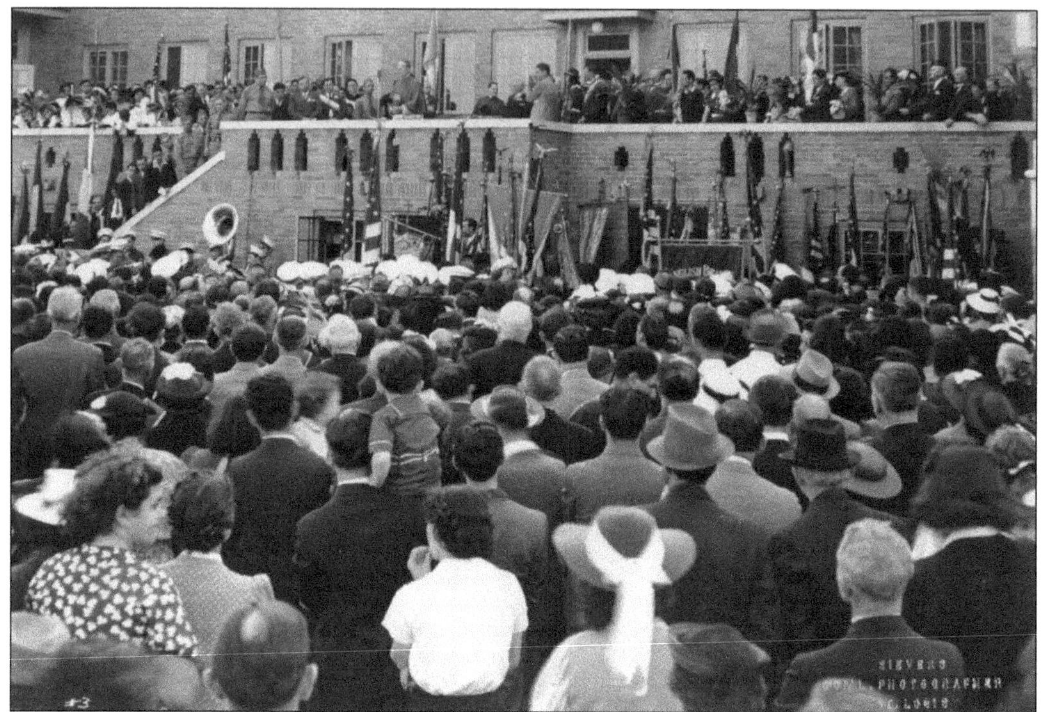

Sacred Heart Villa was dedicated with a grand procession on Mother's Day, May 17, 1940. It was led by members of the Italian World War Veterans, Emilio Rollo Post of the American Legion, followed by various Italian societies. Each organization proudly carried a set of American and Italian flags throughout the procession. The speakers' program took place in the rear of the villa's balcony. (Courtesy of Anthony Garavaglia.)

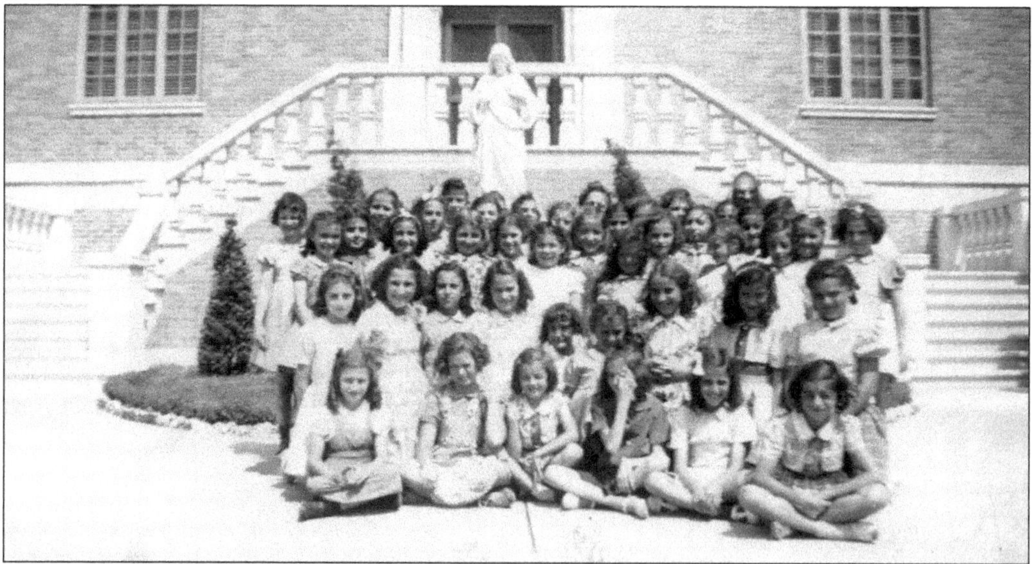

The Sacred Heart Villa day care nursery opened on January 3, 1941. Shown here is one of the early classes at the villa, where young girls learned the art of sewing, among other things. The villa provided education for children from ages three to six, preparing them with a solid base. (Courtesy of Joanne Grimoldi.)

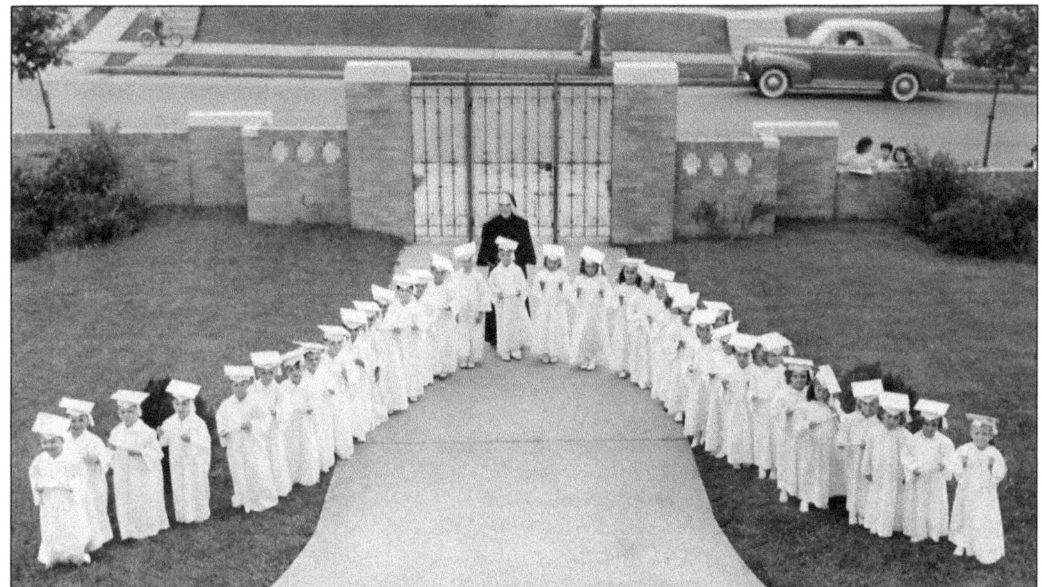

The kindergarten class of 1942 prepares for graduation at the front gates of the villa. In 1956, while continuing to teach the young children, the villa also became home to Cor Jesu Academy, an all-girls Catholic school founded by the Apostles of the Sacred Heart. (Courtesy of Judy Carlson.)

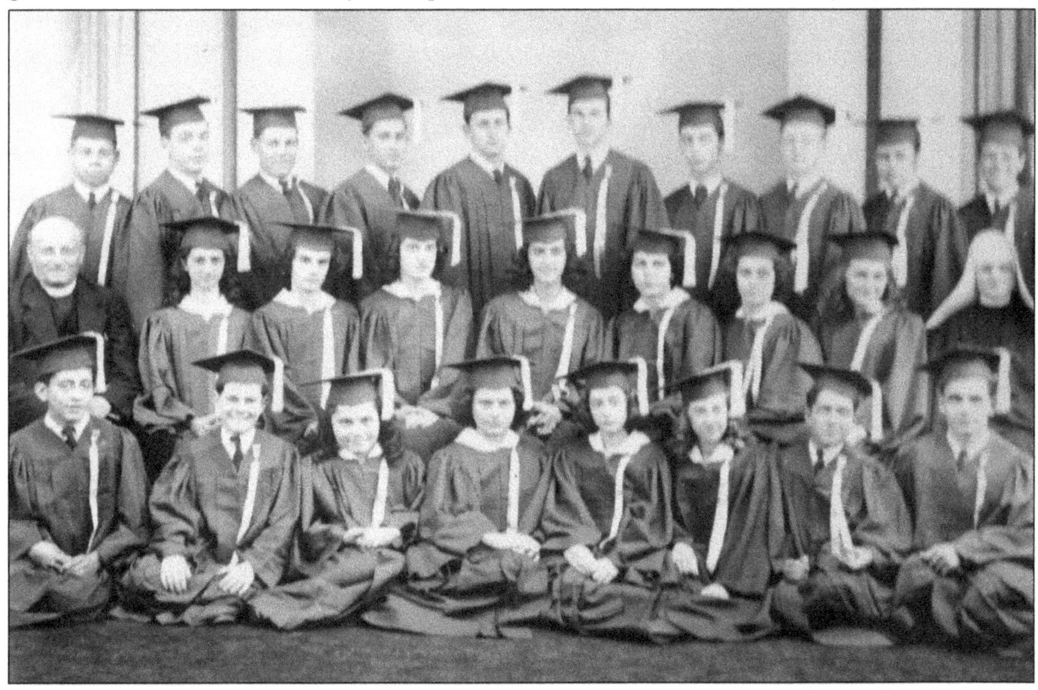

The class of 1943 of St. Ambrose School poses for a portrait. From left to right are (first row) Mike Russo, Louis Berra, Marie Ciami, Mary Gioia, Florence Castiglioni, Angelo Fassani, and Edward Spezia; (second row) Reverend Lupo, Antionette Galli, Rose Mary Cassani, Marie Baroli, Carol Tedoni, Claire Mugavero, Marie Pisoni, Josephine Mola, and Sister Assunta; (third row) Larry Tornetto, Mario Zarinelli, Ange Bianchi, Andrew Diaraghi, Paul Albanelloi, Victor Clavenna, Tony Peleteri, Louis Renerri, and Frank Lisitano. (Courtesy of Victor John Clavenna.)

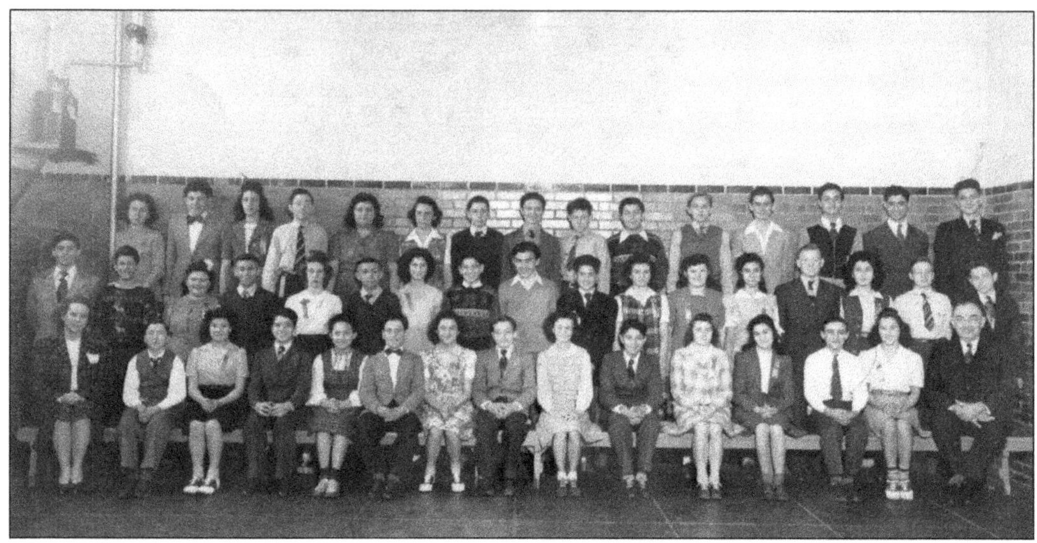

This is the Shaw School eighth-grade graduating class in January 1944. By this time, parents understood the need for education, and these children would move on to high school. Some children attended Southwest High School, and others attended one of the many Catholic high schools in St. Louis. (Courtesy of Johanna Savio Grimoldi.)

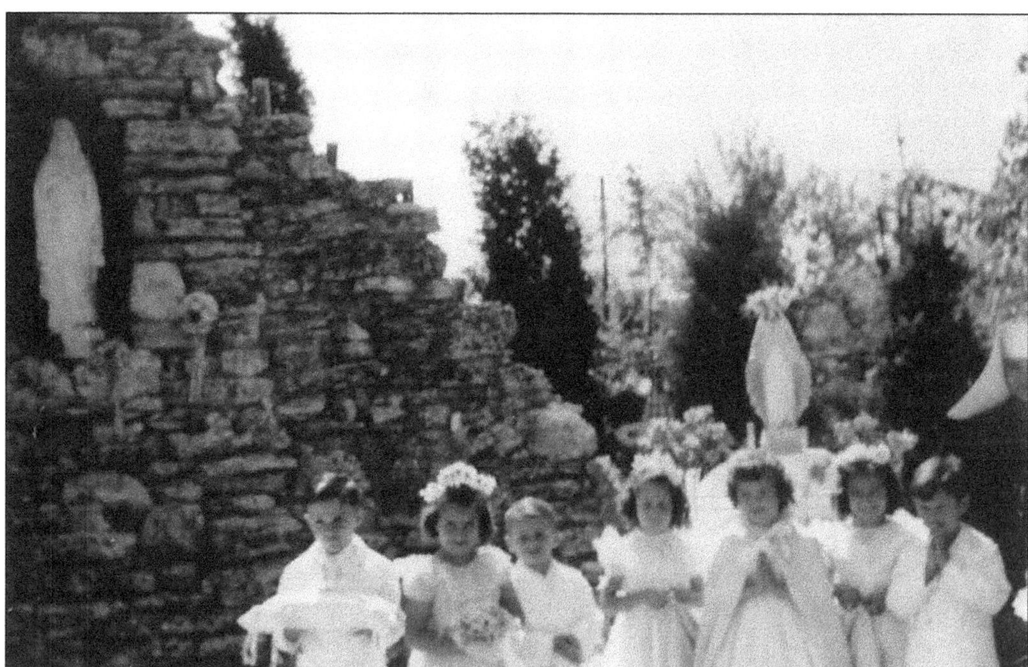

This is the May Crowning in the garden of the Sacred Heart Villa around 1947. This practice was not limited to the villa or the church. Most homes had a statue or a complete grotto in their yard. Many residents would have their own crowning, with the children of family and friends. (Courtesy of Barbara Licata.)

Seven

World War II

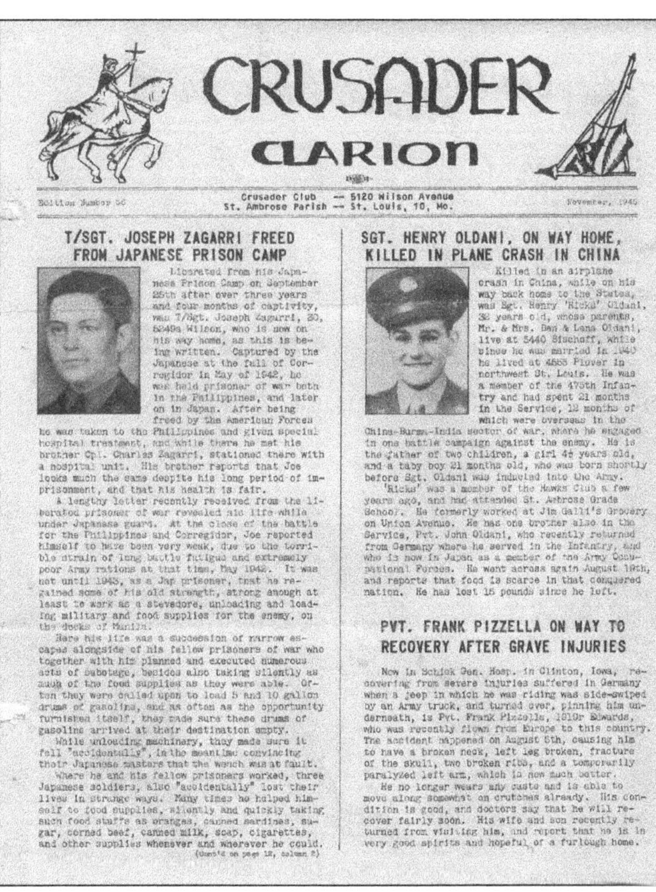

CRUSADER CLARION

Edition Number 56 | Crusader Club — 5120 Wilson Avenue
St. Ambrose Parish — St. Louis, 10, Mo. | November, 1945

T/SGT. JOSEPH ZAGARRI FREED FROM JAPANESE PRISON CAMP

Liberated from his Japanese Prison Camp on September 25th after over three years and four months of captivity, was T/Sgt. Joseph Zagarri, 30, 5249a Wilson, who is now on his way home, as this is being written. Captured by the Japanese at the fall of Corregidor in May of 1942, he was held prisoner of war both in the Philippines, and later on in Japan. After being freed by the American Forces he was taken to the Philippines and given special hospital treatment, and while there he met his brother Cpl. Charles Zagarri, stationed there with a hospital unit. His brother reports that Joe looks much the same despite his long period of imprisonment, and that his health is fair.

A lengthy letter recently received from the liberated prisoner of war revealed his life while under Japanese guard. At the close of the battle for the Philippines and Corregidor, Joe reported himself to have been very weak, due to the terrible strain of long battle fatigue and extremely poor Army rations at that time, May 1942. It was not until 1943, as a Jap prisoner, that he regained some of his old strength, strong enough at least to work as a stevedore, unloading and loading military and food supplies for the enemy, on the docks of Manila.

Here his life was a succession of narrow escapes alongside of his fellow prisoners of war who together with him planned and executed numerous acts of sabotage, besides also taking silently as much of the food supplies as they were able. Often they were called upon to load 5 and 10 gallon drums of gasoline, and as often as the opportunity furnished itself, they made sure these drums of gasoline arrived at their destination empty.

While unloading machinery, they made sure it fell "accidentally", in the meantime convincing their Japanese masters that the wench was at fault.

Where he and his fellow prisoners worked, three Japanese soldiers, also "accidentally" lost their lives in strange ways. Many times he helped himself to food supplies, silently and quickly taking such food stuffs as oranges, canned sardines, sugar, corned beef, canned milk, soap, cigarettes, and other supplies whenever and wherever he could.

(Cont'd on page 12, column 2)

SGT. HENRY OLDANI, ON WAY HOME, KILLED IN PLANE CRASH IN CHINA

Killed in an airplane crash in China, while on his way back home to the States, was Sgt. Henry 'Ricks' Oldani, 32 years old, whose parents, Mr. & Mrs. Ben & Lena Oldani, live at 5440 Bischoff, while since he was married in 1940 he lived at 4653 Plover in northwest St. Louis. He was a member of the 475th Infantry and had spent 21 months in the Service, 12 months of which were overseas in the China-Burma-India sector of war, where he engaged in one battle campaign against the enemy. He is the father of two children, a girl 4½ years old, and a baby boy 21 months old, who was born shortly before Sgt. Oldani was inducted into the Army.

'Ricks' was a member of the Hawks Club a few years ago, and had attended St. Ambrose Grade School. He formerly worked at Jim Galli's Grocery on Union Avenue. He has one brother also in the Service, Pvt. John Oldani, who recently returned from Germany where he served in the Infantry, and who is now in Japan as a member of the Army Occupational Forces. He went across again August 19th, and reports that food is scarce in that conquered nation. He has lost 15 pounds since he left.

PVT. FRANK PIZZELLA ON WAY TO RECOVERY AFTER GRAVE INJURIES

Now in Schick Gen. Hosp. in Clinton, Iowa, recovering from severe injuries suffered in Germany when a jeep in which he was riding was side-swiped by an Army truck, and turned over, pinning him underneath, is Pvt. Frank Pizzella, 1819a Edwards, who was recently flown from Europe to this country. The accident happened on August 8th, causing him to have a broken neck, left leg broken, fracture of the skull, two broken ribs, and a temporarily paralyzed left arm, which is now much better.

He no longer wears any casts and is able to move along somewhat on crutches already. His condition is good, and doctors say that he will recover fairly soon. His wife and son recently returned from visiting him, and report that he is in very good spirits and hopeful of a furlough home.

During World War II, Rev. Charles Koester wanted to keep servicemen from the Hill informed of happenings in the neighborhood. The monthly *Crusader Clarion*, which began publication during the war, was sponsored by the Crusaders Club and supported by generous friends and residents of the community. It was sent free of charge to as many servicemen as possible. The Hill is particularly proud of the 1,027 members of the armed forces who served during World War II. During the war, 23 of these young men gave the ultimate sacrifice for their country. They are remembered on a plaque that hangs in the vestibule of St. Ambrose Church. (Courtesy of Tim Valli.)

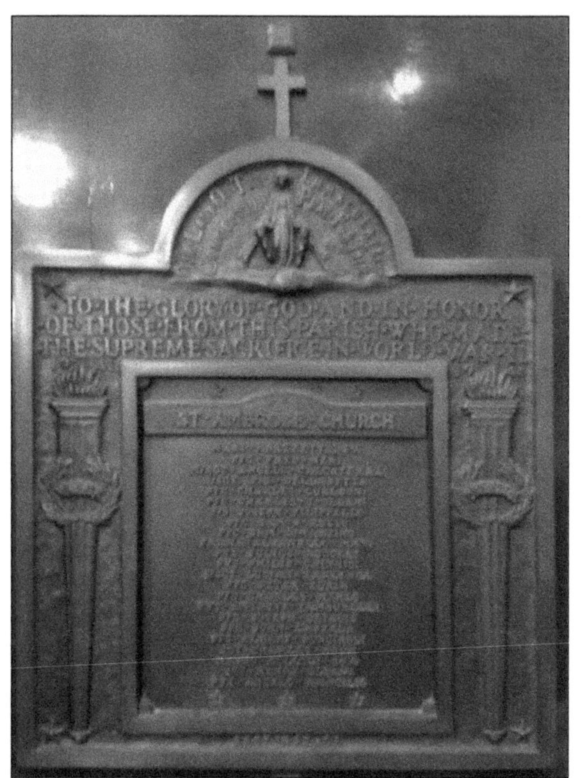

On November 24, 1947, the Rollo-Calcaterra Post of the American Legion paraded down Marconi Avenue to St. Ambrose Church for the special dedication and blessing of this plaque. Listed on the plaque are the names of the young men of the neighborhood who had answered the call to defend the nation with courageous and generous hearts. They had gone gladly, and each is remembered by name, enshrined in the church. (Courtesy of St. Ambrose Church.)

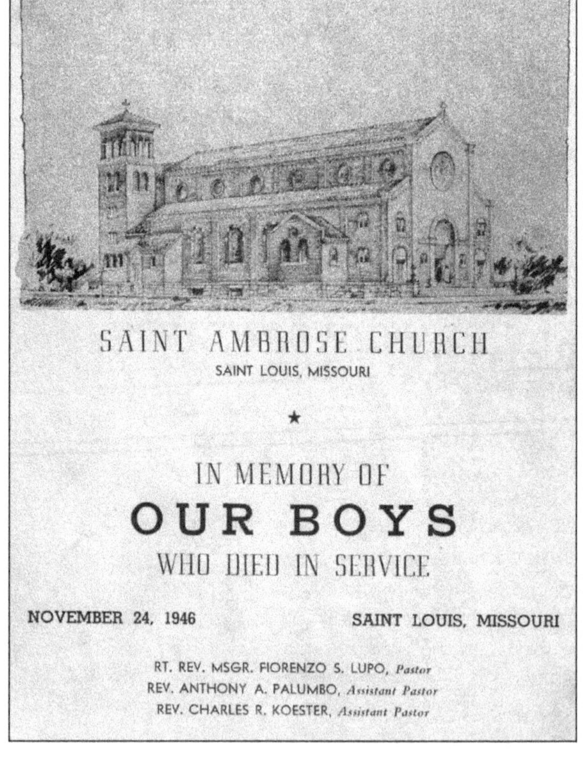

SAINT AMBROSE CHURCH

SAINT LOUIS, MISSOURI

★

IN MEMORY OF

OUR BOYS

WHO DIED IN SERVICE

NOVEMBER 24, 1946 **SAINT LOUIS, MISSOURI**

RT. REV. MSGR. FIORENZO S. LUPO, *Pastor*
REV. ANTHONY A. PALUMBO, *Assistant Pastor*
REV. CHARLES R. KOESTER, *Assistant Pastor*

This commemorative booklet was distributed on the same day that the bronze plaque was dedicated and placed in the vestibule of St. Ambrose Church. It is filled with photographs of the servicemen from the Hill who made the ultimate sacrifice during World War II. Italian American men, women, and societies contributed greatly to the war effort so that democracy could survive. (Courtesy of Tim Valli.)

Louis Belloli stands at the entrance to a building inside one of the concentration camps he helped to liberate. While the men from the Hill were fighting, residents worked in civilian jobs, manufacturing material and parts for the war effort. The Wapello Tribe No. 110, Improved Order of Red Men, was organized on the Hill on August 23, 1904. During World War I, this organization had 25 members serving in various branches of the armed services, and three times that number during World War II. (Courtesy of Dorothy Belloli Downs.)

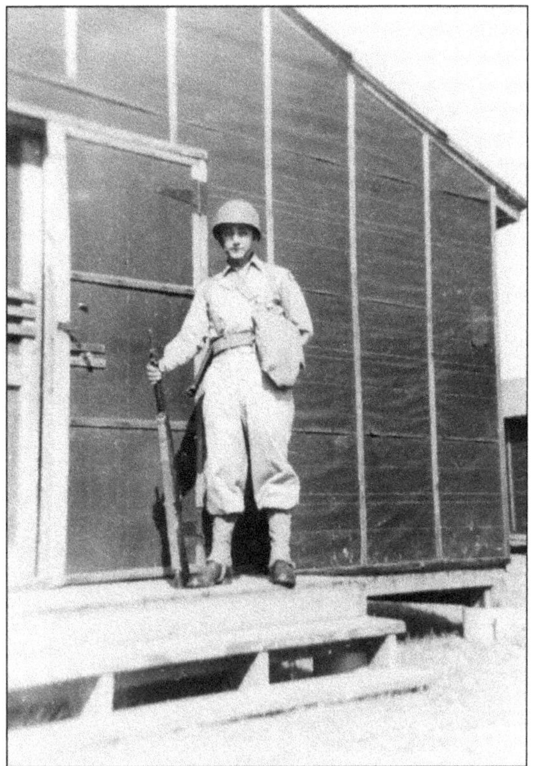

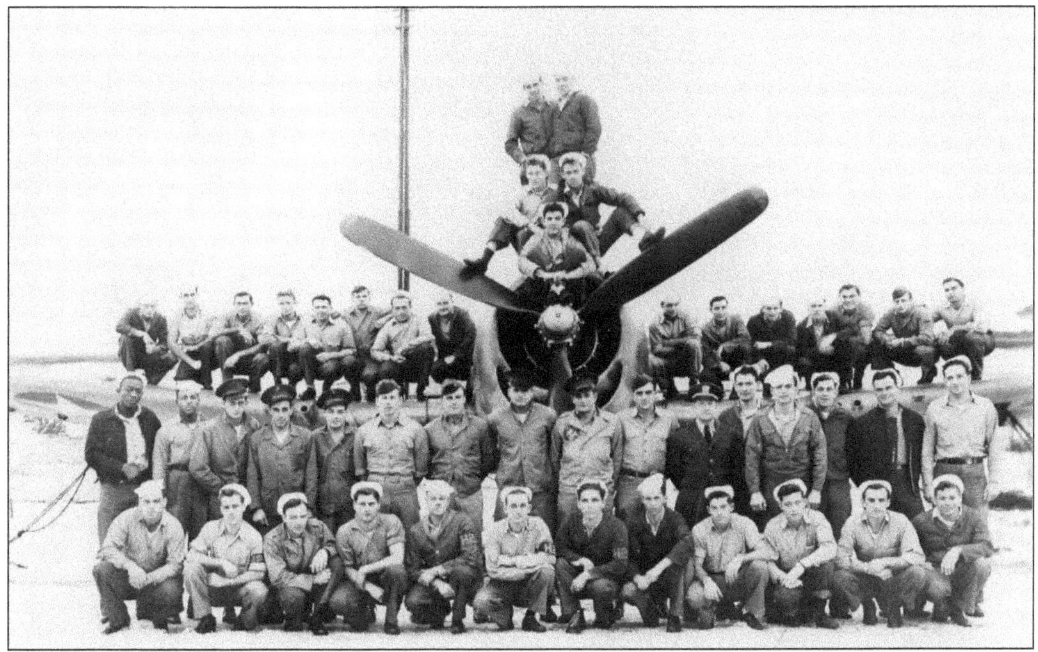

Caesar Torretti, a Hill resident, is in the front row, third from the right. He is posing with the men he served with in the Pacific during World War II, repairing aircraft. The men of the Hill served in all branches of the services, in all parts of the globe. Some men fought near or within the towns that their families came from. (Courtesy of Barbara Torretti.)

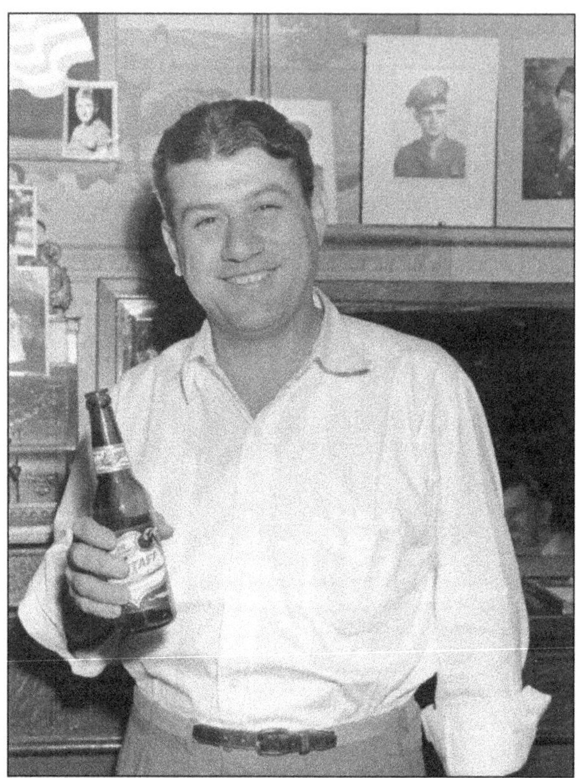

Charlie Grassi stands near the register at Charlie's Place (later to be named John and Rose's) where local soldiers' pictures were proudly displayed. This was a common practice among the establishments on the Hill. The 1940 census shows Charles Grassi living at 1931 Edwards Street with his wife, Rose, and daughter, Ann. (Courtesy of Anna Jo Hof.)

Hill residents celebrate on the day Italy joined the Allies, a turning point for the war in Europe and a joyous occasion for Italian-Americans. Upon the surrender of Japan, Henry Ruggeri opened his restaurant and tavern early, and crowds came out to celebrate. (Courtesy of Anna Jo Hof.)

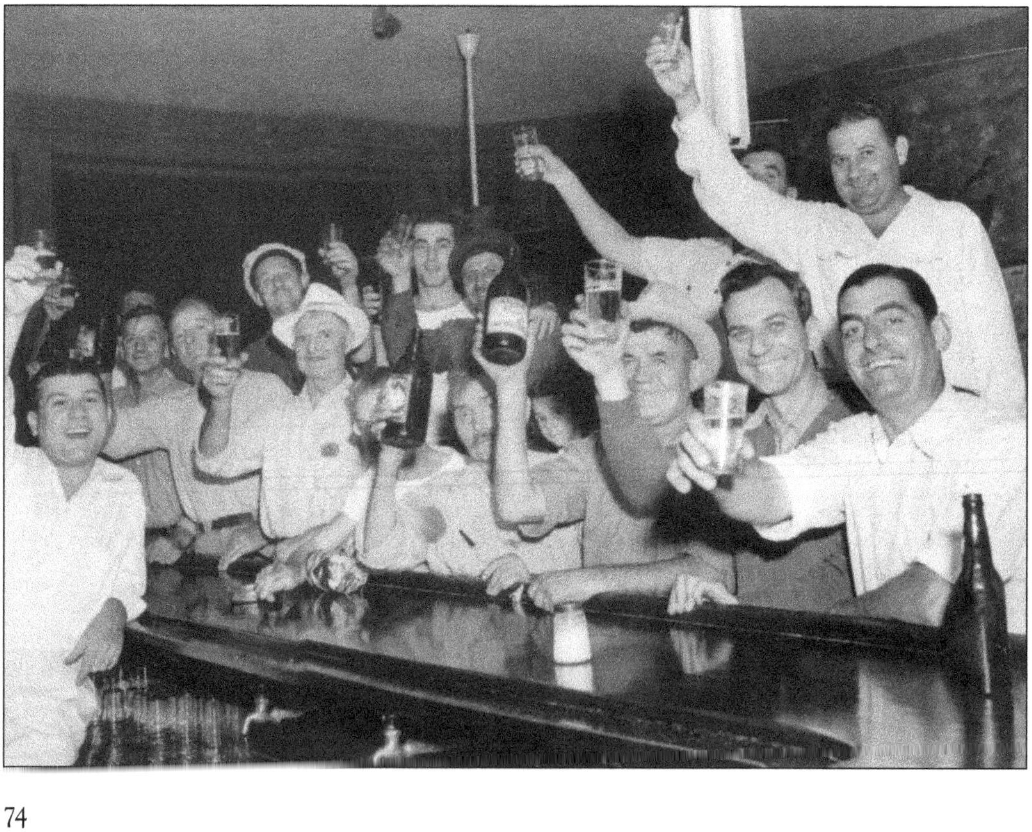

Eight

Clubs, Social Organizations, and Sports

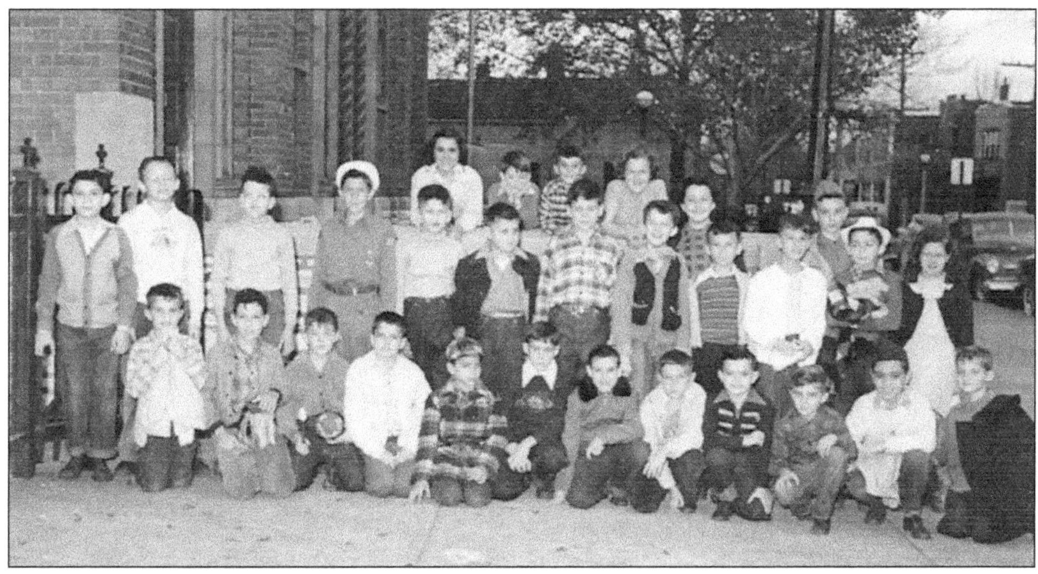

Troop 212 of the Boy Scouts of America was organized at St. Ambrose in May 1936. The church and leadership of St. Ambrose embraced and encouraged organizations dedicated to the welfare of neighborhood youth. Participation in organizations like Girl Scouts, Boy Scouts, choir, and social and athletic clubs kept the young out of trouble and focused on activities good for the mind, soul, and body. Rev. John T. Weinberg was the assistant at St. Ambrose from 1931 to 1936. He worked extremely well with the young. He founded the Crusader Club as well as Troop 212. Geographic isolation, the local economy, the Roman Catholic Church and schools, athletic clubs, and mutual-aid societies all contributed to the Hill maintaining its ethic identity. (Courtesy of James Merlo.)

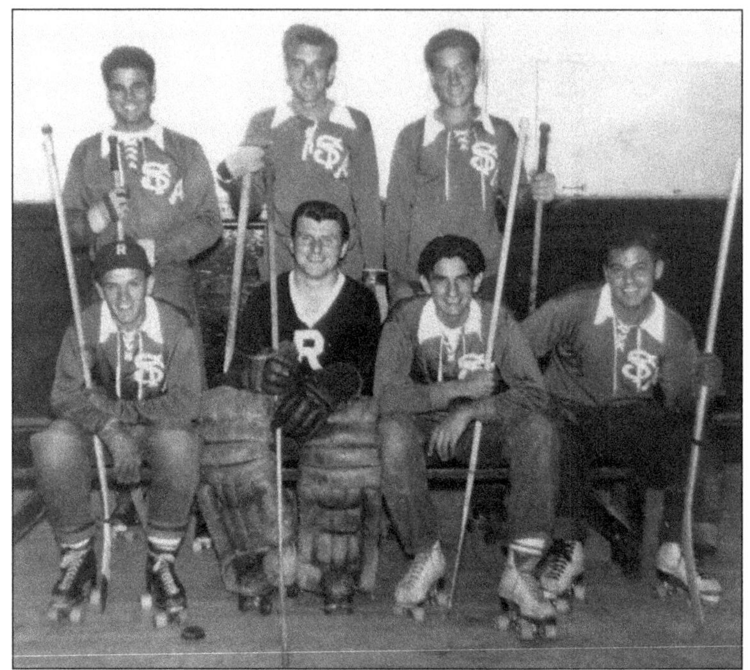

In this photograph of a roller-hockey team from the late 1930s, the goalie is proudly wearing a Ravens shirt. Identified are Sam DeGregorio, John Colombo, Barry Berra, Frank Caputa, and Sam Antonora. Sports allowed the athletes of the Hill to be introduced to American culture through their participation in games, while also continuing to reinforce the preservation and identification of their ethic culture. (Courtesy of Shari Ann Hoelzer.)

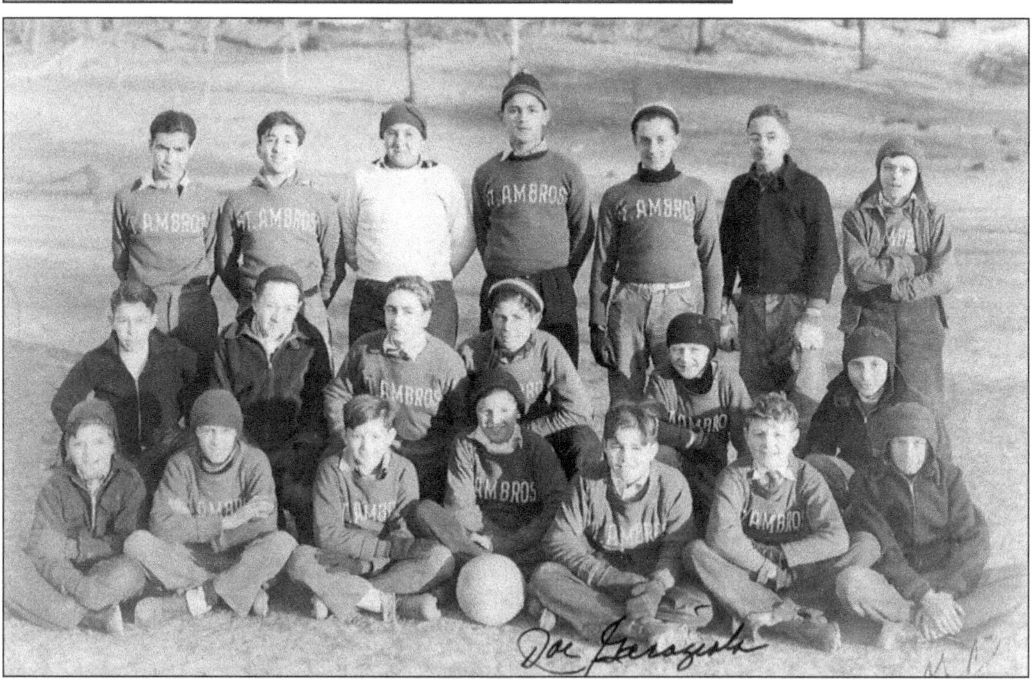

The St. Ambrose soccer city champions of 1937–1938 gather for a photograph. They are, from left to right, (first row) Louis Garavaglia, John Miriani, Bill Bartoni, Alert Ponciroli, Joe Garagiola, Henry Garegnani, and Paul "Whitey" Colombo; (second row) John Cerutti, Jon Oldani, Charles Marnati, Henry Garavaglia, Charles "Skip" Torretta, and Paul Berra; (third row) John Pedroli, Charles Barrale, Angelo Pastori, Raymond Barreni, Louis Ravetta, Ray Rapisardo, and Henry Merlo. Joe Garagiola was a future St. Louis Cardinals player and radio announcer, as well as a regular on NBC's *Today Show*. (Courtesy of James Merlo.)

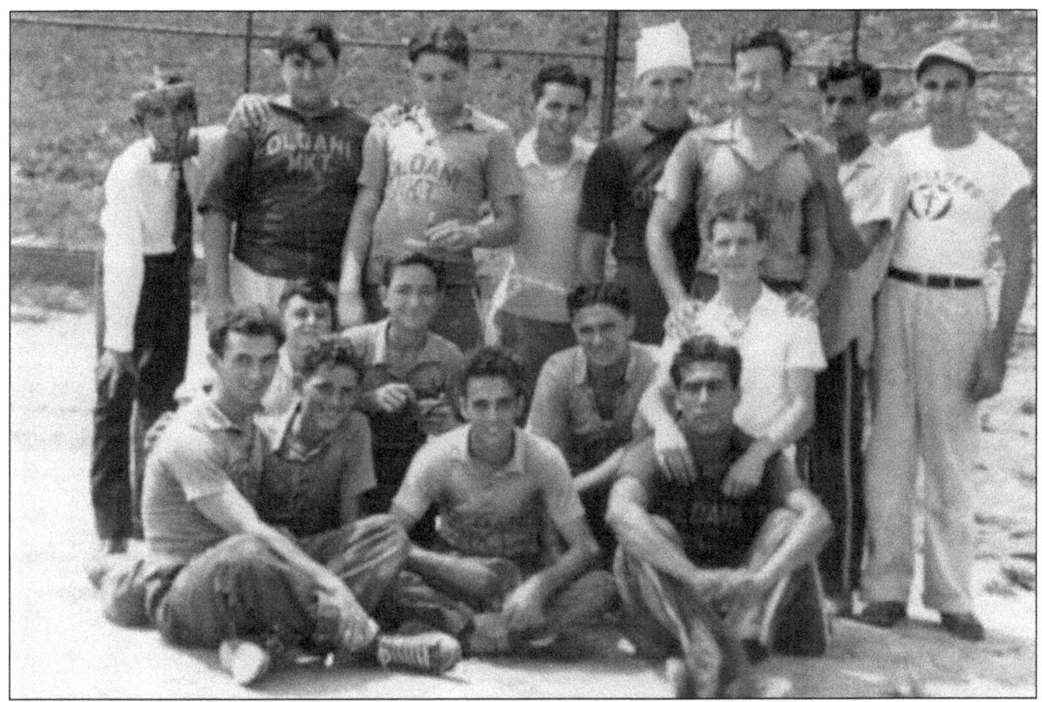

Many small businesses on the Hill sponsored sports teams, like the Oldani's Market team shown here. The Vikings played under the sponsorship of Savoy Gardens Tavern. Sponsorship was not just for the local markets or taverns. Correnti Cleaners sponsored an amateur soccer team. It was later sponsored by Joe Simpkins Ford dealership in 1947 and played a major role in US soccer. (Courtesy of Dave Tedoni.)

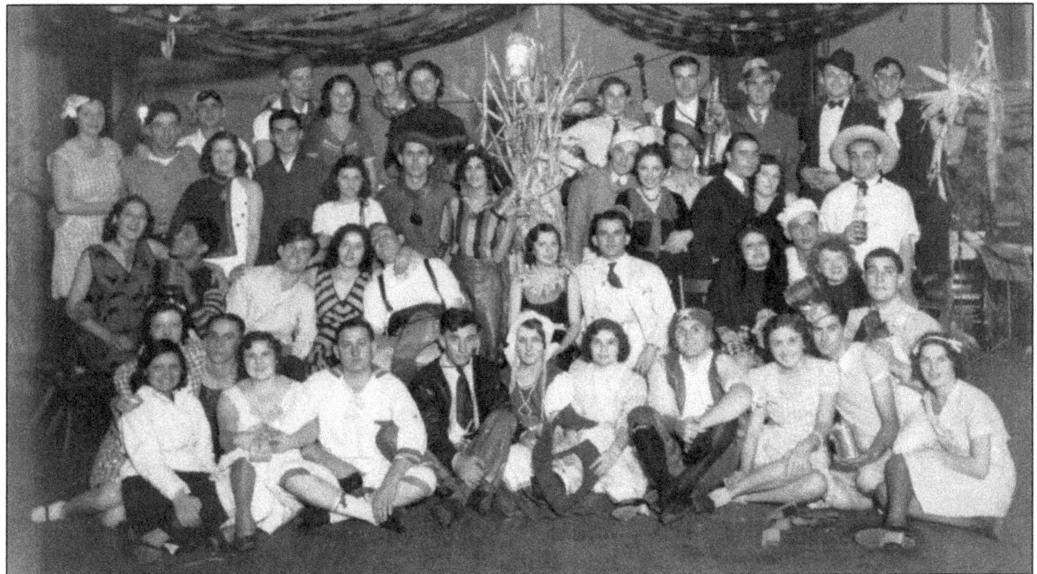

This is a 1930s costume party for the members of the Hawks Club. Sports provided an arena for the people of St. Louis to see a broader perspective of Italian Americans, unlike stereotypical depictions in the broader culture. Sports also introduced Hill residents to American traditions. (Courtesy of Fay Berra Venegoni.)

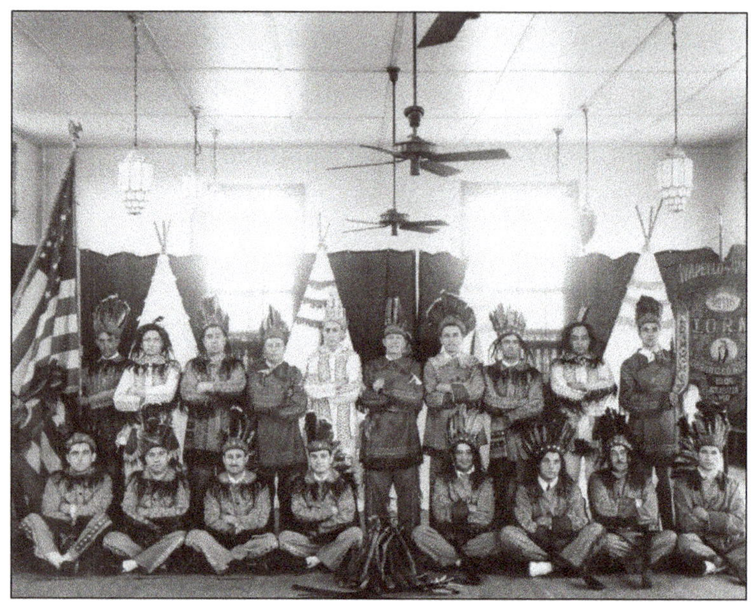

The Wapello Tribe No 110, Improved Order of Red Men existed on the Hill. Such groups benefited the neighborhood as a whole. The following mutual-aid societies existed in 1943: North Italian-American Mercantile Company, Big Club, Societa Castelltermini, Megara Augusta Society, North-Italian-American Mutual Aid Society, and many others. (Courtesy of Judy Marcallini.)

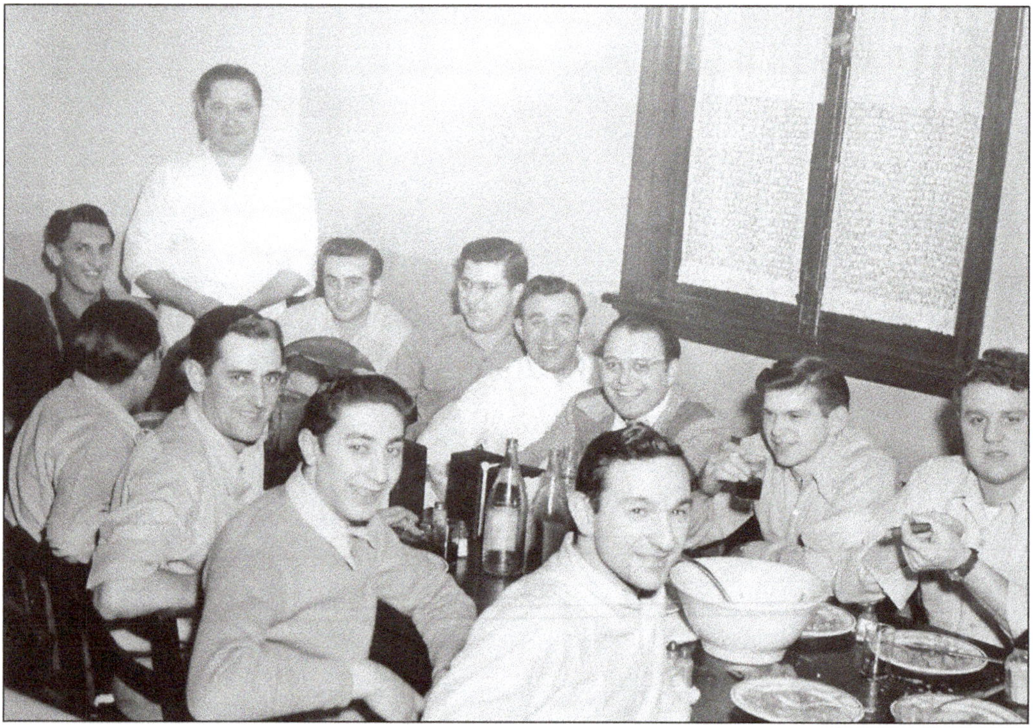

The Crusaders Club was organized and founded by Rev. John Wienberg on Easter Monday, 1935. Reverend Wienberg died in an accident in December 1936 and Reverend Palumbo succeeded him as spiritual director of the club. Identified in this photograph are, counterclockwise from front center, Paul Torno, Anthony Garagavlia, Mario Ravetta, Angelo Pastori, John Mariani, Achilli Berra (owner), Charles Ronzio, Emil Carabelli, Caesar Valli, Glenn Smith, Louis Cassani, and Rex Garegnani. (Courtesy of Armando Passetti.)

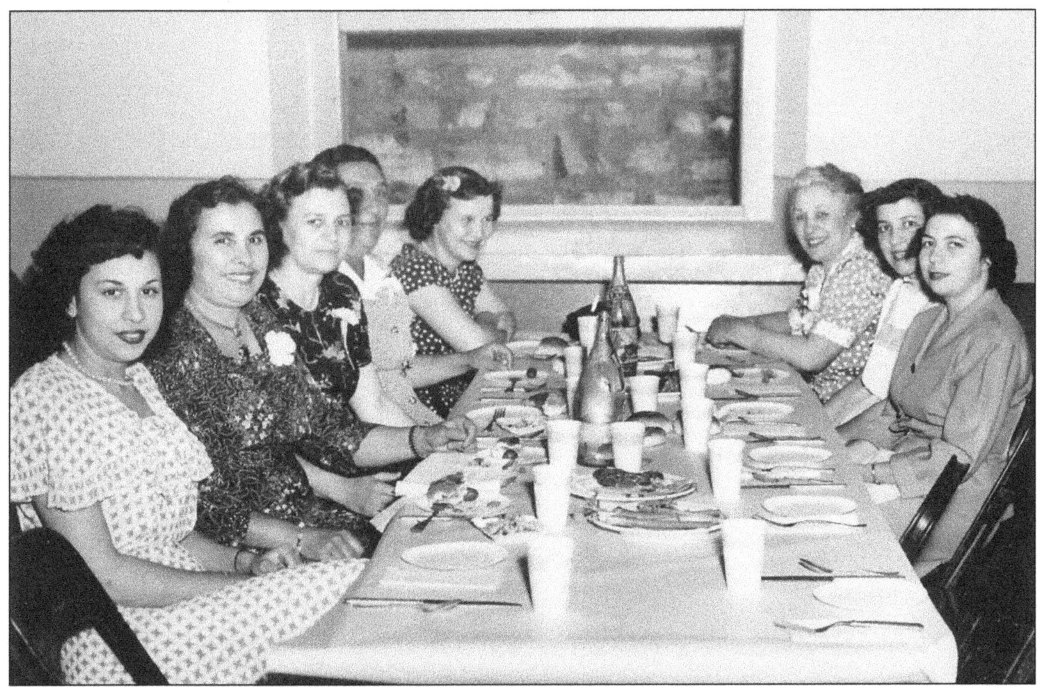

The Grail Club was organized by Rev. Adrian I. Dwyer in April 1938 for the girls of the parish. The club did not have any original officers as such, but initially consisted of leaders and members. It later became a custom to elect regular officers. (Courtesy of Armando Passetti.)

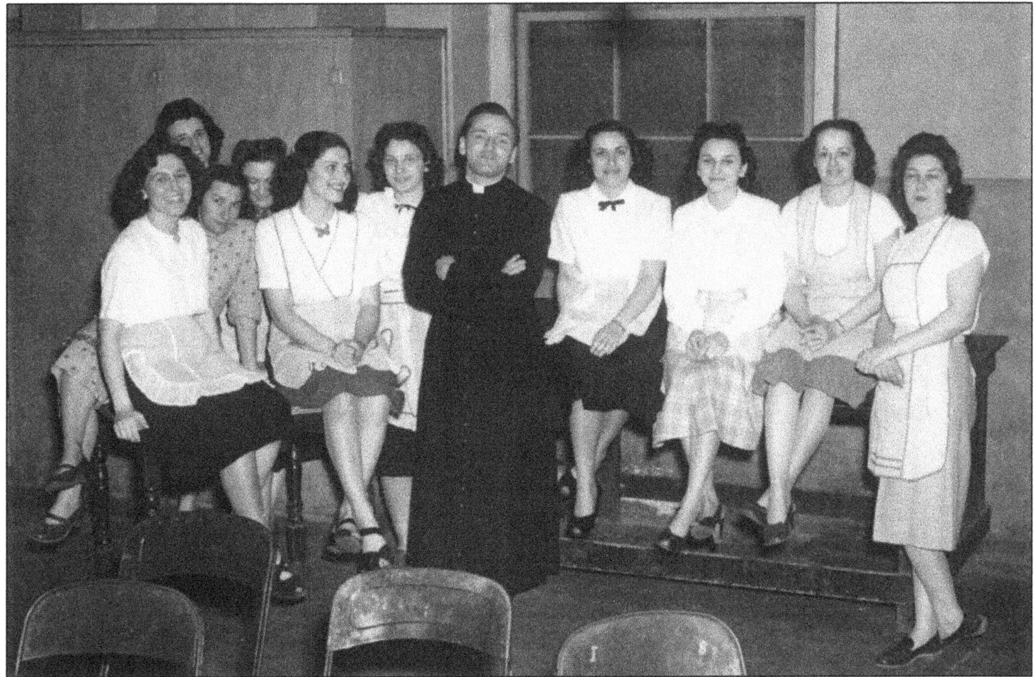

The Grail Club was organized by Rev. Adrian Dwyer in April 1938 for the purpose of encouraging spiritual ambitions and providing intellectual and physical recreation for its members. (Courtesy of Armando Passetti.)

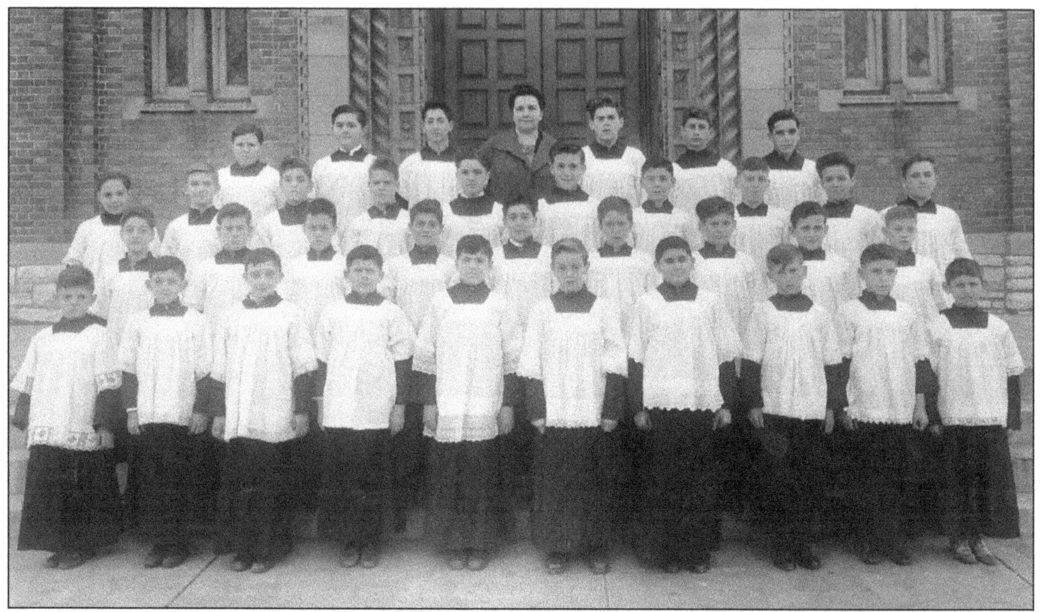

Rose Oldani (back row, center) was the organist and choirmaster for a number of years at St. Ambrose Church. She played the organ for weddings and funerals and taught piano from her home on Columbia and Southwest Avenues. (Courtesy of James Merlo.)

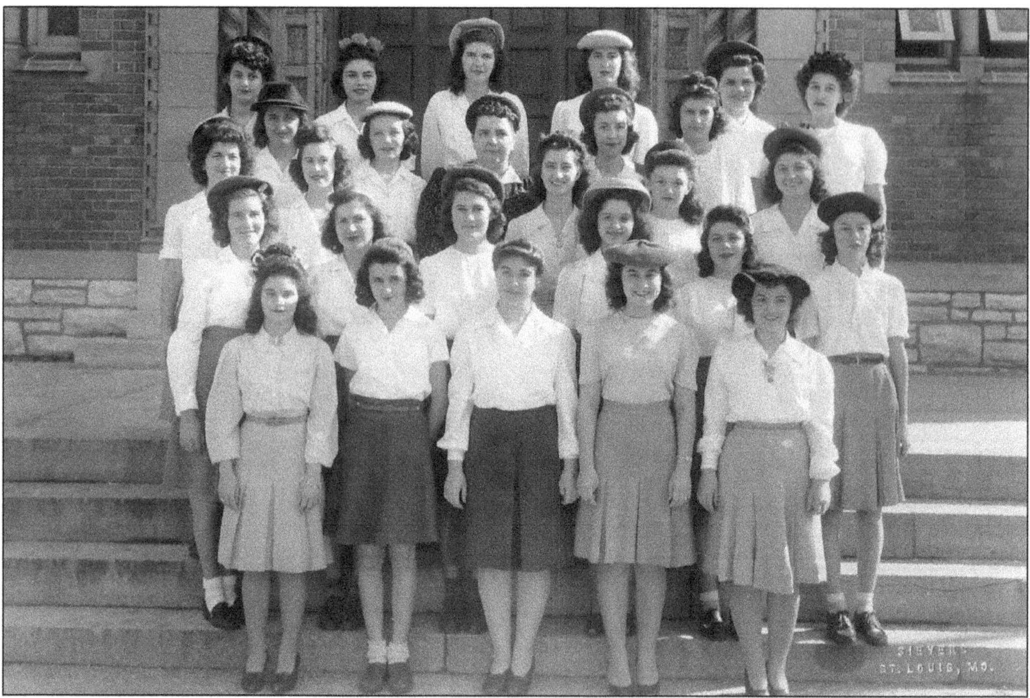

This is the St. Ambrose Young Ladies' choir. Identified are (first row) L. Mancuso, C. Mariani, J. Carnaghi, M. Puricelli, and A. Ferrario; (second row) D. Puricelli and J. Crespi; (fourth row) J. Garavaglia, I. Ceriotti, Rose Oldani (organist and choir director), R.M. Garavaglia, and M.A. Berra; (fifth row) A. Di Franco, R. Zarinelli, P. Bertani, A. Colombo, E. Oldani, and L. Novarra. (Courtesy of James Merlo.)

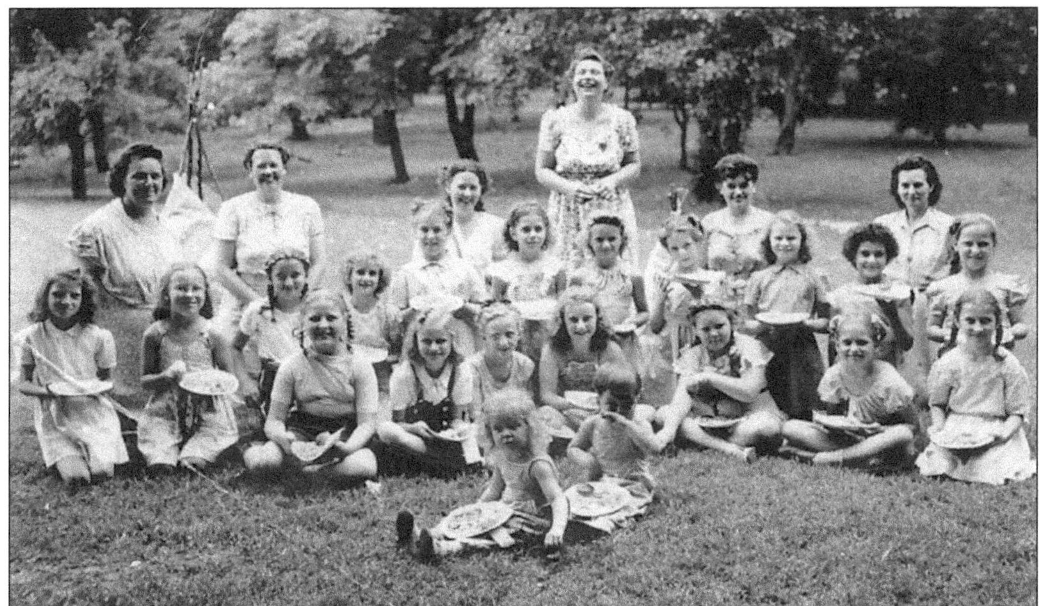

This group of Brownies holds a meeting at Tower Grove Park. Such activities provided an entry for the young into American culture, allowing them to feel welcome among people outside the Hill. (Courtesy of Judy Carlson.)

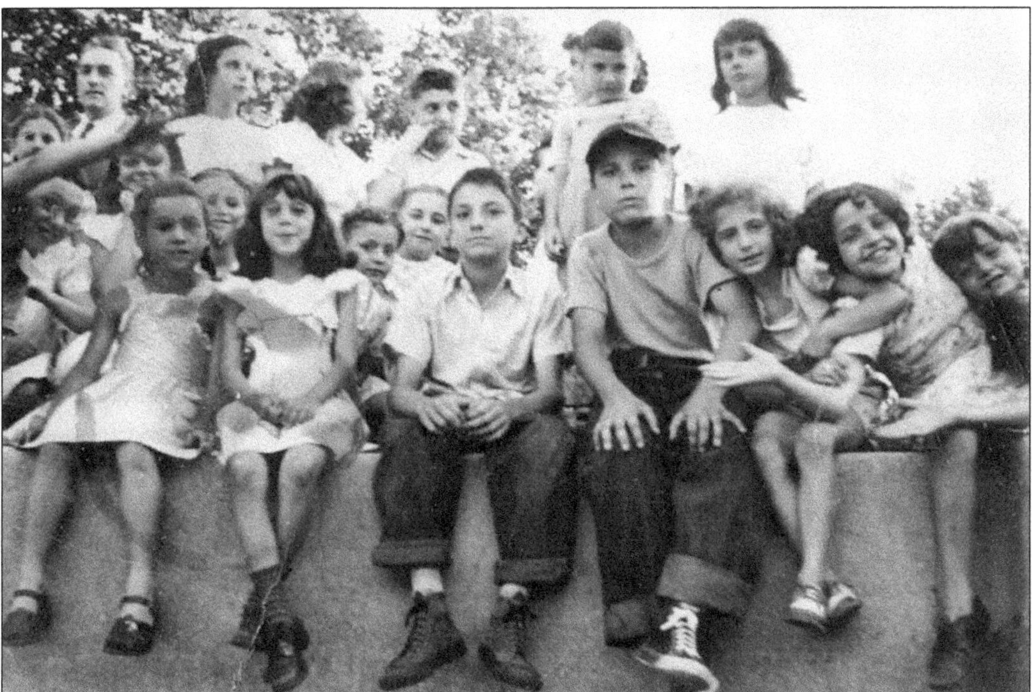

Children sit on the edge of the pool at Shaw Playground around 1947. In addition, the school had a playground and open spaces to hit a tennis ball or play baseball. This was a common meeting place for the children of the neighborhood outside of St. Ambrose. The school continues to operate today in the same location, on the corner of Macklind and Columbia Avenues. (Courtesy of Judy Carlson.)

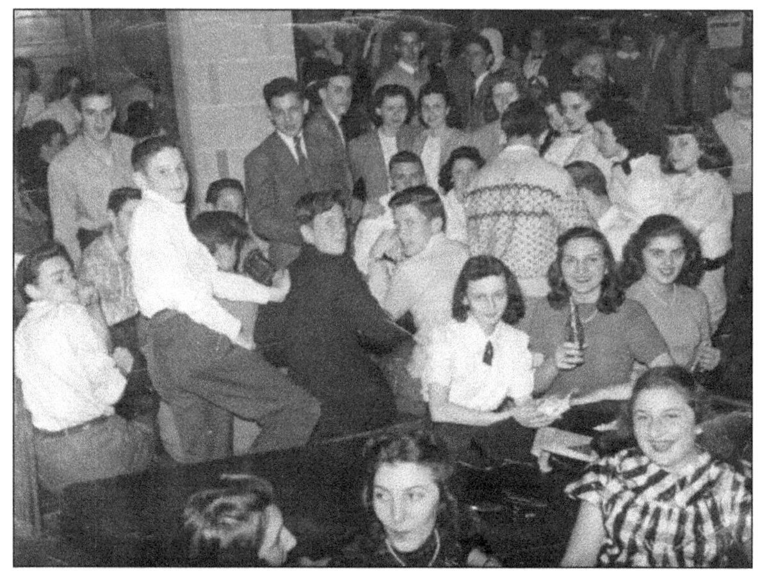

These children from the Hill are attending Teen Town night at Holy Innocents Parish about 1947. Many children in this generation would become familiar with American culture and move into neighborhoods surrounding the Hill. The priest chaperoning the event would tap the teens dancing too closely and tell them to leave space for the Holy Ghost. (Courtesy of Joanne Grimoldi.)

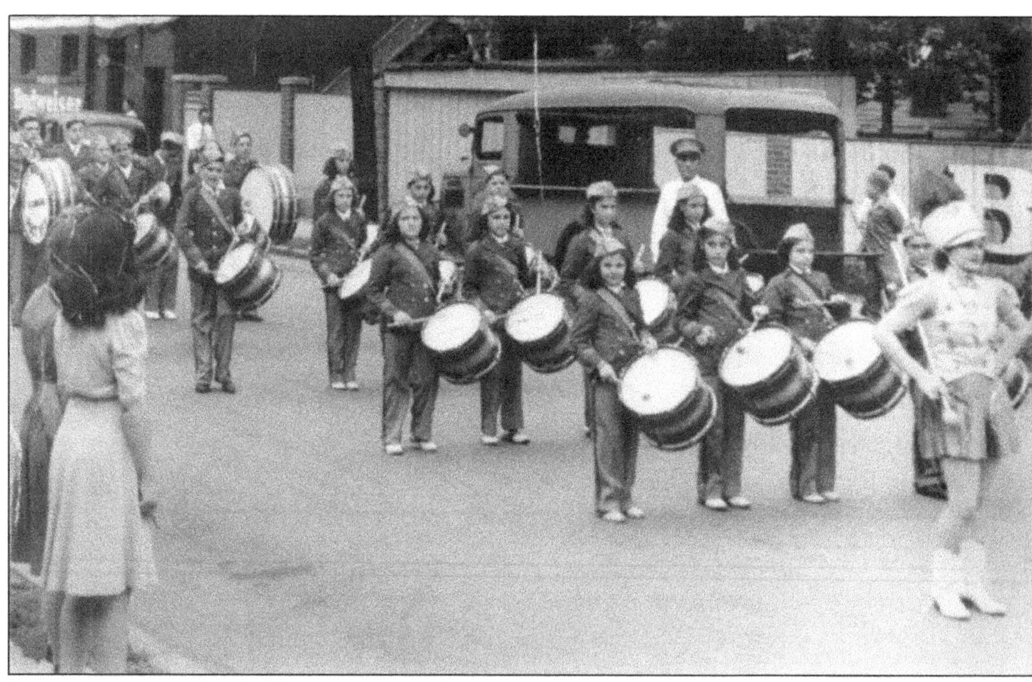

It was customary for children receiving their First Communion to march in the Corpus Christi Procession. Members of the armed forces, the police, scouts, and other organizations escorted the procession. Music was provided by a choir or band; the Drum and Bugle Corps would perform for many of the processions on the Hill. Here, it marches in the Corpus Christi Procession in 1947. The Drum and Bugle Corps was sponsored by the Italian Veterans of World War I and was led by John Barni. (Courtesy of Joanne Grimoldi.)

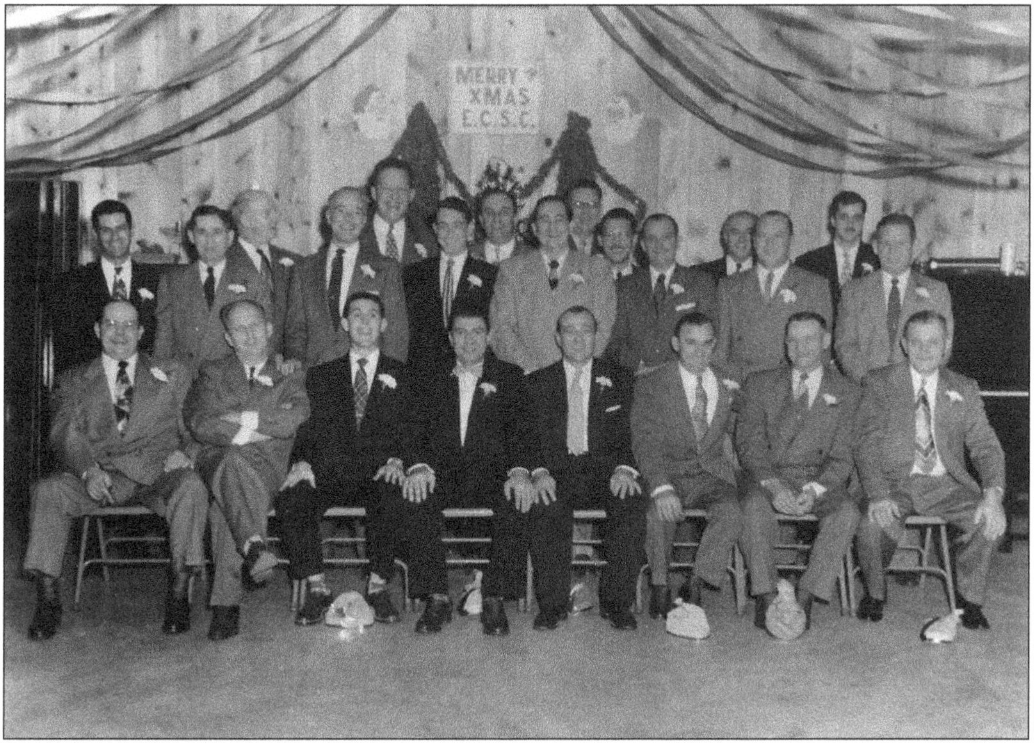

The men from the Hill who worked at McQuay Norris had a Christmas club. They would save part of each paycheck in order to purchase presents for their families and have a Christmas party. McQuay Norris built a large plant that extended from Marconi and Bischoff Avenues to Marconi and Southwest Avenues. A manufacturer of piston rings and engine parts, the firm became a major employer for the residents. (Courtesy of Barbara Torretti.)

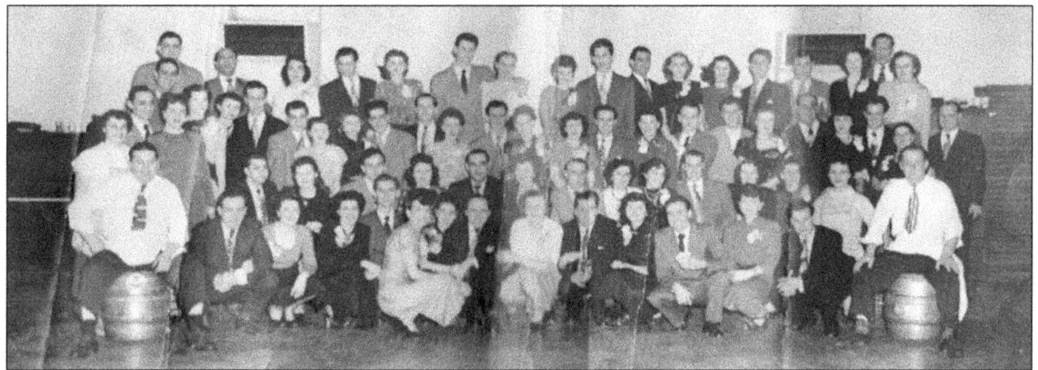

The Fawns Banquet in 1949 was an evening of fun, dancing, and music. Many men's clubs had a wives' auxiliary, and banquets such as this were an opportunity for husbands and wives of the clubs to get together. College became an alternative for Hill residents after World War II, with help from the GI Bill and athletics programs. (Courtesy of Anna Jo Hof.)

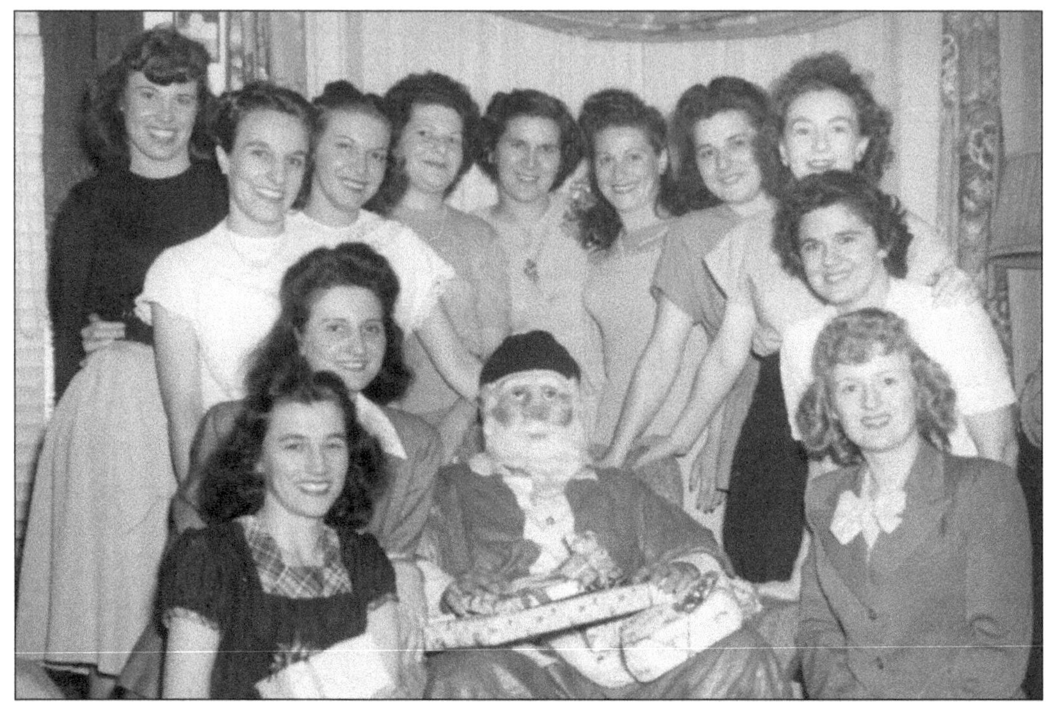

Members of the Rametts get together for a baby shower. Many clubs would arrange a night out at the Big Club Hall. Members of clubs or organizations stayed together long past the young adult years; many surviving members continue to meet today. (Courtesy of Martina Garagiola Bettlach.)

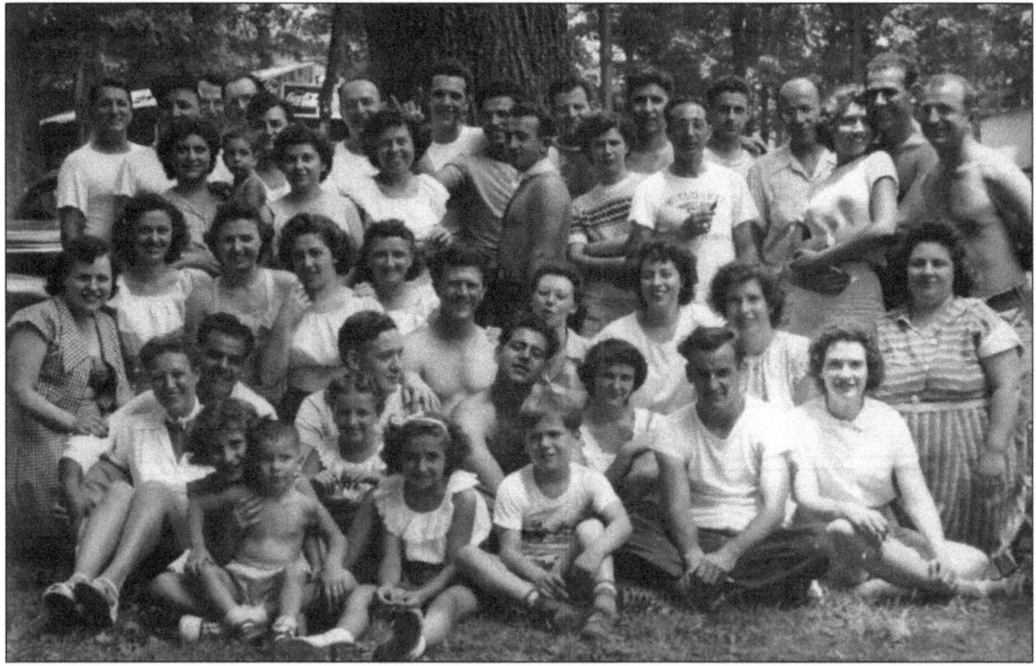

Shown here is a Royal Falcons family picnic about 1950. The end of the war did not change the camaraderie felt within these clubs. Annual picnics, community events, and St. Ambrose Church were common places to meet. (Courtesy of Martina Garagiola Bettlach.)

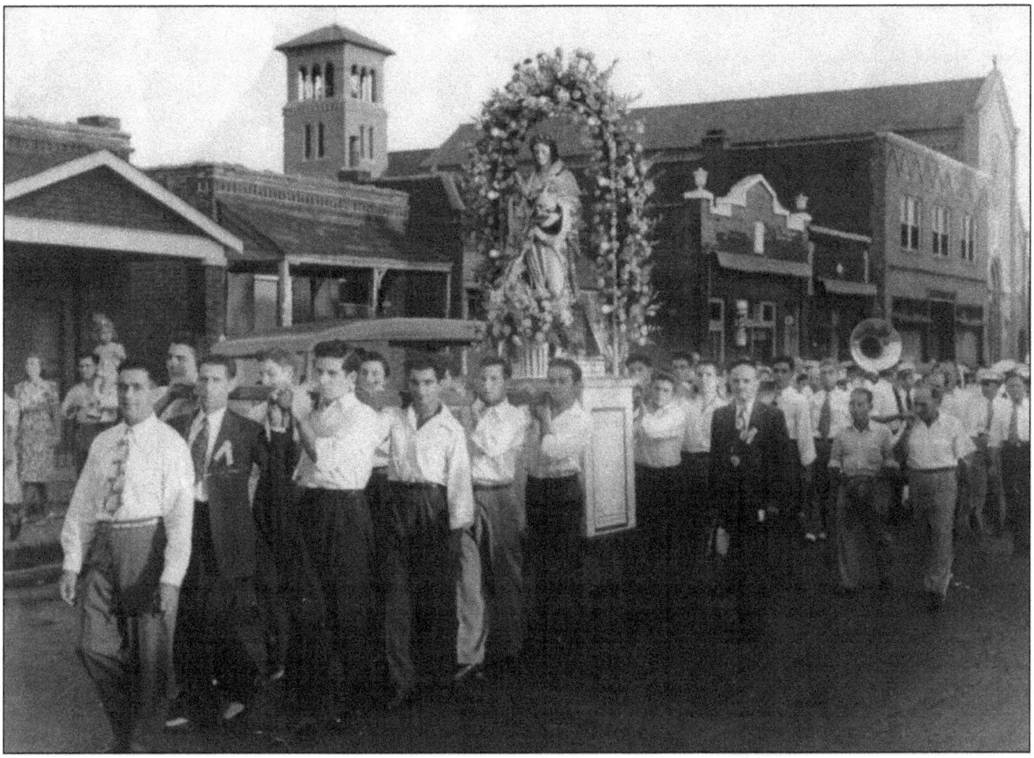

This procession was in honor of Santa Rosalia, patron saint of Palermo, Sicily. Many feast days were celebrated on the Hill, some for the patron saints of the towns in Italy where residents came from. Other feasts, like Corpus Christi, are special for all Catholics. Though some saints' days may have been regional in Italy, everyone participated on the Hill. (Courtesy of Rich LoRusso.)

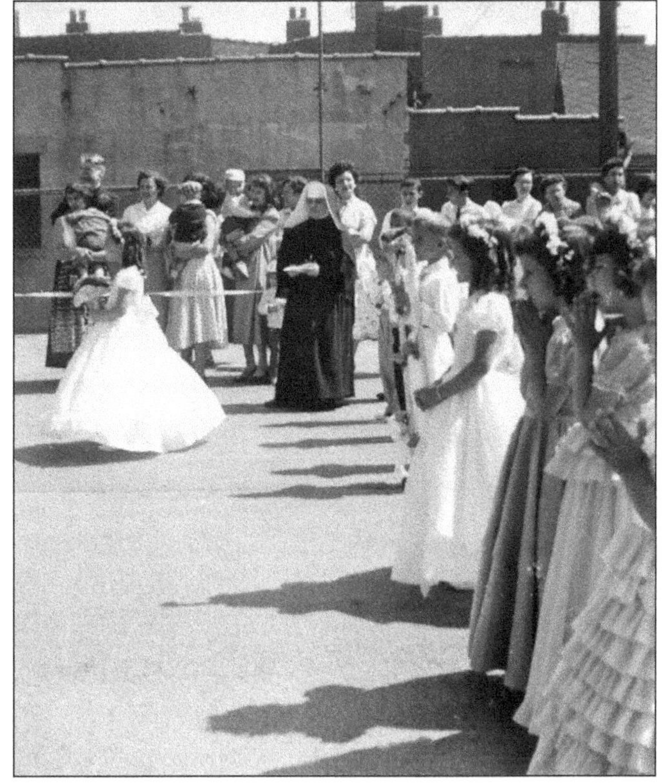

St. Ambrose School honors the May Crowning tradition before one of the weekly all-school Masses. These children are participating in the annual crowning of the statue of the Blessed Virgin by the May Queen. A student representing the whole community is chosen to place a crown on Mary, the mother of Jesus. (Courtesy of Faye Berra Venegoni.)

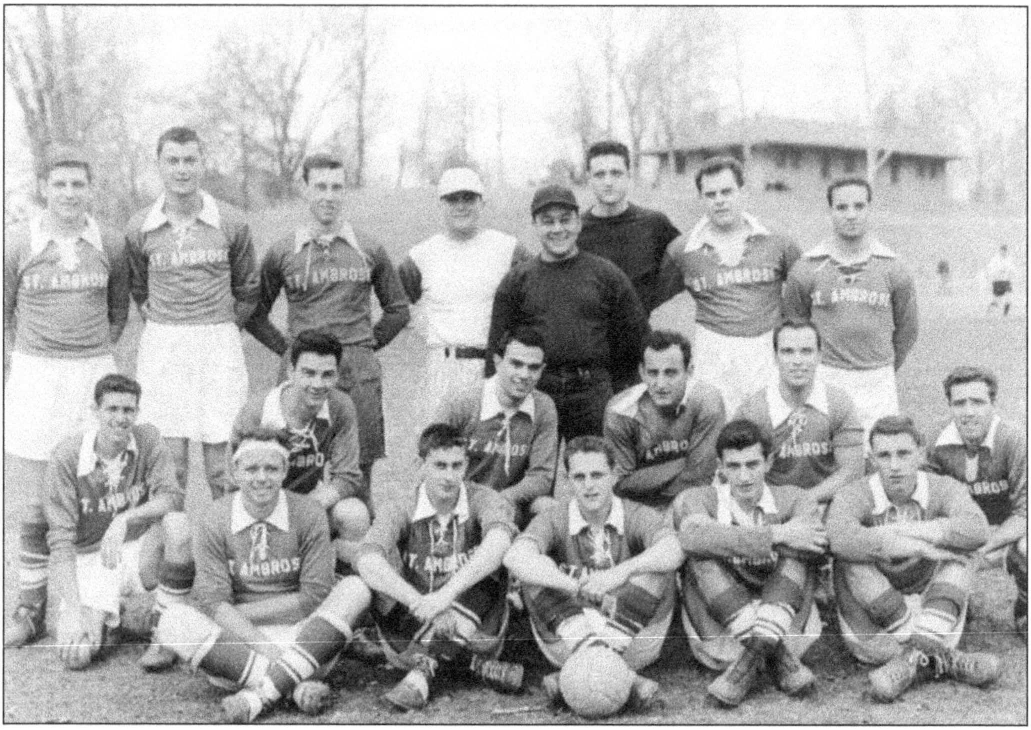

The enthusiasm for soccer gave emphasis to the ethnic identity of the Hill. This is only one of the St. Ambrose successful senior men's soccer teams. From left to right are, (first row) Ray Kurcher, Charlie "Chaleen" Miramonti, Frank "Red" Fararra, Rich "Skinny" Pozzini, and Vasco Gasperoni; (second row) Ray Farina, Ray Puricelli, Joe Reno, Al Nazoli, Charlie "Mott" Calcaterra, and Aldo Farina; (third row) Bob "House" Garavaglia, Gene Cucchi, Jim Krull, Pat Delesandro, "Bubbles" San Fillipo, Herman Valli, Ron Colombo, and Sam Sapienza. (Courtesy of James Merlo.)

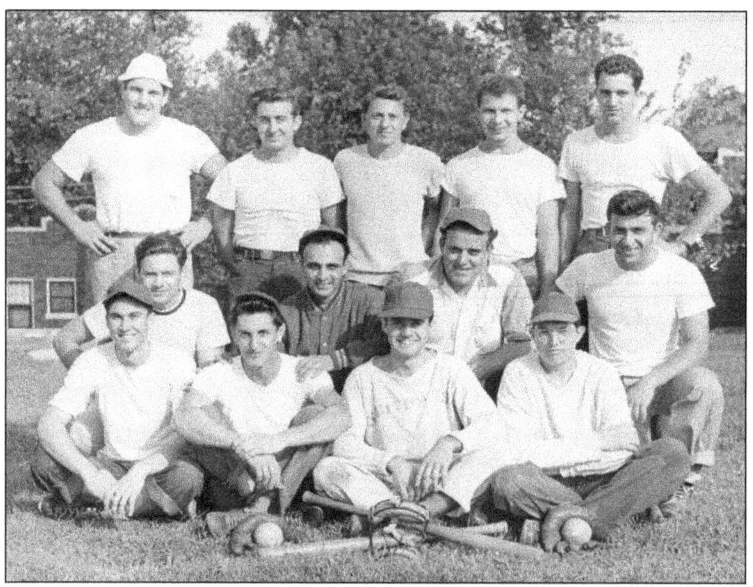

Young men played together on many baseball teams in the neighborhood. Shown here are, from left to right, (first row) Vic Clavenna, John Mirani, Roy Russo, and Pete Ferrario; (second row) John Macchi, Joe Traina, Silvo Milani, and Caesar Valli; (third row) Joe Oldani, Leo Garavaglia, Lino Balloni, Louis Bottini, and Joe Rapisardo. (Courtesy of Lance Bottini.)

Frank "Creepy" Crespi played for the St. Louis Cardinals from 1938 to 1942. He played in 146 games in 1941 and 93 games in 1942 and appeared in one World Series game, against the New York Yankees in 1942. He was drafted into the Army in 1943. Though he qualified for a deferment as the sole supporter of his elderly mother, he refused it, saying he wanted to fight for his country. (Author's collection.)

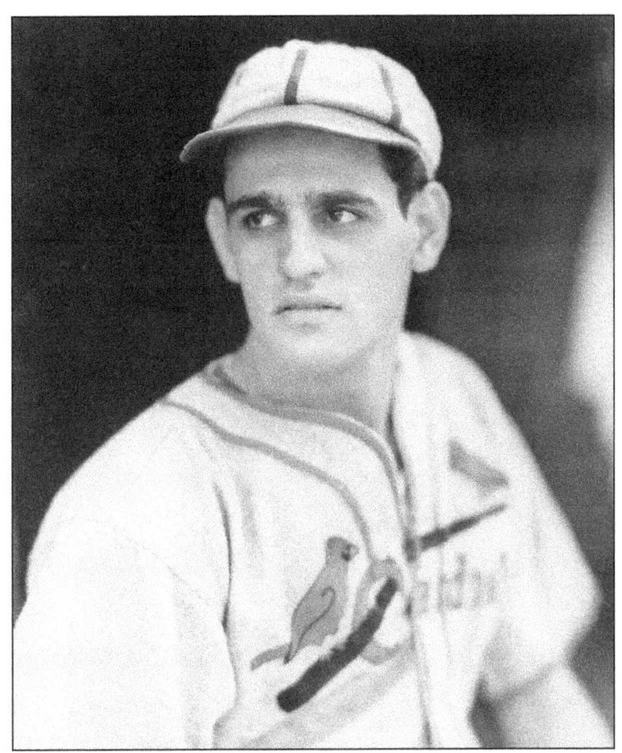

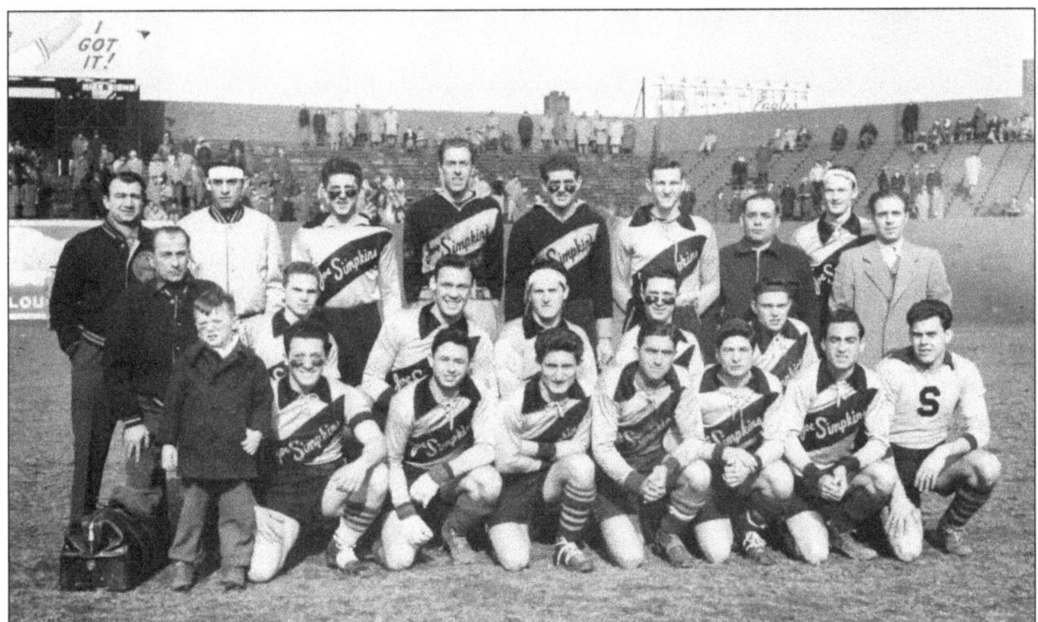

Joe Numi coached the Simpkins soccer team, winners of the US soccer championship in 1948. In 1950, Numi coached the Simpkins team in winning the league title and the National Challenge Cup. Among the team's players, Robert Annis, Gino Pariani, Charlie Colombo, Frank Borghi, and Frank Wallace would play on the 1950 World Cup team. This team inspired a book written by Geoffrey Dougals, *The Game of Their Lives*. A movie of the same name followed in 2005. (Courtesy of Missouri Bakery.)

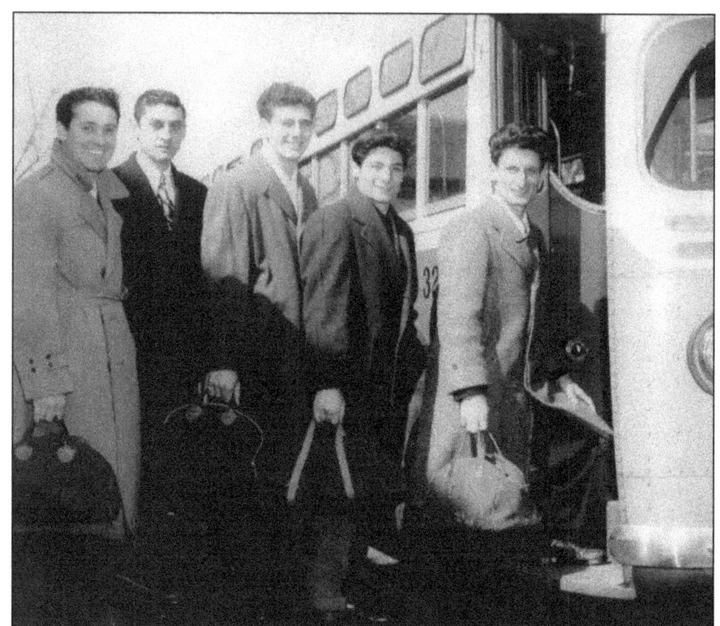

Loading the bus for another soccer game are, from left to right, Mike Montani, Leo Lang, Frank Borghi, John Barrale, and Gino Pariani. These men would represent the Hill in the United States and around the world. By 1955, six men from the Hill would play professional baseball, and 12 would play professional soccer. (Courtesy of Marcia Barrale DeSpain.)

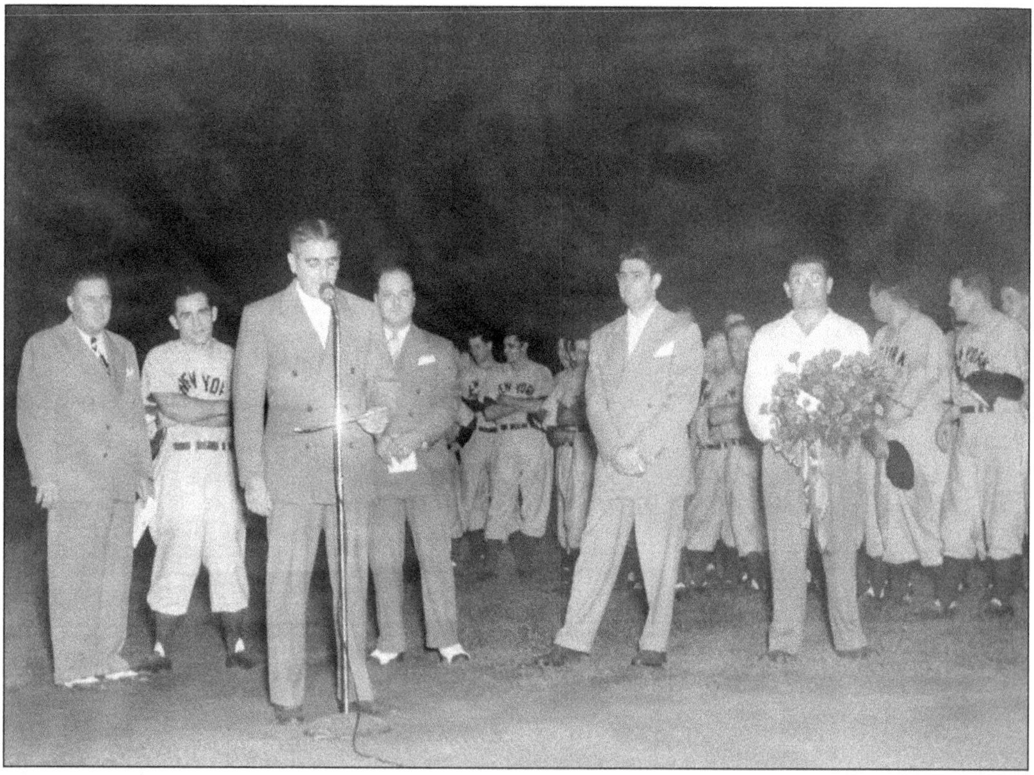

This photograph was taken at Sportsman's Park in St. Louis during Lawrence "Yogi" Berra Night at the ballpark. The New York Yankees were in town playing the St. Louis Browns. The Hill was honoring Berra, a native son, that night. It was on this occasion that Berra (second from left) said, "I want to thank all those who made this night necessary." Paul Calcaterra is at the microphone, and Mike Grassi is holding the flowers. (Courtesy of Lance Bottini.)

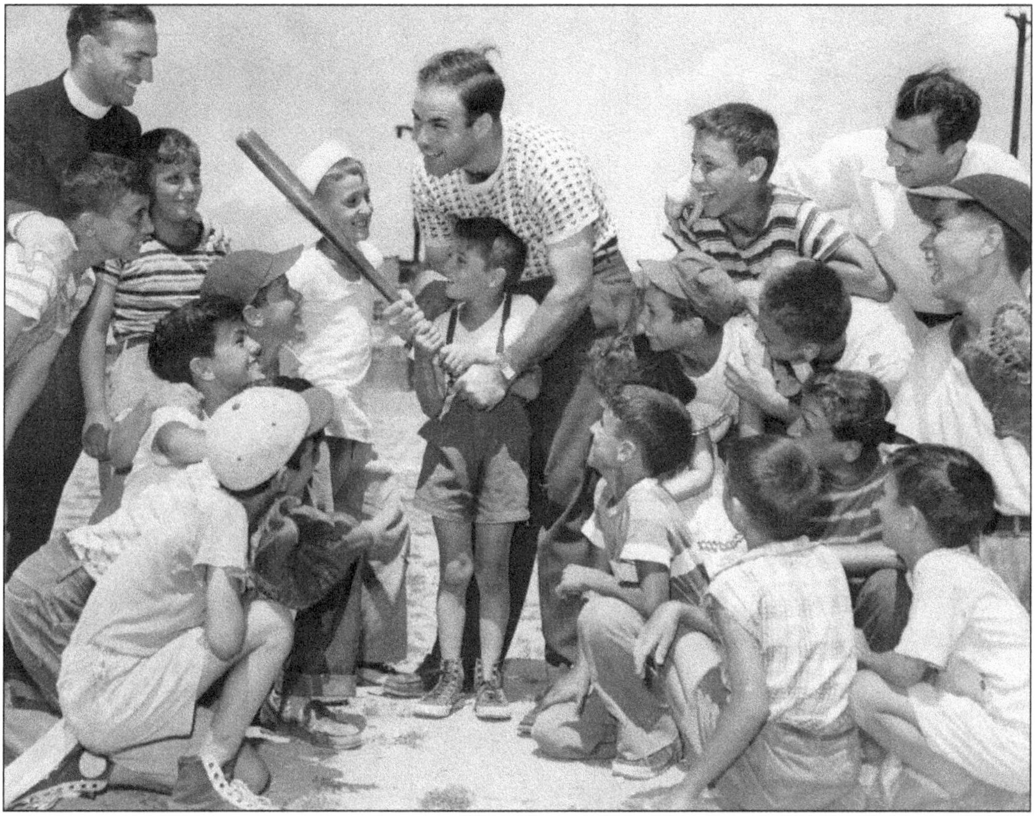

Reverend Charles Koester (upper left) watches as Joe Garagiola gives some batting tips to the neighborhood boys at one of the parks on the Hill. Garagiola was signed by the St. Louis Cardinals at age 16. He played his rookie year in 1946, when the team won the World Series. On January 2, 1971, Pope Paul VI appointed Rev. Koester as the titular bishop of Suacia and the auxiliary bishop of St. Louis. (Courtesy of Robert Garagiola.)

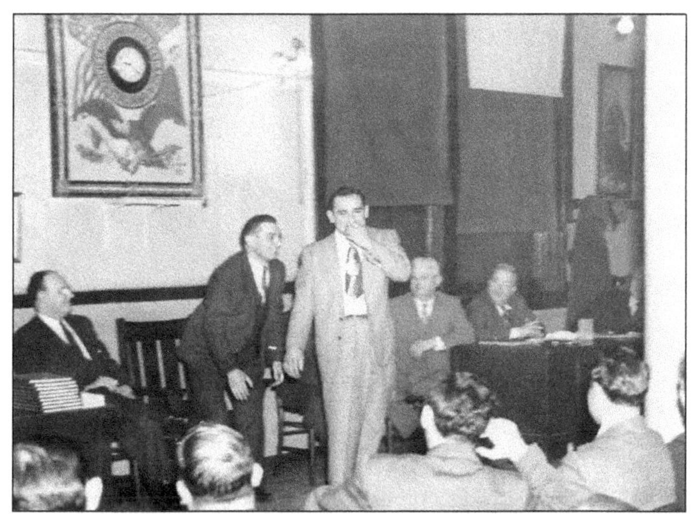

Yogi Berra appeared in 21 World Series as a player, coach, and manager and is regarded as one of the greatest catchers in baseball history. Here, he addresses members of the Fratellanza Society. The clock was created and designed by John Pellarin, made by C. Sivestri, and presented to Fratellaza on its 75th anniversary. It is an example of lasting beauty in terrazzo. (Courtesy of the Fratellanza Society of St. Louis.)

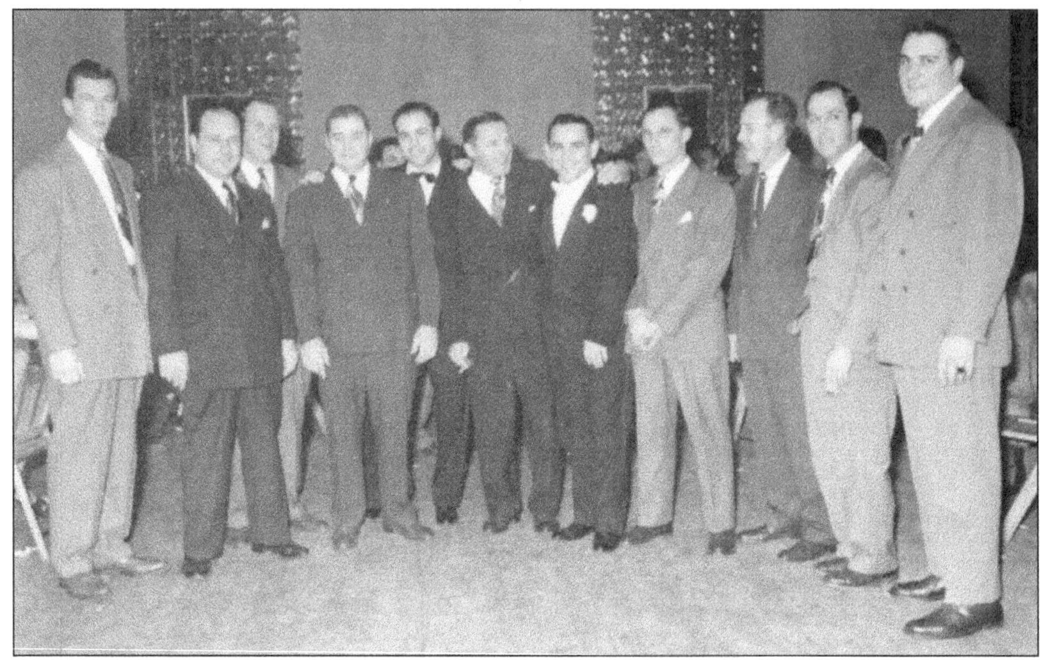

Yogi Berra (fifth from right) and his wife, Carmen, were married in 1949. They held the wedding reception at the Big Club Hall. The last man on the right is Berra's friend Ben Pucci, who grew up on the Hill and played professional football. He joined the Cleveland Browns in 1948, and the team posted a perfect record and won a third straight championship. Pucci organized a Shaw grade-school reunion for many years and included his club, the Stags. (Courtesy of Martina Garagiola.)

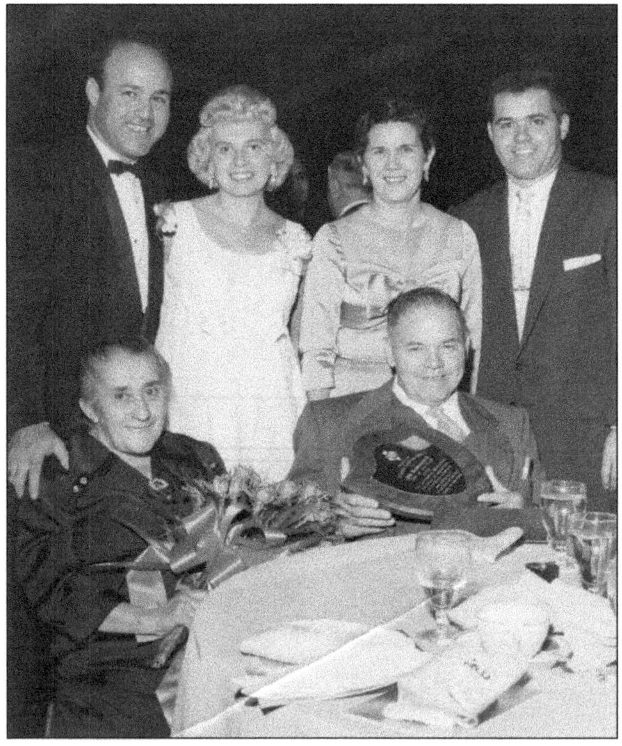

Gathered here are, standing from left to right, Joe Garagiola, his wife Audrey, Mickey Garagiola, and his wife Adele Riva. Seated at the table are the Garagiola parents, Angelina and John. Joe started his broadcasting career working at KMOX Radio from 1956 to 1962, announcing Cardinals games. In 1991, he was honored by the National Baseball Hall of Fame with the Ford C. Frick Award for outstanding broadcasting accomplishments. (Courtesy of Robert Garagiola.)

Nine

WEDDINGS

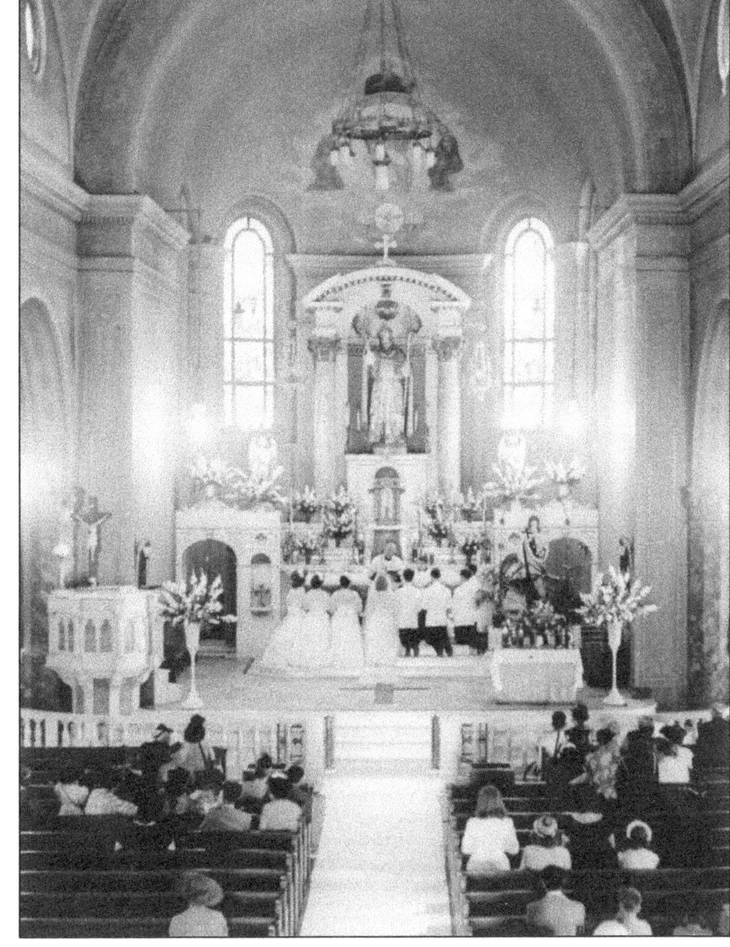

The interior of St. Ambrose Church is seen here sometime prior to 1961. When a girl was about 11 years old, her mother would begin preparing a *trousseau*, or hope chest. In earlier years, weddings would last for two or three days. There would be a simple ceremony at St. Ambrose and a party to follow at the bride's home or the Big Club Hall. Friends and relatives would show up on the first day, and there would be music, singing, and dancing. The next couple of days would include visits to the newly married couple's home, where gifts would be exchanged. The final day was shared with close relatives. St. Ambrose Church remains a popular place for weddings today. (Courtesy of Denise Pfleger.)

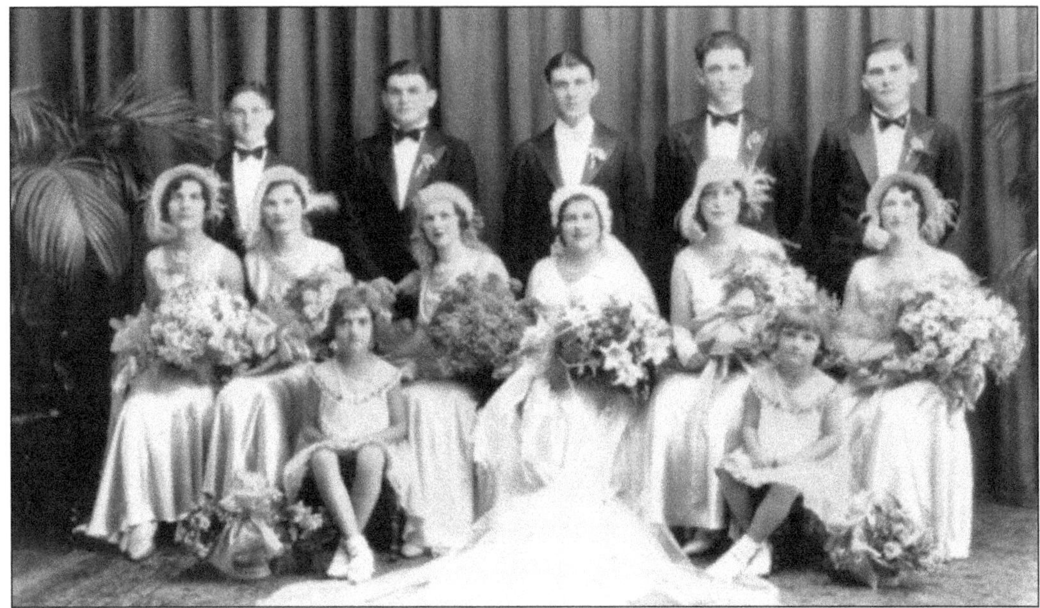

On September 6, 1930, Rose Spezia and Charles Grassi were married at St. Ambrose Church. The family traditions continued in the next generations. Anna Jo Grassi and Thomas Hof were married on November 26, 1960; Diane Murphy and Thomas Hof were married on May 11, 1984; and Abigail Hof and Peter Phillips were married on October 31, 2009. (Courtesy of Abigal Phillips.)

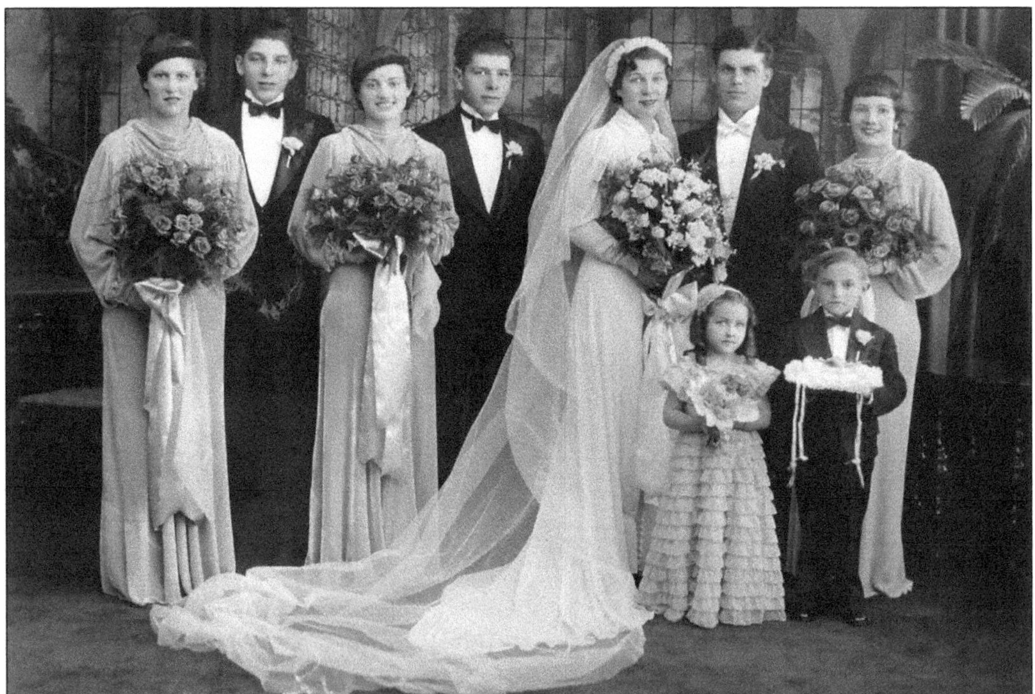

The groom, John Denando, came to the United States at 19 and later married Lena Purcelli in 1937. Denando would become one of the founders of the Italia America Bocce Club. He was an example of one of the many immigrants who used his tile-setting skills to build the club, like other craftsmen including plumbers, carpenters, and electricians. (Courtesy of John Denando.)

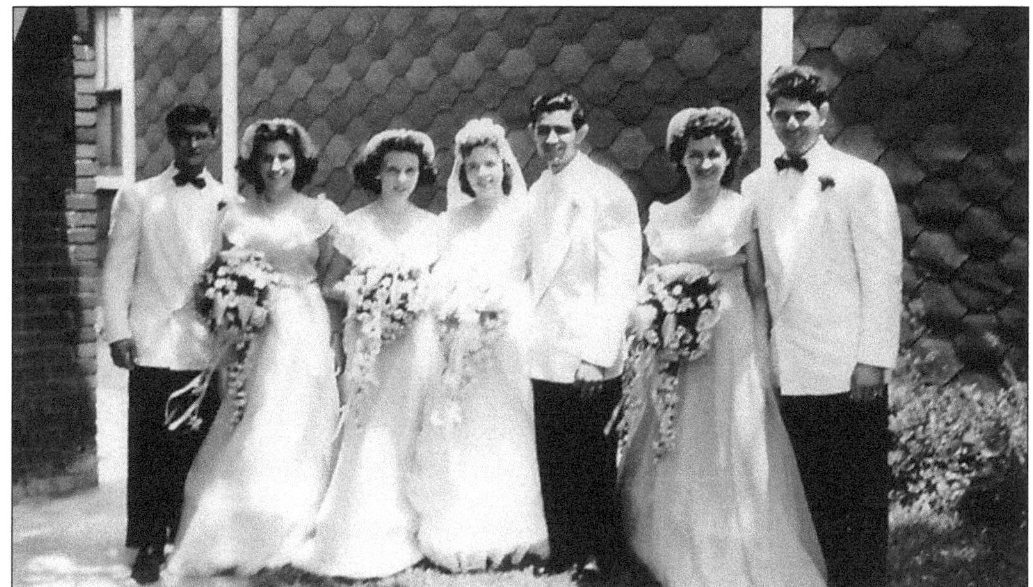

Shown here is the wedding of Rosemary and Ernie Respi Jr. (center). At the far left is Junior's brother Ambrose, and to the right of Junior are his sister Clementine and her husband, Rico Garavaglia. According to the 1940 census, the groom's family lived at 5320 Bischoff Avenue. The head of the household was Ernest Respi Sr., who worked as a laborer in a stone quarry. (Courtesy of Barbara Torretti.)

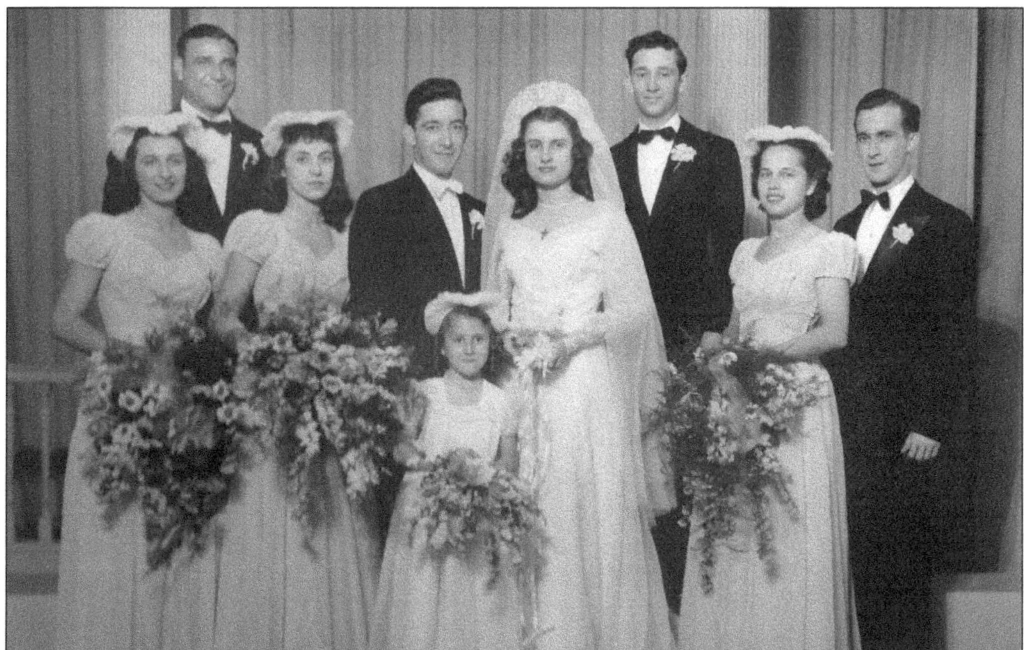

Shown here at center on their wedding day are Caesar Torretti and Angeline Pera. Both were children of immigrants. Caesar was a member of the Wildcats, the Holy Name, and the Christmas Club. He was employed by McQuay Norris and was active in the United Auto Workers. Angeline Pera was a member of Madre Christiani and the Kittens Club. The groom's parents were Caesar and Louise Torretti, who lived at 2333 Marconi Avenue. (Courtesy of Barbara Torretti.)

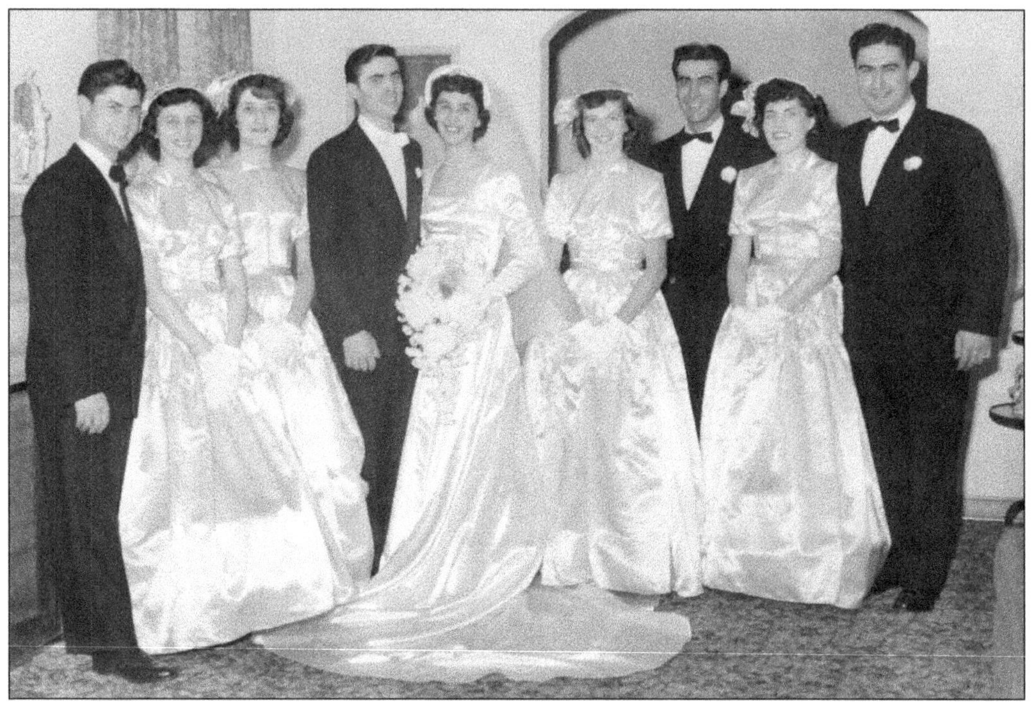

The members of the Mastrantuono wedding party are, from left to right, Joe Mastrantuono, Marie Cissi, Marie Barroli, Bill Mastrantuono, Carol Tedoni Mastrantuono, Rosemary Tedoni, Tom Tedoni, Rita Gualdoni, and Louis Aiazzi. The differences between people whose ancestors came from Northern and Southern Italy were diminishing by this time. Some may have continued to say they were Sicilian or Italian, but the community was becoming one. (Courtesy of Dave Tedoni.)

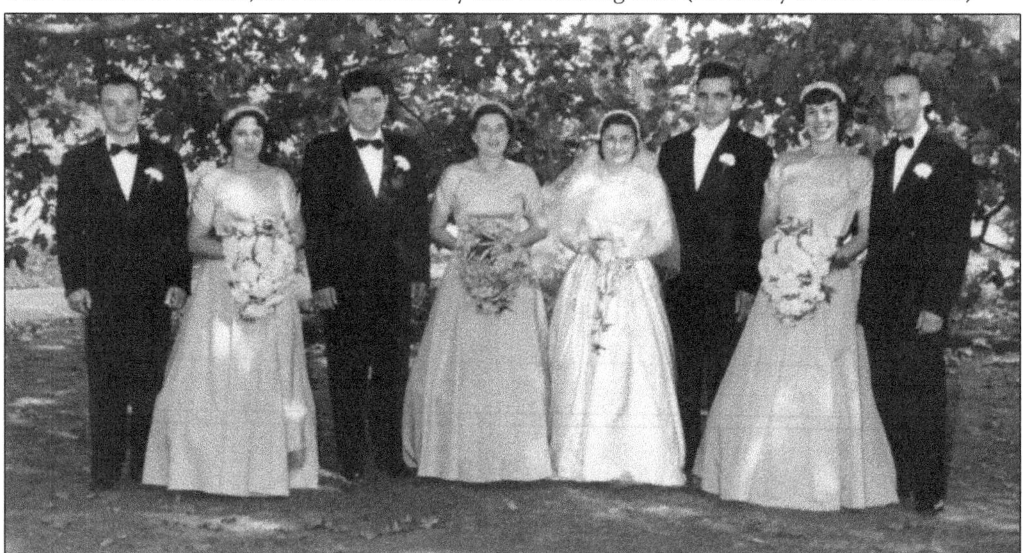

Shown here is the wedding party of Anthony Grimoldi and Johanna Savio Grimoldi. Both had fathers who fought in World War I for the United States. Anthony's father was born in the United States and, while serving in the war, he suffered from a mustard-gas attack. Anthony came to the United States in 1947 as an American citizen born in Cuggiono, Italy. (Courtesy of Johanna Savio Grimoldi.)

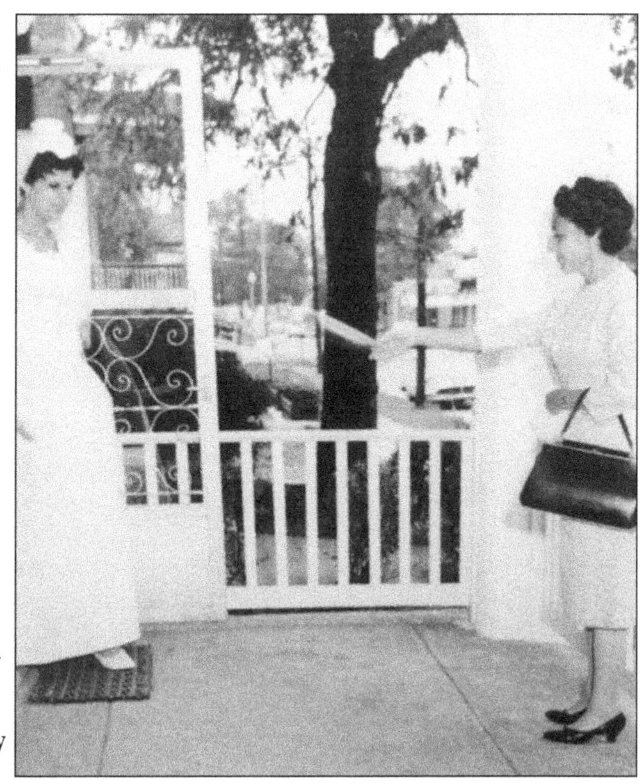

A friend of the family is performing the traditional breaking of the plate and surprising the bride for good luck. It was customary to surprise the bride by breaking a plate. If she was surprised, this was meant to imply that the couple would have many happy years together. (Courtesy of Kay Marzorati.)

The groom, Victor Mancuso, born in Sicily, married a Lombard, Thelma Pizzella, in 1947. Victor was a member of the Fawns Athletic Club and a veteran of World War II. Thelma was a member of the Grail and worked at Style Craft, making parts for the armed forces. (Courtesy of Thelma Pizzella Mancuso Bene.)

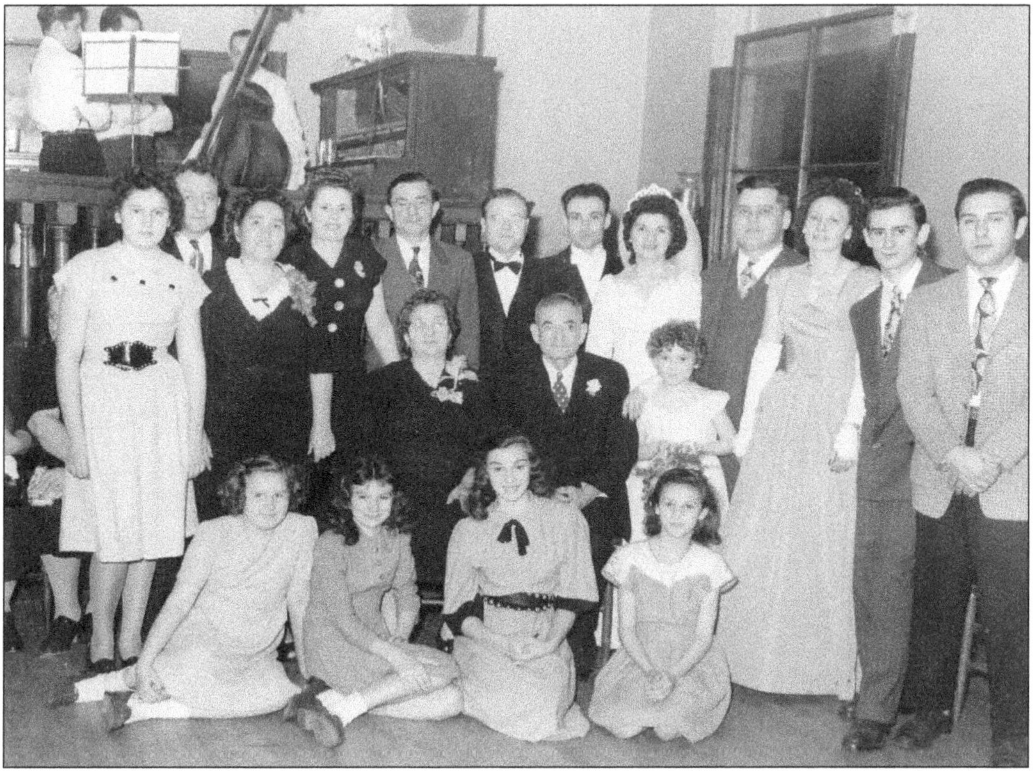

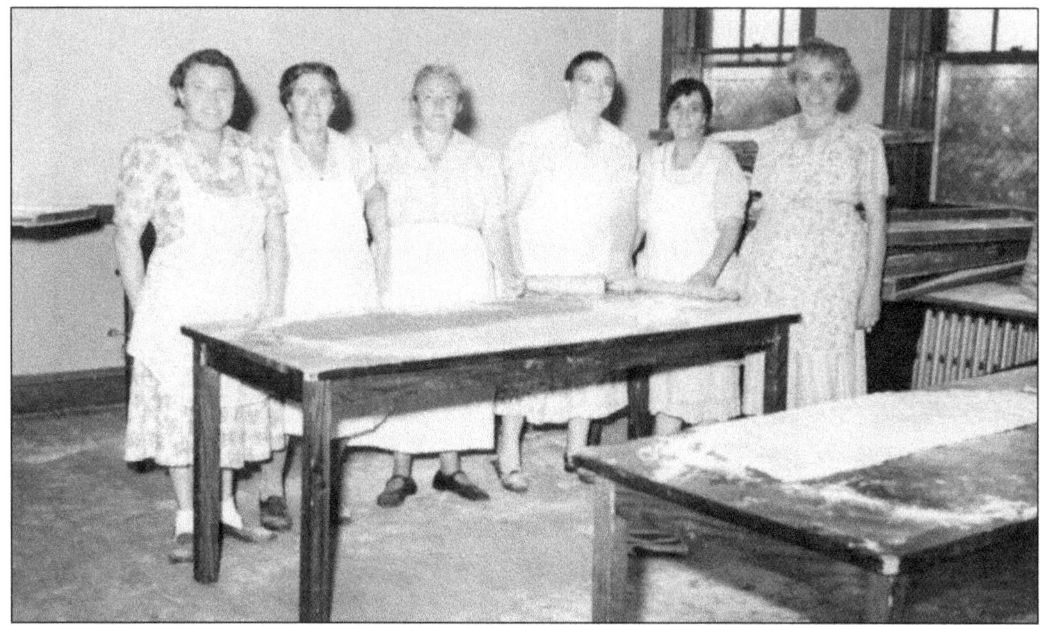

The North Italian American Club, founded in 1897, was the first society to be organized on the Hill by a group of young Lombards, headed by Luigia Caloia. They built a two-story structure at the corner of Shaw and Marconi Avenues. This became the "Big Club Hall," a club house, tavern, banquet center, and place for business and political meetings over the decades. These ladies are preparing ravioli for the next wedding at the Big Club Hall. (Courtesy of Joe Gorla.)

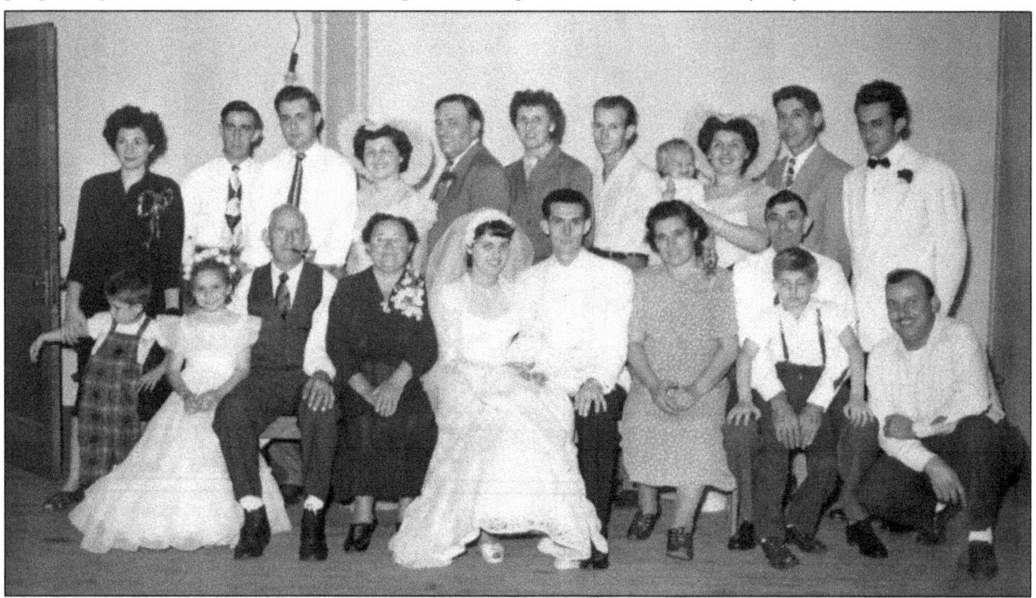

Joe Gorla and Agnes Colombo, both children of Italian immigrants living on the Hill, are seen here in the first row at center on their wedding day. Gorla's father passed away when he was nine. His mother worked as a seamstress, and his grandmother lived in their home to help take care of the family. Gorla attended Wade Elementary School, graduated from Southwest High School, and served in the Army during World War II. He coached soccer, baseball, and basketball at St. Ambrose School from 1951 to 1978. (Courtesy of Joe Gorla.)

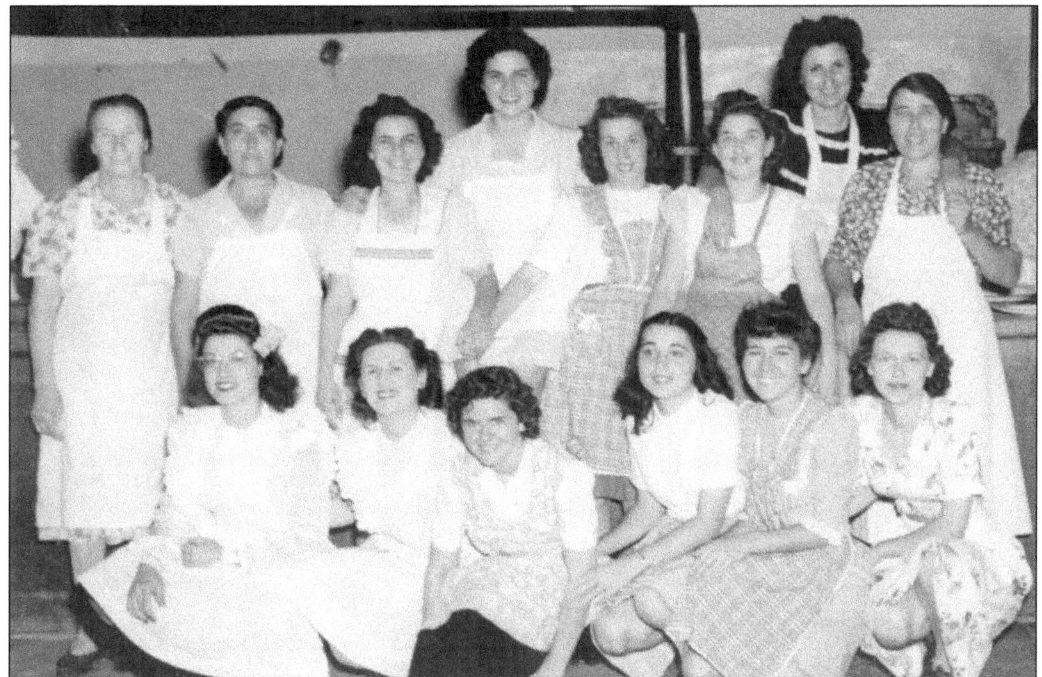

With an increase in the number of weddings in the 1940s and 1950s, the Big Club Hall needed servers. These young ladies of the neighborhood were ready to work for modest pay in a safe environment close to home. (Courtesy of Johanna Grimoldi.)

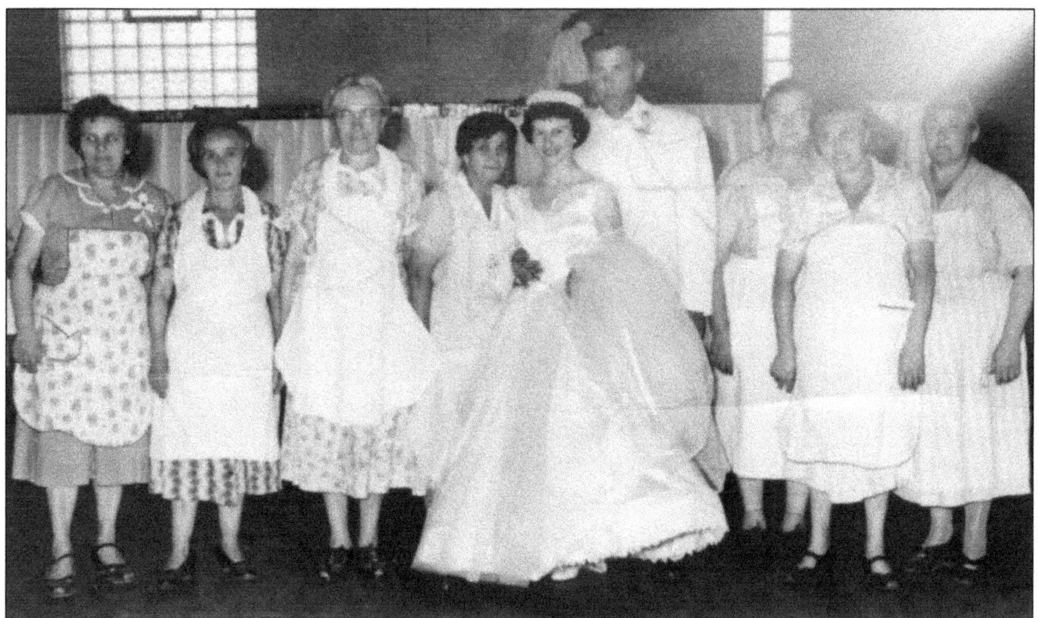

Shown here is one of the first groups of women to cook for a wedding at the Big Club Hall. They are, from left to right, Gina Ruggerioli, Emelia Garavaglia, unidentified, Rosa Oldani, an unidentified bride and groom, Gina Noe, and two unidentified women. These ladies cooked for three days to prepare for a wedding. A typical meal would include salad, antipasti, ravioli, beef, and chicken. (Courtesy of Anne Garavaglia Agusti.)

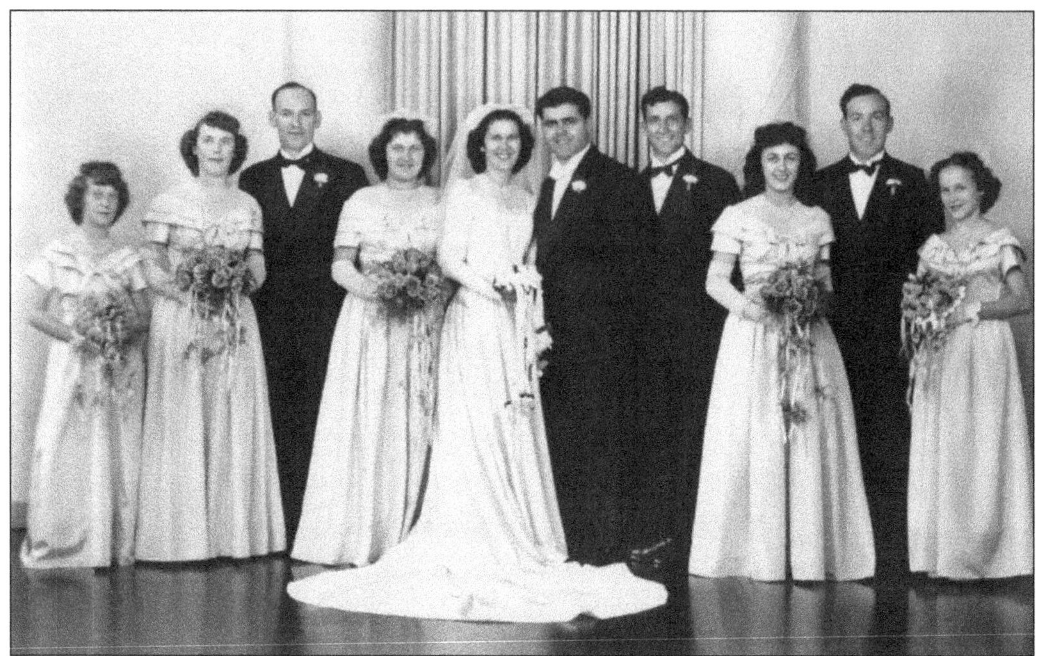

Shown here is the wedding party of Mickey Garagiola and Adele Riva. Garagiola served in the Navy during World War II and was a longtime ring announcer and commentator for the St. Louis Wresting Club. He was inducted into the St. Louis Wresting Hall of Fame. (Courtesy of Martina Garagiola Bettlach.)

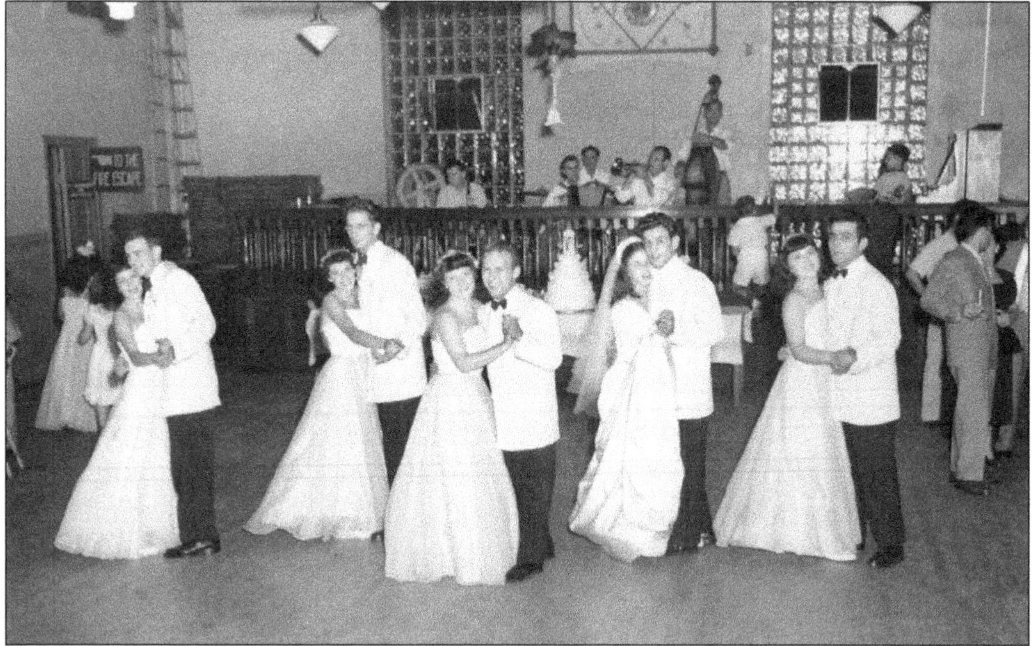

The Cacciatore wedding party joins the bride and groom on the Big Club Hall dance floor. Frank Cacciatore married Marge Fitsgibbons, an American girl not of Italian descent, from Epiphany Parish. They met at one of the Teen Town events held at the parish. Just two weeks after the weeding, Frank was serving his country in the Korean War. (Courtesy of Marge Fitsgibbons Cacciatore.)

Ten

LIFE AFTER WORLD WAR II

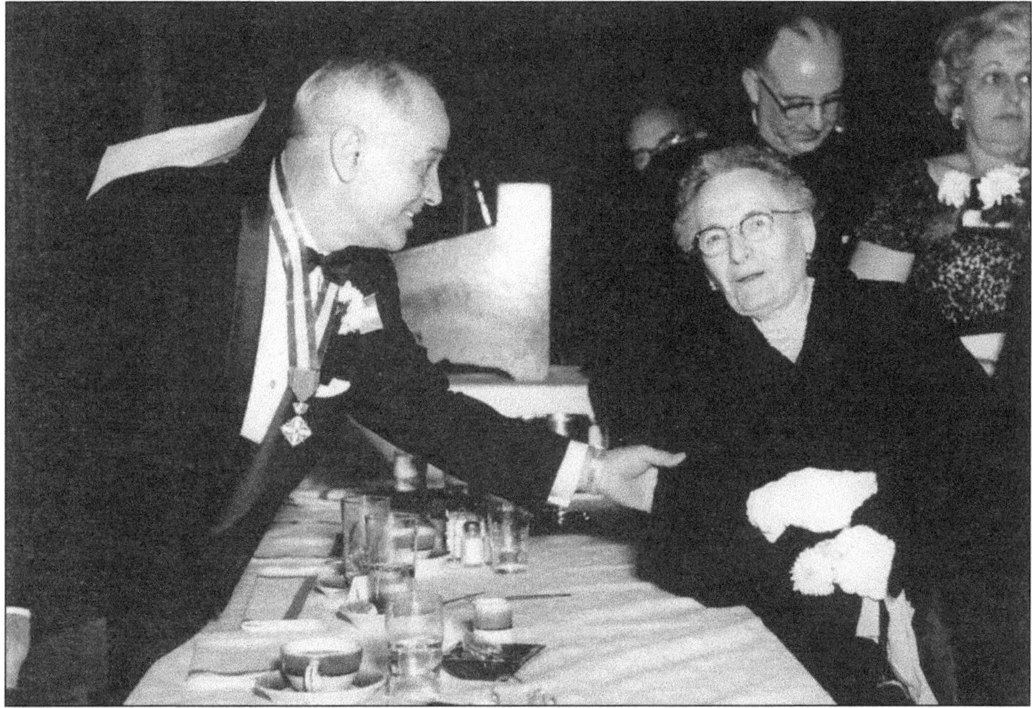

Fred Giacoma (left) was the executive vice president at Southwest Bank, and Mrs. Volpi (right) was the Hill's midwife. Prior to World War II, the majority of children on the Hill were delivered by Mrs. Volpi and her sister, Mrs. Valli. In Italy, before immigrating to America, they had passed an examination that licensed them as midwives. Second-generation Italian Americans were educated, experienced with interacting with others outside the Hill, and attracted to the middle-class lifestyle. Women who had worked during the war began dating and marrying men from outside the Hill area. Veterans began to purchase new homes, the construction of which created new jobs. Home ownership also encouraged further development. The areas around the Hill, such as Blue Ridge Heights, became populated by many of this generation. The Hill would welcome a new wave of immigrants from war-torn Italy, putting more demands on housing. (Courtesy of Armando Passetti.)

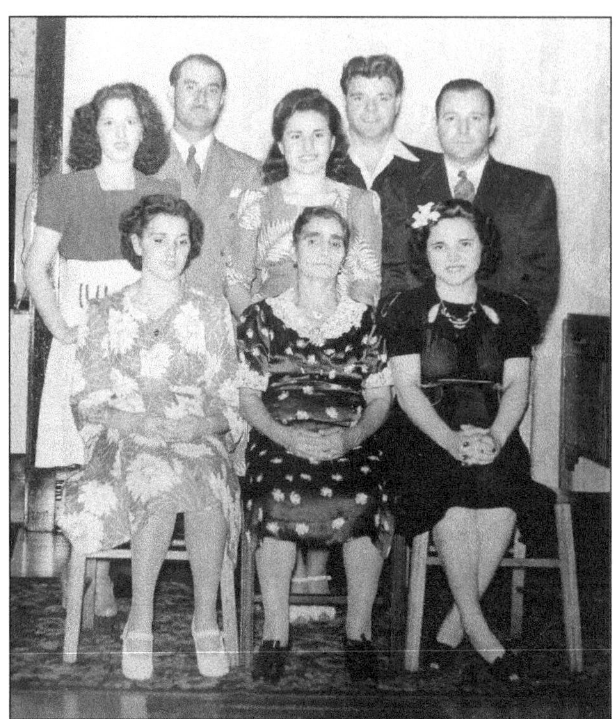

Rosa VanCardo Novara (first row, center) poses with her children. After World War II, younger residents no longer felt isolated and restricted to taking factory jobs on the Hill. This generation had greater opportunities for education and employment. But the Hill remained solid in its traditions, and the residents remained proud of their heritage and wanted others outside of the Hill's boundaries to know it. (Courtesy of Suzie Spavale Hession.)

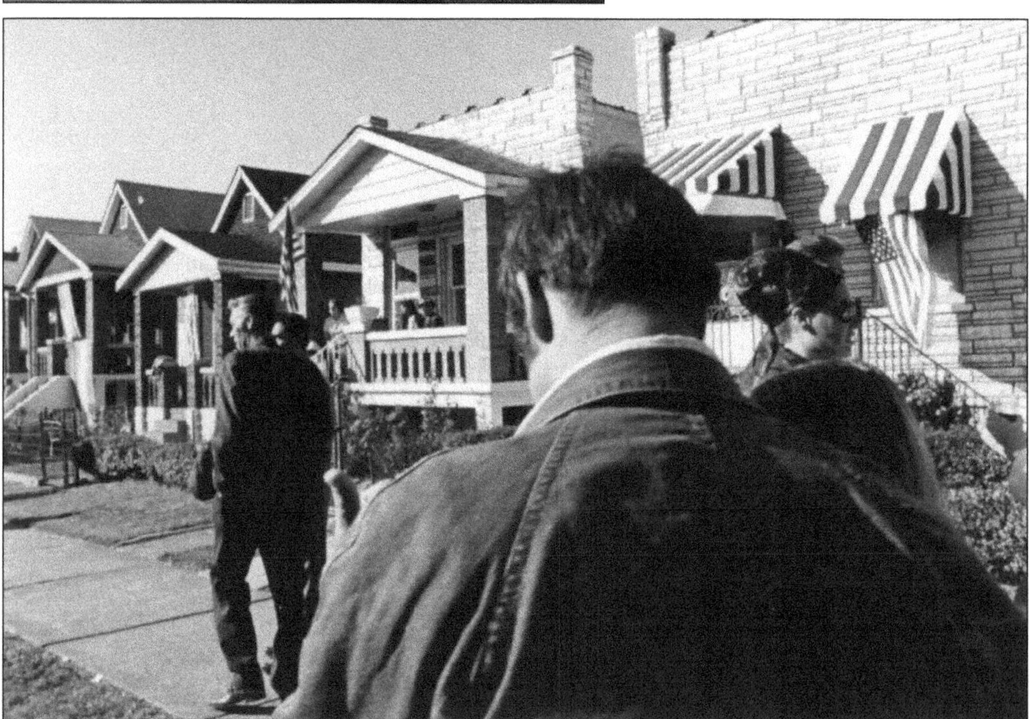

The older homes on the Hill were small, and conditions were crowded for large families. New home construction could not keep pace with the increasing number of marriages and the resultant needs of newlyweds. Veterans could apply to the Veterans Administration and the Federal Housing Authority for home loans. (Courtesy of Gino Mariani.)

On September 6, 1956, Sacred Heart Villa became the home to Cor Jesu Academy, a Catholic girl's high school under the administration of St. Anita Marie Giampetro, its founding principal. As enrollment increased, a larger facility was required. In 1965, the present campus was opened on a 13-acre tract of land near Grant's Farm in southwest St. Louis County. (Courtesy of Cor Jesu Academy.)

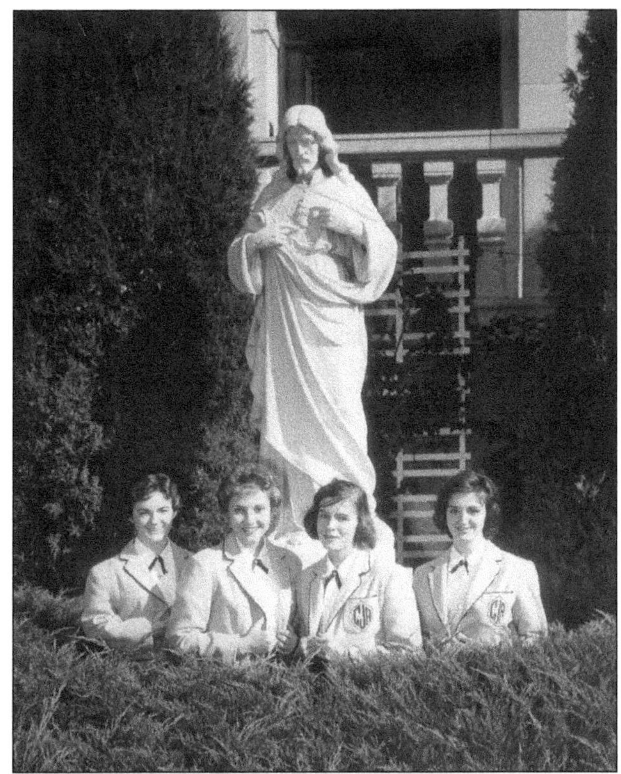

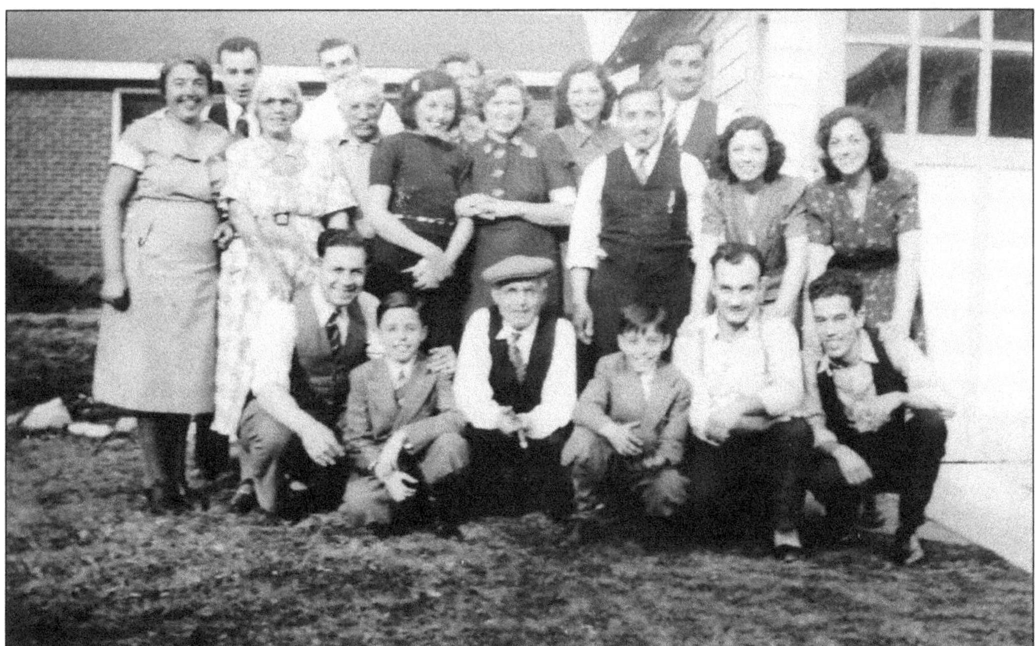

Georgio Matranga (first row, center) and his family came to St. Louis in 1902 from Palermo, Sicily. Georgio worked at the Laclede Christy clay mines. Family members included eight children, seven of whom were born on the Hill, in a house that was located where St. Ambrose School is today. (Courtesy of Paula Toronetto Gusamano.)

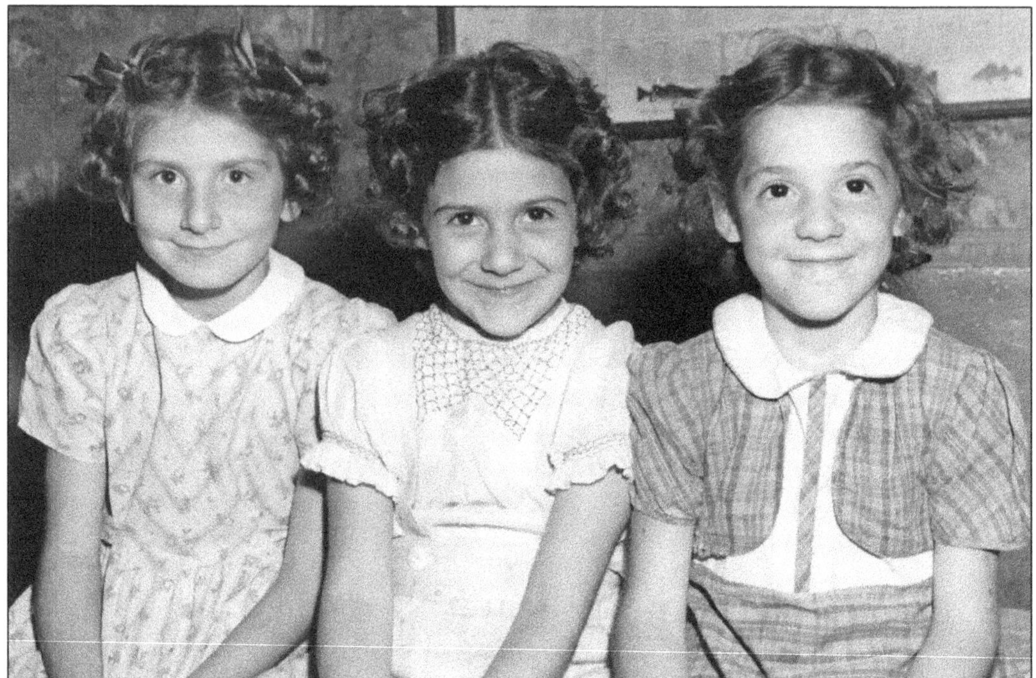

Many homeowners on the Hill added basements with separate front and back doors, as individual families often lived on separate floors of the home. This was done out of convenience for an elderly parent, or for a recently married child, or for economic reasons. In an example of separate families living under the same roof, Frances Ruggeri (left), Anna Jo Grassi (center), and ReRe Grassi became best friends forever. Relationships extended beyond bloodlines; everyone was a person's cousin, aunt, or uncle on the Hill. (Courtesy of Chris Stephens.)

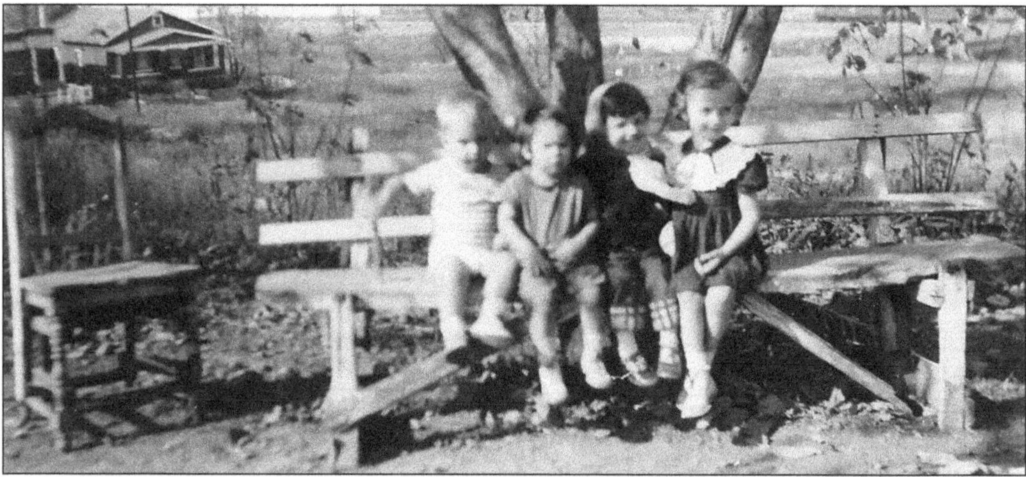

Barbara Torretti recalls life on the Hill: "Growing up on Northrup Avenue was like living in an Italian village. We heard Italian dialect every day. My grandfather and his friends would sit on this bench and smoke their strong Italian cigars and converse in Italian for hours. Cousins lived a few doors down on each side, and my grandfather's friends from the 'old country' also lived nearby. Some families had one car, and other families had none, so there was very little traffic on our block. We spent a lot of time playing and riding our bikes in the street, or playing in what was at that time an open field on the north side of Northrup." (Courtesy of Barbara Torretti.)

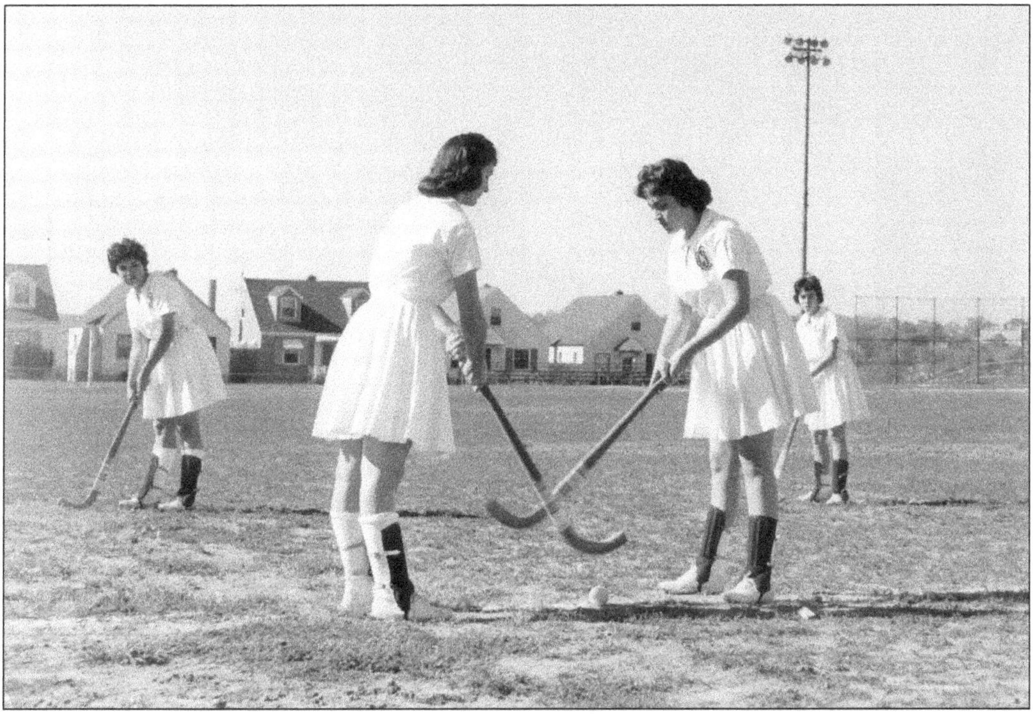

These girls from Cor Jesu Academy are playing field hockey at Berra Park during gym class. The one tract of land on the Hill that was improved and offered for development was the area west of Macklind Avenue between Shaw and Daggett Avenues. It was used as a trash dump prior to the 1950s. Most of the homes were sold before they could be completed. Some of them can be seen in the background. (Courtesy of Cor Jesu Academy.)

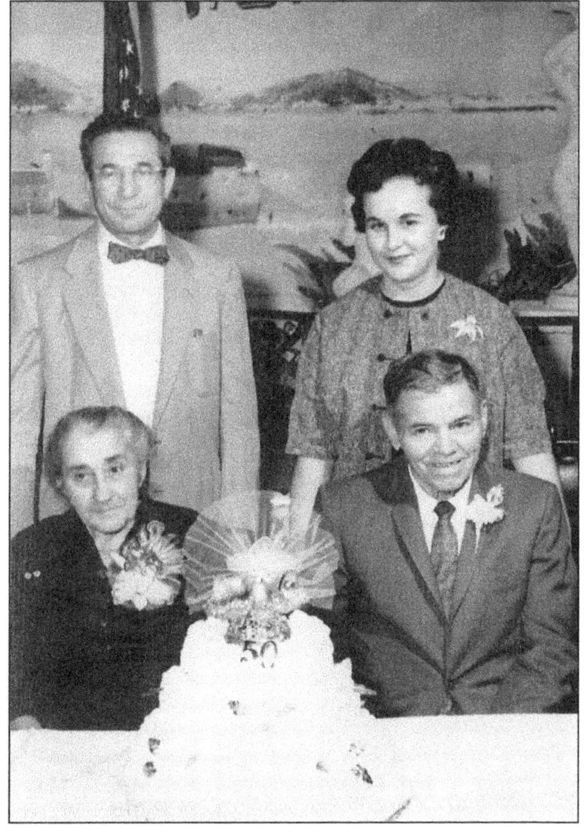

John and Ann Clavenna (standing) celebrate the anniversary of lifelong friends and neighbors Angelina and John Garagiola. Love of old friends and neighborliness did not change after the war, and St. Ambrose Church would remain the pillar of the Hill. Downtown Little Italy saw its residents moving away. Most of its parishioners relocated to north St. Louis County or the Hill. By 1982, the two Italian churches downtown would be closed. (Courtesy of Victor John Clavenna.)

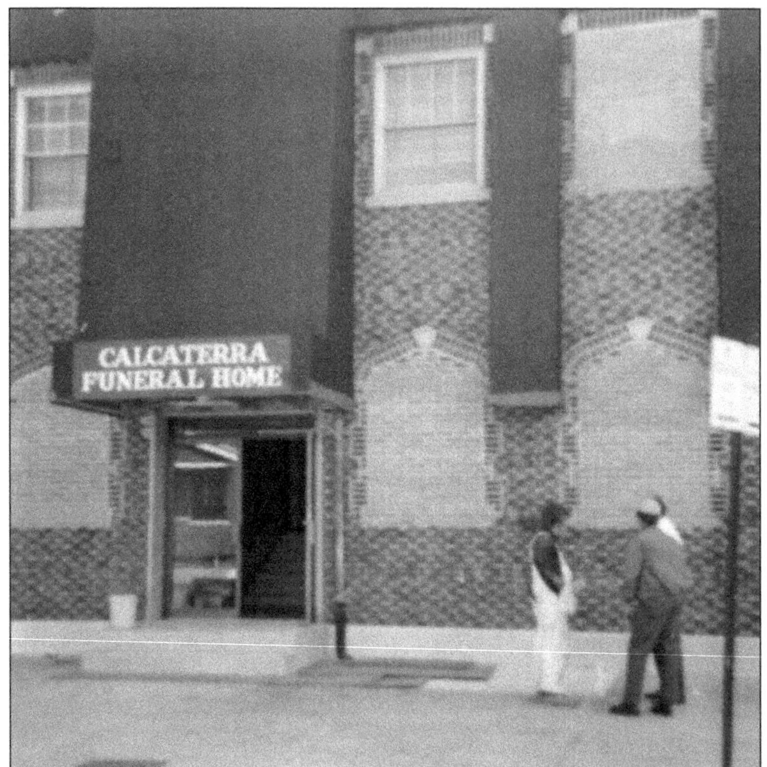

The Calcaterra Funeral Home, near the corner of Daggett and Marconi Avenues, was owned by Paul Calcaterra. It was remodeled around 1970. Paul Calcaterra was active in many of the Italian societies, and organized athletic teams sponsored by the funeral home. (Courtesy of Gino Mariani.)

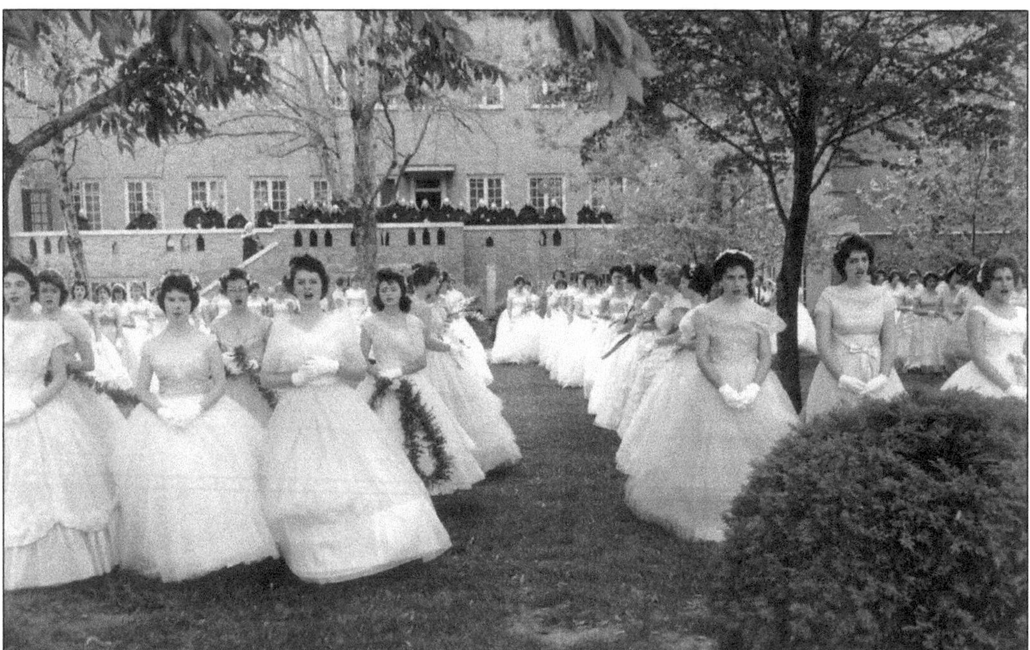

The high school students from Cor Jesu Academy celebrate the May Crowing at Sacred Heart Villa. Processions became smaller in size and number over time. There was less emphasis on individual patronage to saints or townships. The new prevailing attitude was that residents were all Italian, worshipping under one Roman Catholic Church. (Courtesy of Cor Jesu Academy.)

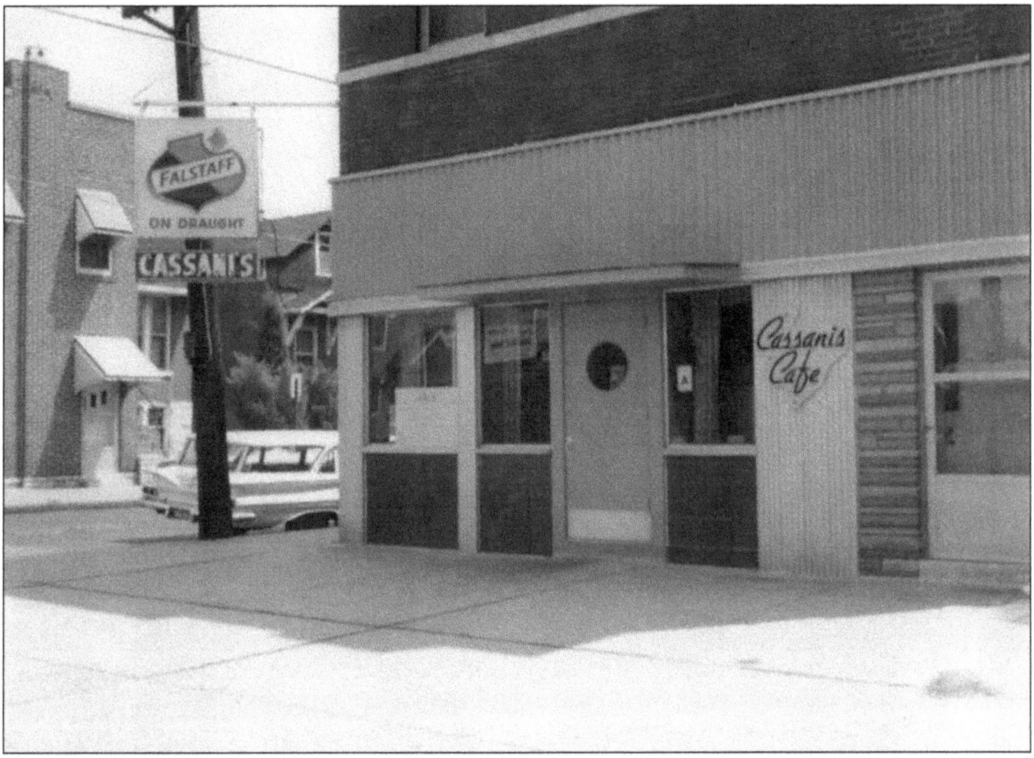

Long before there were gourmet restaurants on the Hill, there was barbecue. Cassani's storefront is seen here after it was remodeled in 1959. The barbecue and fish fry on Fridays remained a neighborhood favorite. Residents could smell the food as the cooks at Cassani's began preparing the ribs on Friday, but they had to wait until Saturday for a taste. (Courtesy of Gino Mariani.)

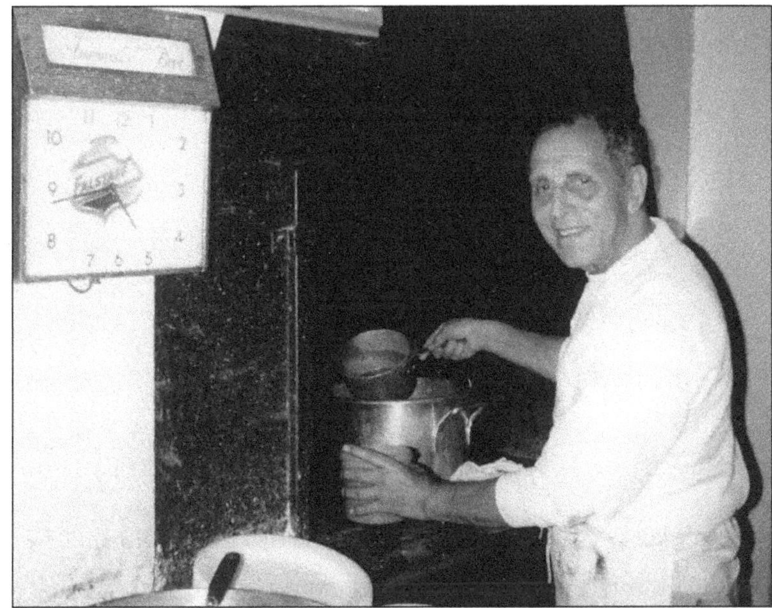

For over 40 years, John "The Barbecue Man" Martarona tantalized his customers at Cassani's. He served scrumptious St. Louis–style ribs, offered up ambrosia in the form of a beef sandwich, and made manna in the guise of an Italian hamburger. This gastronomic genius did not have mere customers, but friends. They traveled from afar to partake of his gifts. (Courtesy of Lawrence Beville.)

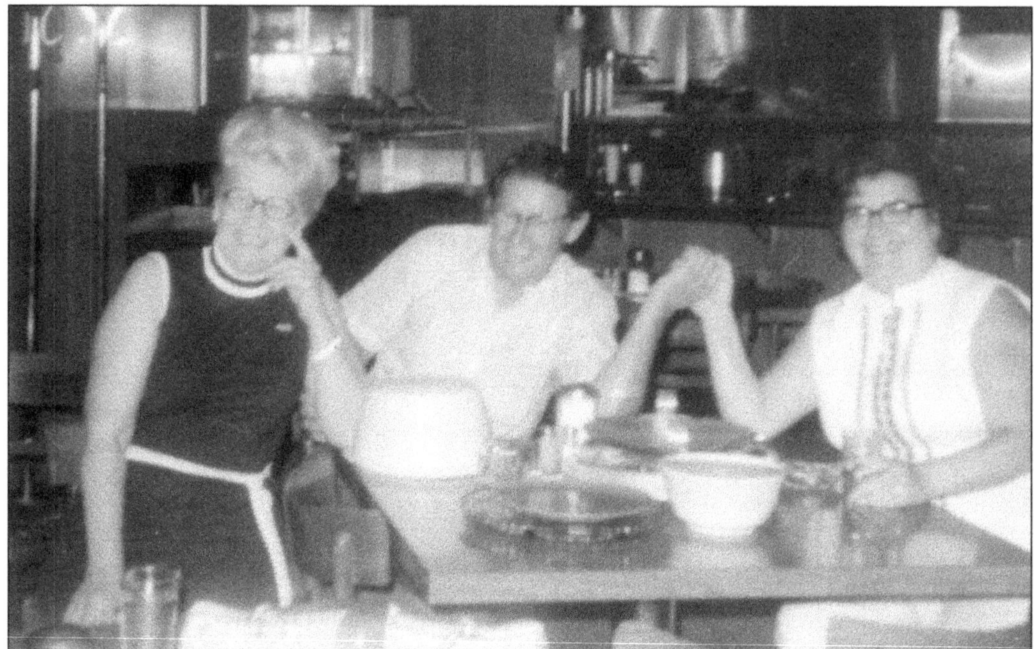

Cassani's would later become Galimberti's, but the barbecue remained the same—perfect. This is the interior of Galimberti's in 1971. Shown here are Fannie Berra (left), her husband, Louis, and Marie Galimberti. (Courtesy of Faye Berra Venegoni.)

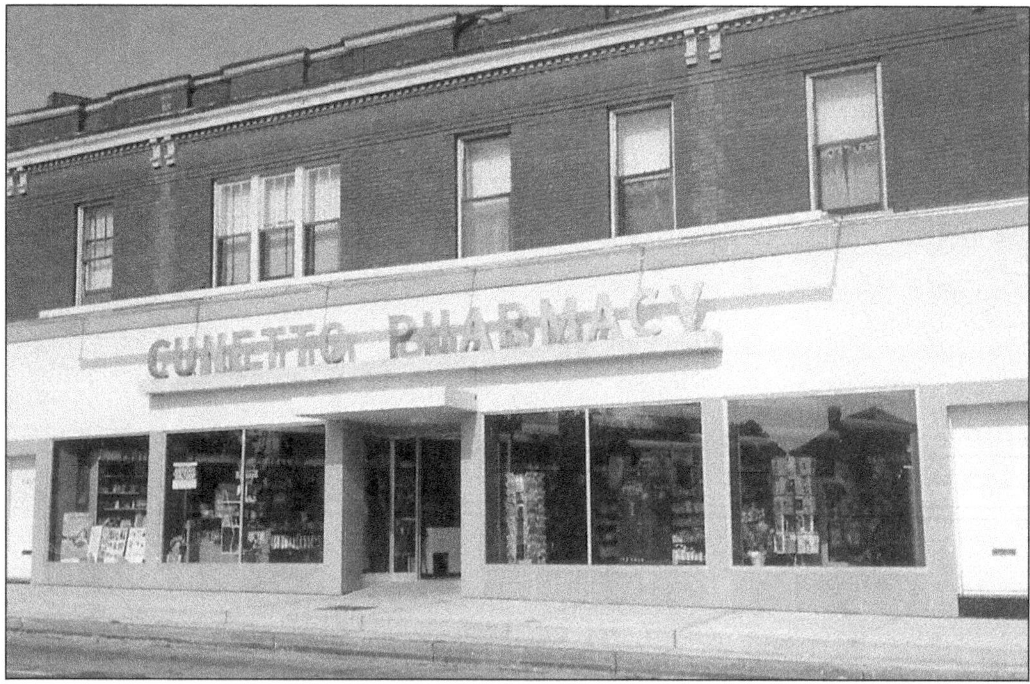

The Cunetto family sold the pharmacy in 1972, but they were determined to stay on the Hill. Vince Cunetto and his family opened Cunetto House of Pasta in October 1974, and it remains in the same location today. The restaurant is still in the family, owned and operated by Vince's son, Frank Cunetto. (Courtesy of Frank Cunetto.)

Frank Mario "Chick" Severino Sr. was a civil servant, columnist, and cartoonist. An example of his work is shown here. His parents emigrated from the town of Casteltermini, Sicily. He served in the US Army during World War II, in the European theater. Upon returning from the war, Severino met and married Ann Marie Marcolla, and they raised five sons. The Severino family had emigrated from Casteltermini, Sicily, and the Marcolla family came from Vigo Di Ton (Trentino), Italy, in the 1930s. (Courtesy of Mary Agosti Thompson.)

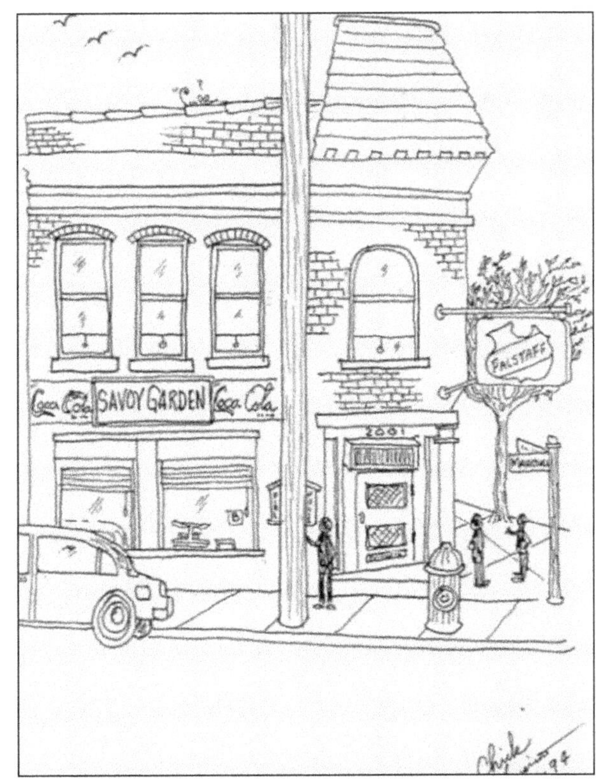

Phyllis Gairani is standing in front of Gairani's Corner Confectionary, which opened in 1951 and closed in 1965. Mrs. Gairani would hand out grab bags to the kids when they stopped in after school. Other local businesses in the area included Vago's Superette, Rumbolo's Market, Consolino's, and Serra Drug Store. (Courtesy of Phyllis Gairani-Vthoulkos.)

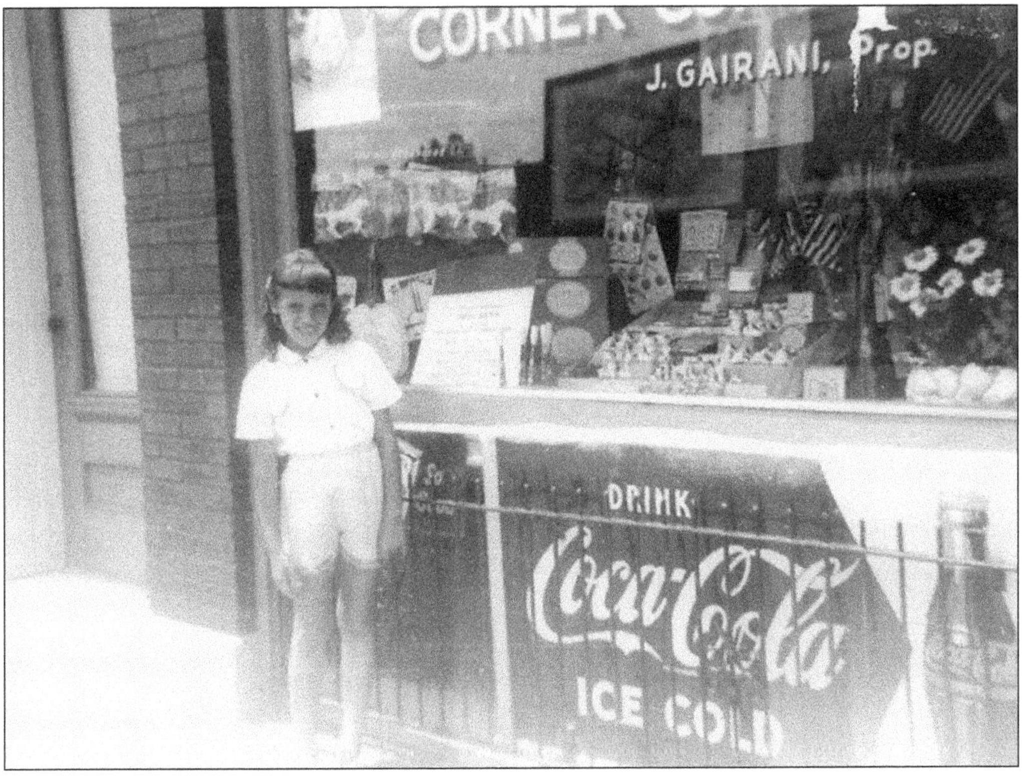

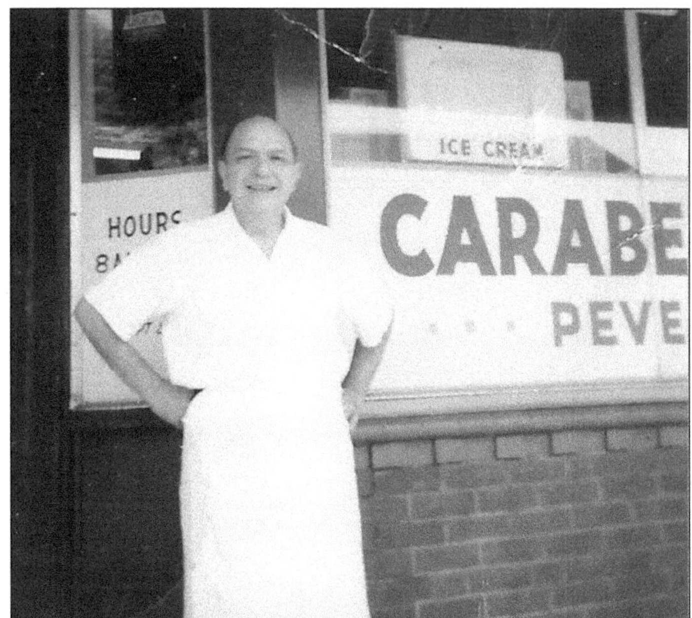

Felice Carabelli is standing in front of his grocery store at 5400 Elizabeth Avenue. Children would be sent to the store with a grocery list, and the parents would come to settle the bill later. Kids were often put to work cleaning or carrying items for the owners of these local shops, but they were always rewarded. (Courtesy of Victor John Clavenna.)

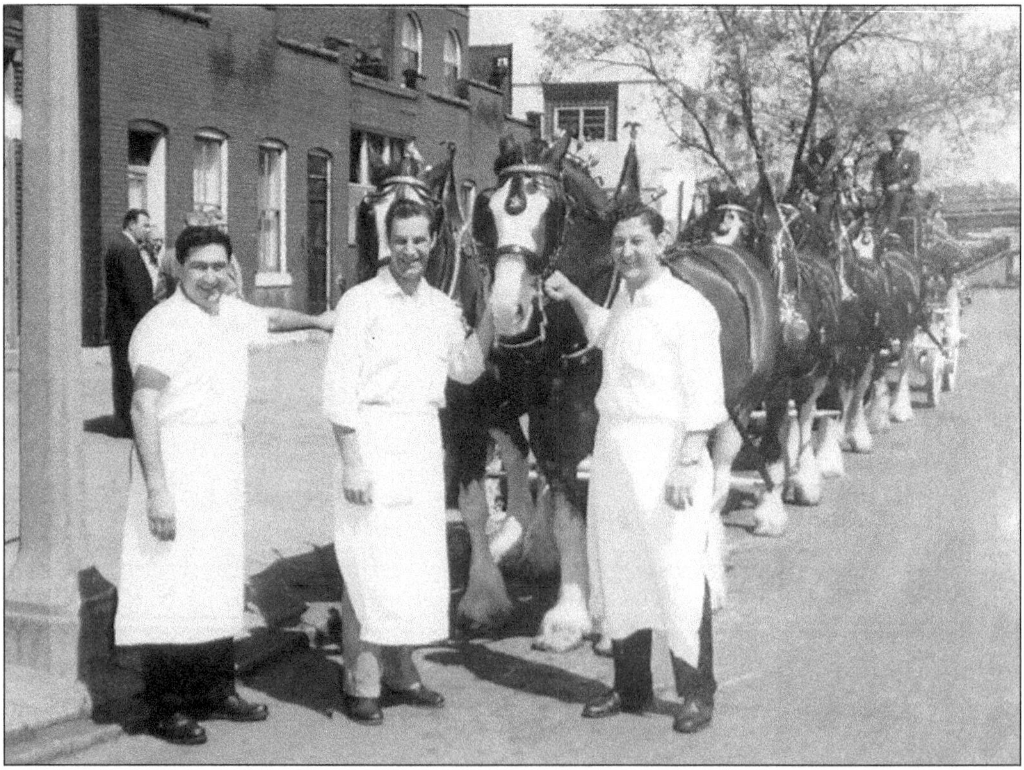

Rigazzi's, founded in 1957 by John Riganti and Lou Aiazzi, is still in operation. It has been under the Aiazzi family's ownership most of this time. Rigazzi's is famous for its Frozen Fishbowl, a 32-ounce glass that was modeled after a giant glass of ice cream the family bought at the 1904 World's Fair. Shown here from left to right are Louis Aiazzi, Martin Colombo, and John Riganti. (Courtesy of Rigazzi's Restaurant.)

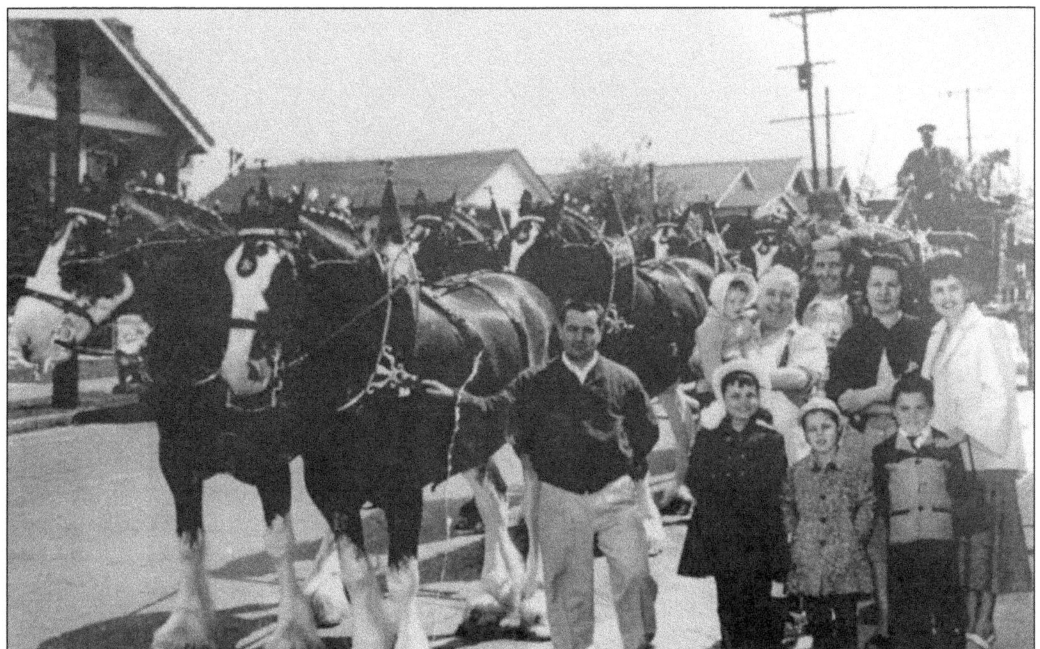

Mama Toscano's originally started as Toscano's Market. The local grocery store provided the Italian community with fresh-cut meats, lunchmeats, cheeses, and canned goods. The building has been in the Toscano family (pictured) for over 90 years. (Courtesy of Catherine Toscano Peluso.)

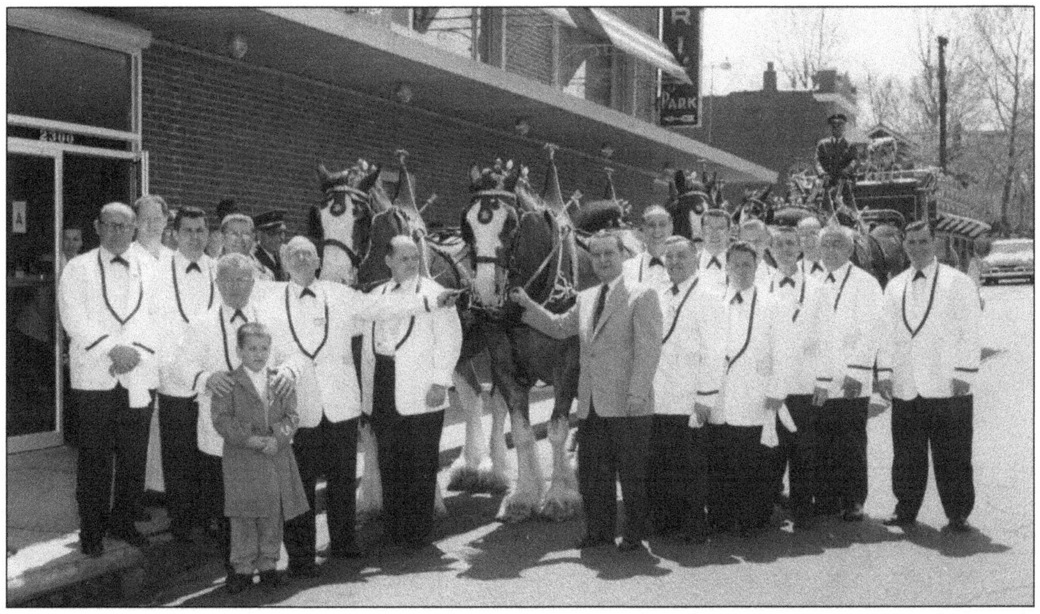

The staff of Ruggeri's Restaurant and the owner, Henry "The Chief" Ruggeri (center, dark suit), pose in 1968 with the Budweiser Clydesdales in front of the restaurant. Anthony Ruggeri opened the business in 1904, and it won many national awards. The restaurant was the originator of the charcoal broiled steak, which made the establishment famous from coast to coast. (Courtesy of Martina Garagiola Bettlach.)

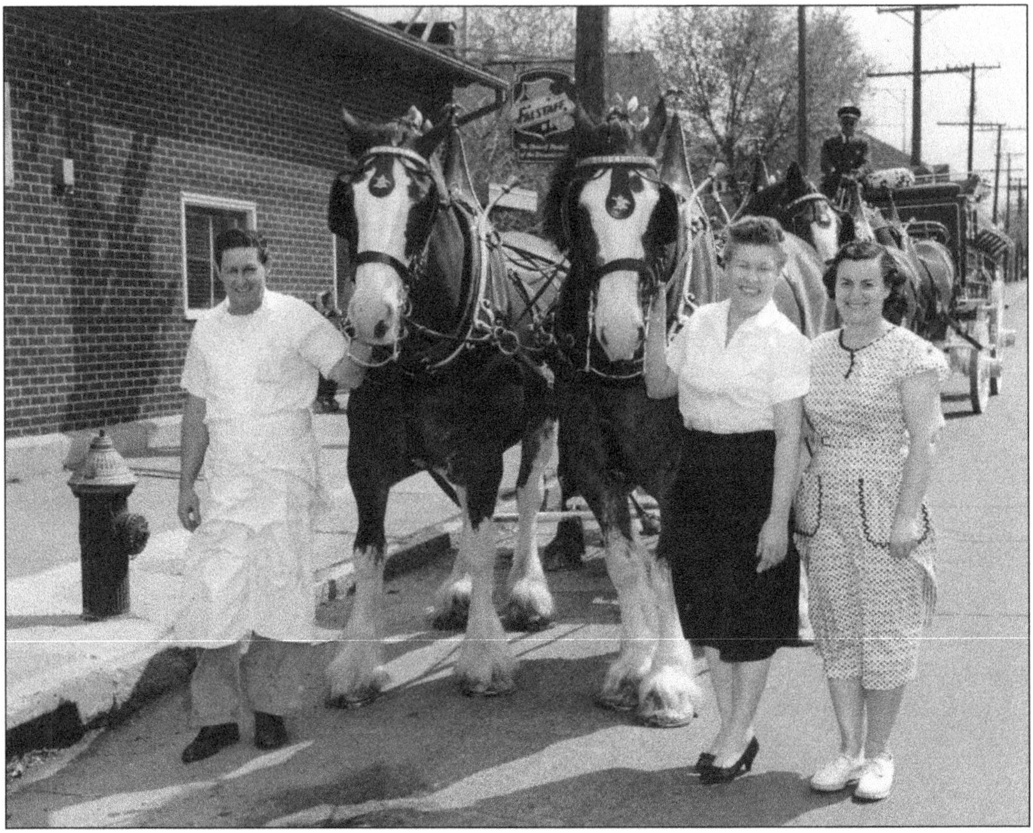

Berra's Café was owned by, from left to right, Louis Berra and wife Fannie Berra, Mary Berra, and her husband Lance Berra (not pictured). Their specialty was home cooked food, along with the friendly atmosphere. The restaurant was most noted for lunches made available to workers, who would line up out the door waiting to be served. (Courtesy of Faye Berra Venegoni.)

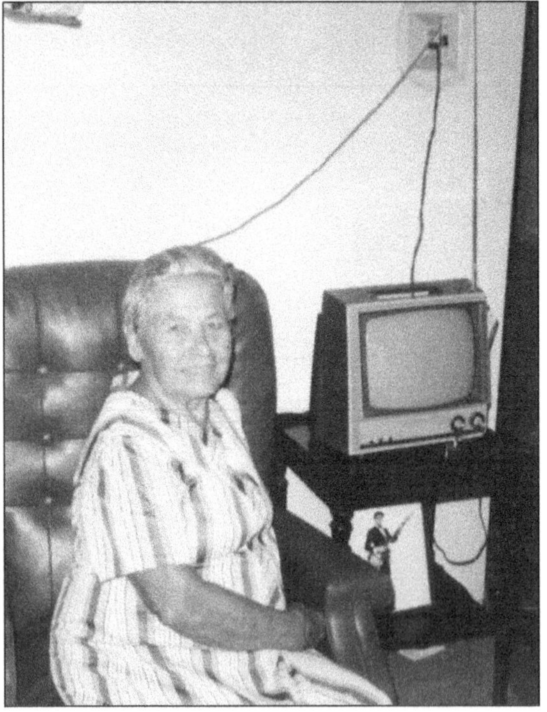

Leonarda Gianino, known as Dona Narda to residents, came to the United States in 1913. Her husband, Pete, and children, Carmella and Frank, lived at 2020 Marconi Avenue. Pete Gianino worked as a laborer in the clay-pipe industry. Leonarda Gianino retired at 56 years of age after working 43 years at Liggett and Meyers, cutting, mixing, and racking tobacco. (Courtesy of Gino Mariani.)

In June 1954, Sam and Dora DiGregorio moved to St. Louis with their two small children, Giuseppa and Francesco. In June 1971, Sam started a small corner grocery store on the Hill. DiGregorio's is still family owned and operated. Shown here are, from left to right, Sam, Dora (holding Giuseppa), Francis, and her husband, Roland DiGregorio, brother of Sam. (Courtesy of Rosemary DiGregorio Parentin.)

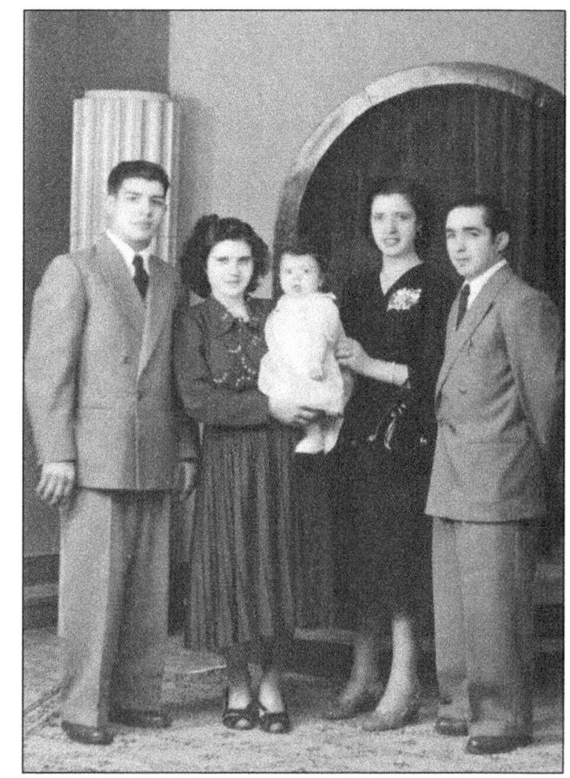

The Budweiser Clydesdales trot past DiGregorio's Market at the corner of Marconi and Daggett Avenues. Sitting next to the driver is longtime caretaker of the horses, Sam DeGregorio. (Courtesy of DiGregorio's Market.)

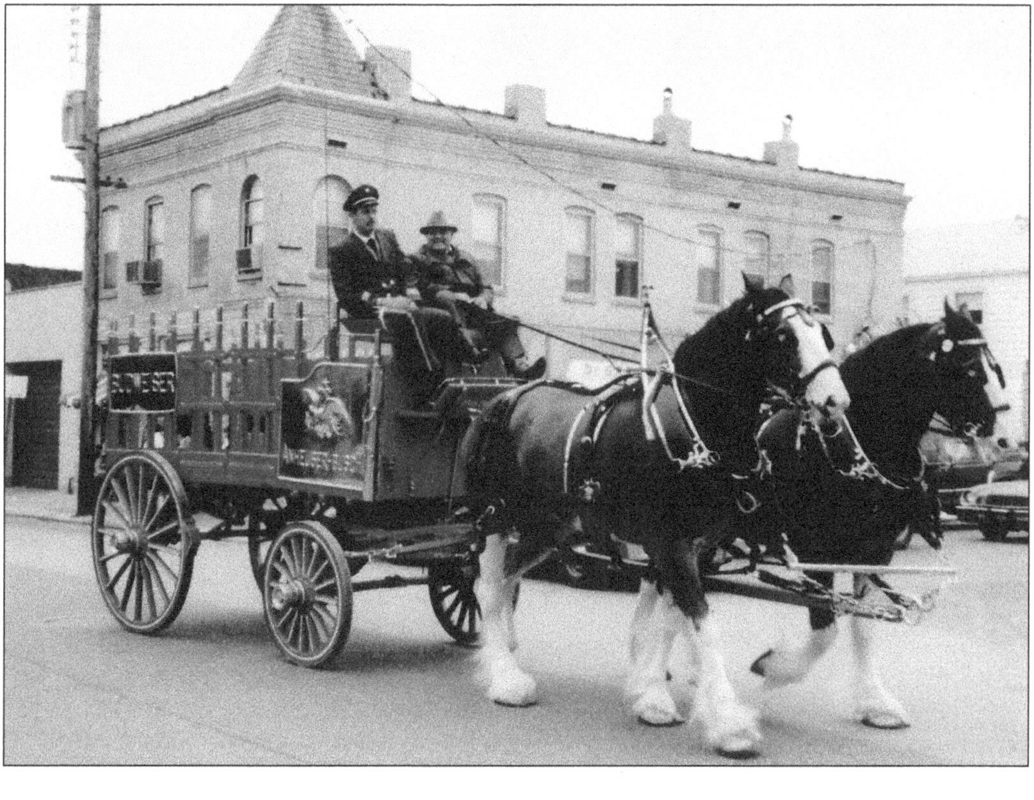

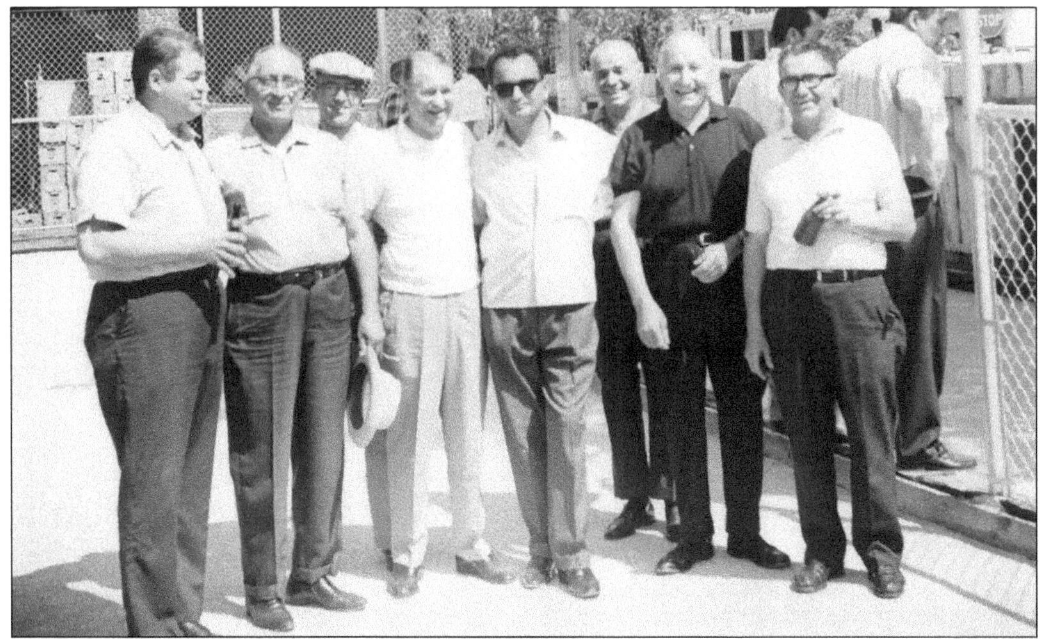

John and Rose's bocce courts were an icon on the Hill. This was the place to meet old and new friends and to network with executives from Southwest Bank and other neighborhood companies. Most important, it was the place to play some serious bocce. The courts began getting a little noisy and competitive for the neighbors. (Courtesy of Gino Mariani.)

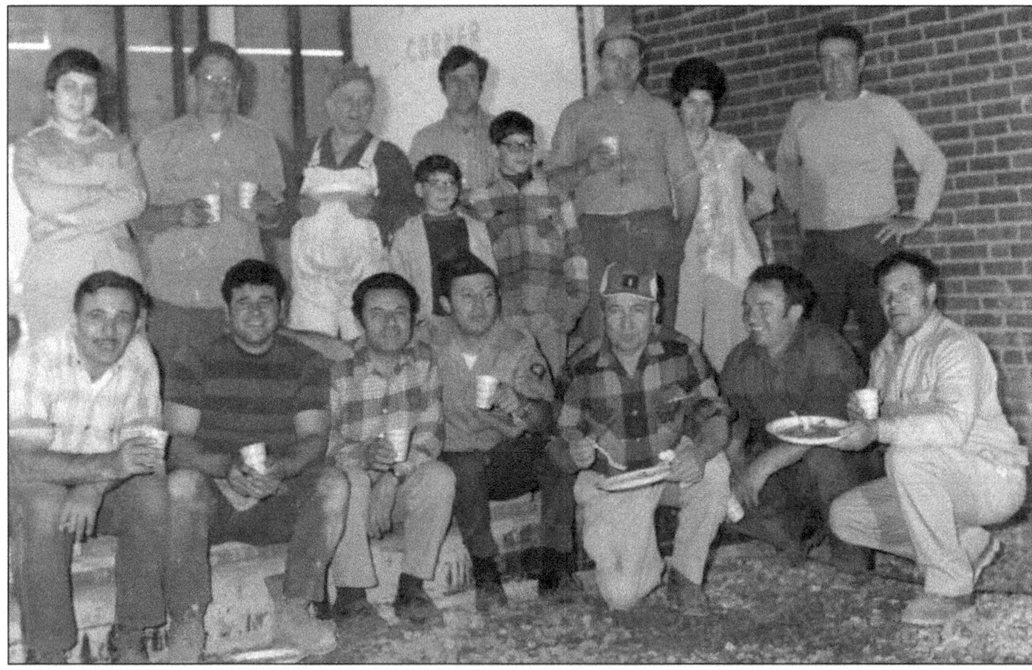

This group played bocce at John and Rose's on the Hill. A close group of friends were enthusiastic about forming a club of their own, so they pooled their resources and talents to purchase a building at 5627 Manchester Road, just off the Hill. They labored for one year in their spare time before the building was opened in 1975. (Courtesy of Italia America Bocce Club.)

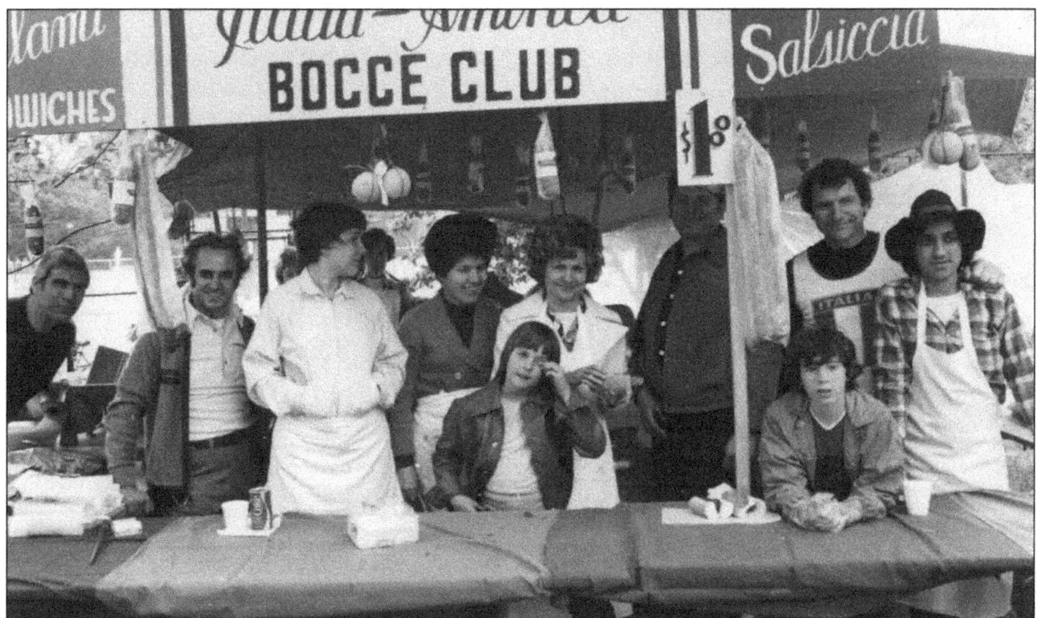

This was the first fundraiser for the bocce club to be built on Manchester Road. Later, in 1991, the club members rebuilt a large facility on the Hill, a few steps from St. Ambrose. Today, the Italia America Bocce Club has five beautiful courts, a dining room, and 400 members. (Courtesy of the Italia America Bocce Club.)

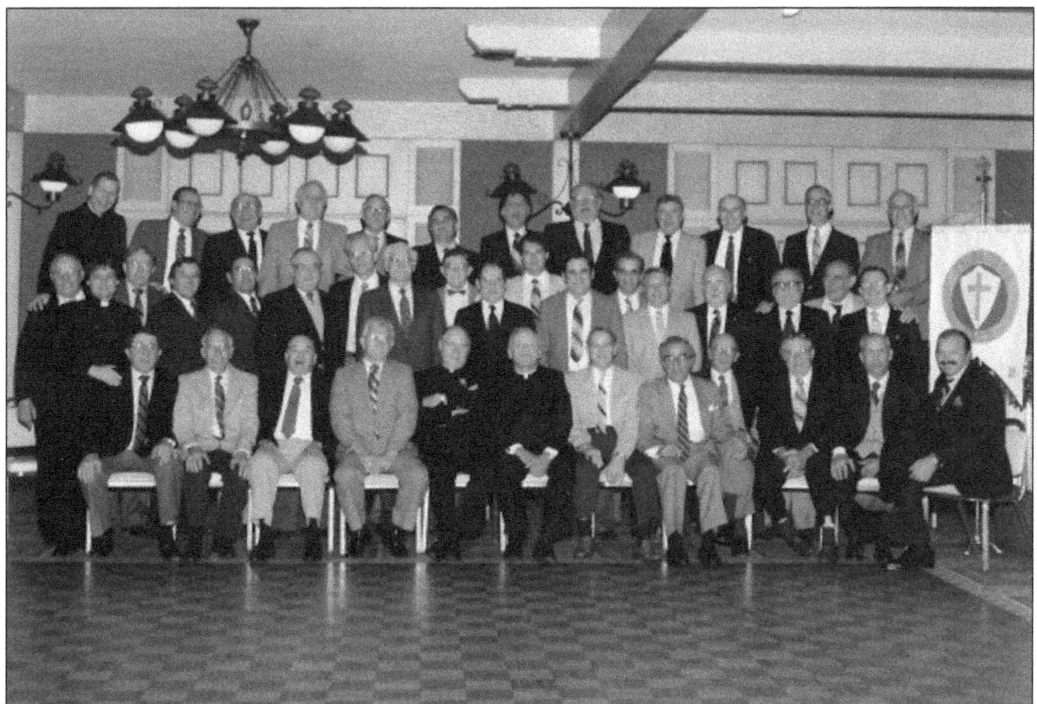

The Crusaders Club continues to meet monthly. The club has a limit of 50 members and a long list of prospective individuals wishing to join. When an opening occurs, men are nominated by existing members and must receive a majority vote for acceptance. (Courtesy of Tim Valli.)

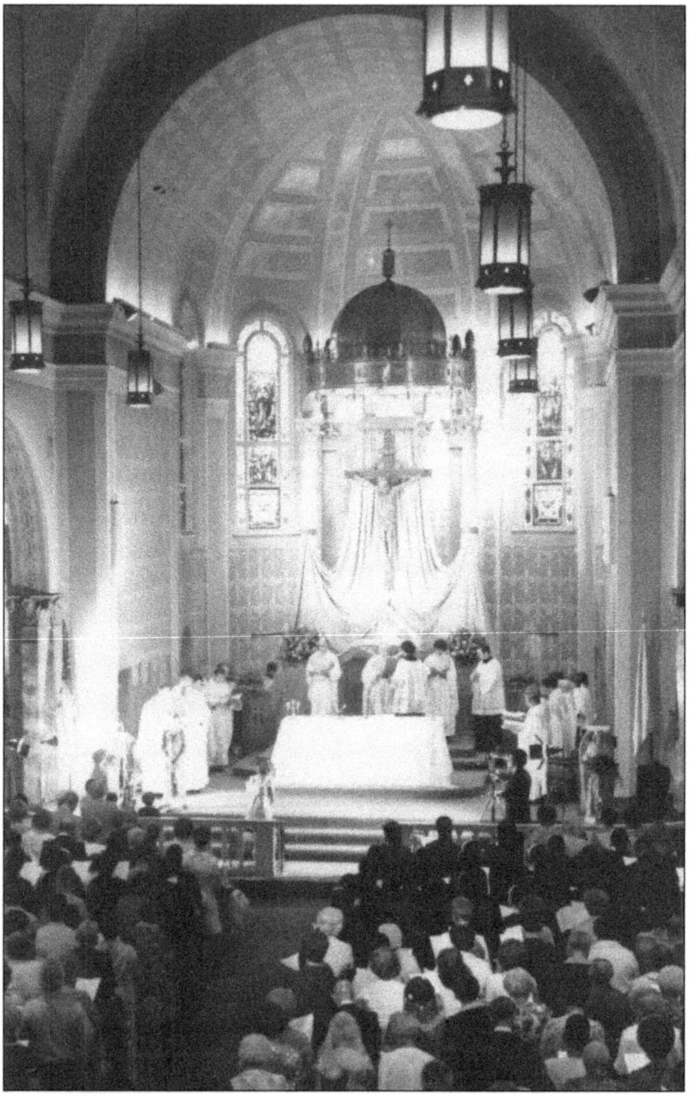

In the 1960s, St. Ambrose Church was remodeled, and the statue of St. Ambrose was replaced with a large crucifix. St. Ambrose held a 75th-anniversary celebration, with a large procession followed by Mass and then a special dinner. The church remains as pictured here at the 75th anniversary Mass. In the 1960s, urban flight threatened the Hill. Neighborhood leaders got involved and helped to stabilize the area. (Courtesy of Gino Mariani.)

The first Hill Day celebration was held on August 15, 1965. It coincided with the centennial of the City of St. Louis. Thousands were entertained with music, dancing, food, and crafts. A parade with beautifully decorated floats proceeded down the streets of the Hill prior to the celebration. The day ended with a spectacular fireworks display at Berra Park. (Courtesy of James Merlo.)

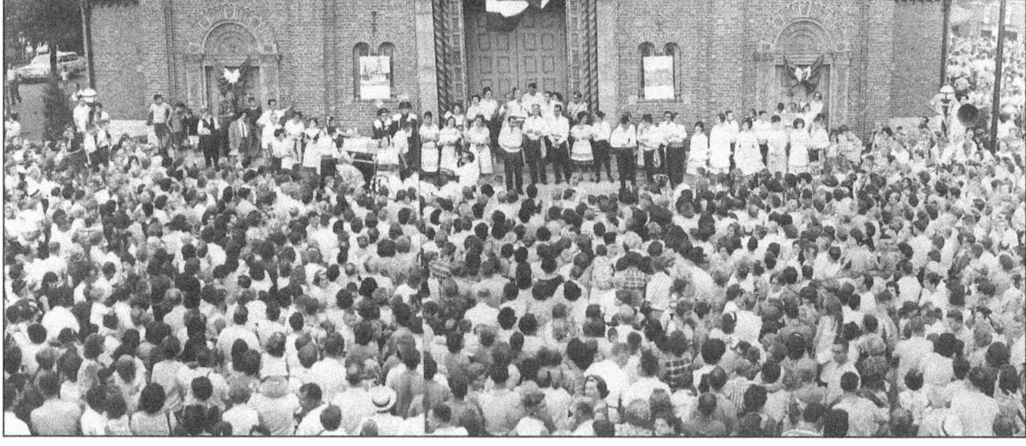

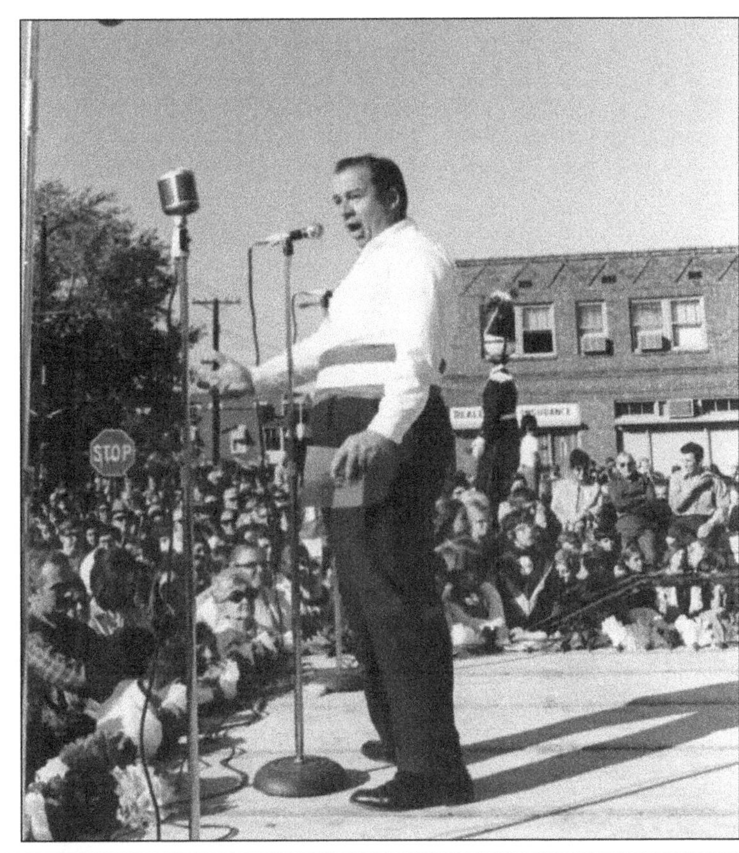

Tony Bossi entertains the crowd on Hill Day. Other performances included Italian folk dancing and singing. The crowd, in excess of 75,000 people, enjoyed Italian art, culture, customs, traditions, religious events, and folklore handed down from one generation to the next. (Courtesy of Gino Mariani.)

These Hill Day performers are, from left to right, Robert "Bootsie" DeMattei, Joe Gorla, Al Migneco, and James Merlo. Booths on the streets around St. Ambrose Church offered Italian dishes like ravioli, Italian sausage, pasta, and meatballs. (Courtesy of Gino Mariani.)

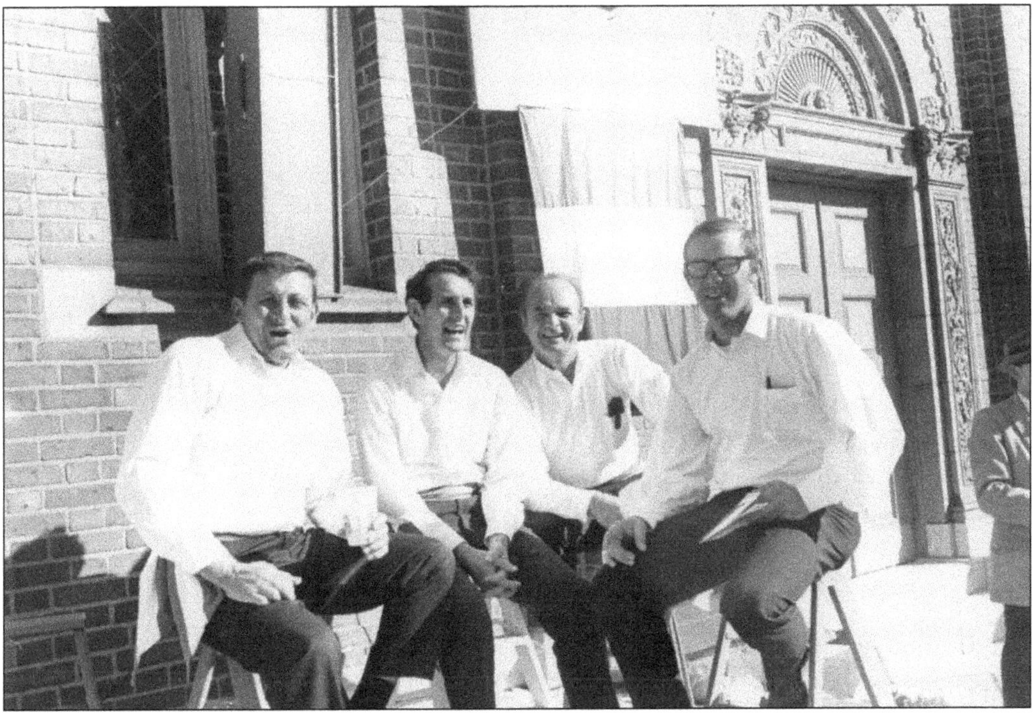

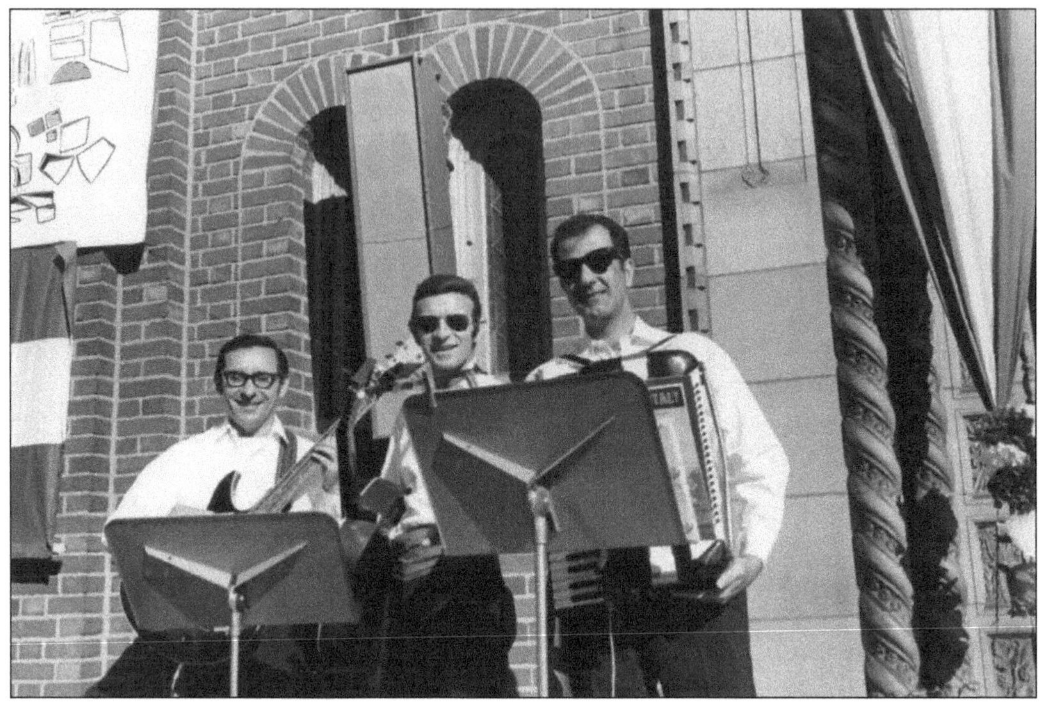

Posing here are Hill Day musicians (from left to right) Al Gaia, Charles "Skip" Torretta, and Salvatore Finocchiaro. These men would entertain crowds around the Hill and perform programs at St. Ambrose Church with dramatic clubs. They also performed at the Big Club Hall. (Courtesy of Gino Mariani.)

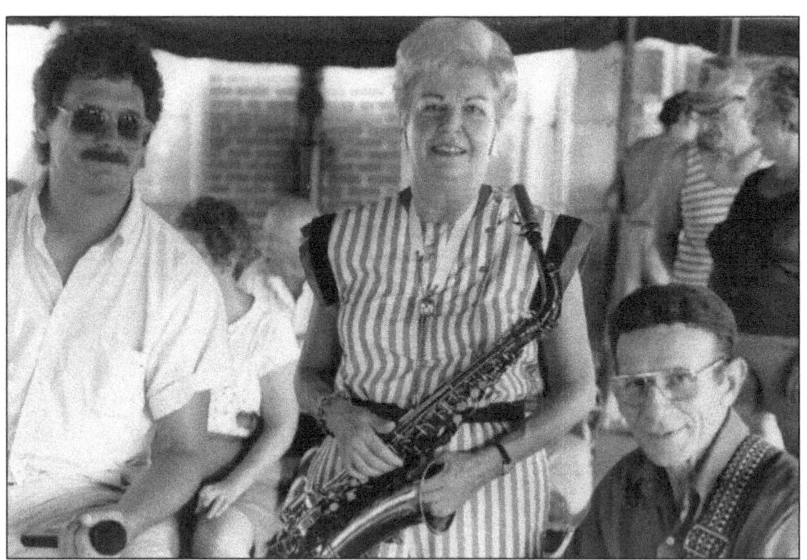

Keith Ballentine (left) has been entertaining Hill residents and Italian Americans for years. Not only is he a talented musician, he also hosted his own cable show, *Casa Cucina*, about everything Italian. (Courtesy of Gino Mariani.)

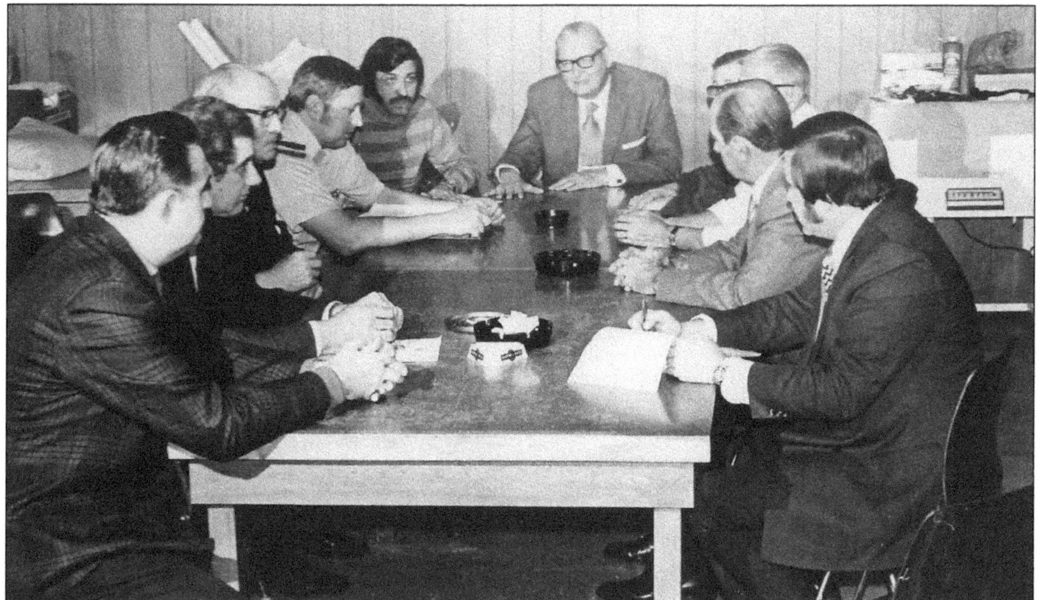

The board members of Hill 2000 are shown here in 1972, working on plans for neighborhood improvement. Today, Highway 44 separates Northrup and Pattison Avenues from the southern parts of the Hill. On the south side of Pattison, 100 homes were destroyed. Hill 2000, led by Rev. Salvatore Polizzi, unsuccessfully fought to get the highway rerouted. They did succeed in having a pedestrian overpass installed, after a committee from the Hill presented the US Department of Transportation with a check for $50,000. The overpass allowed residents to continue to walk to work and to worship at St. Ambrose Church. (Courtesy of Gino Mariani.)

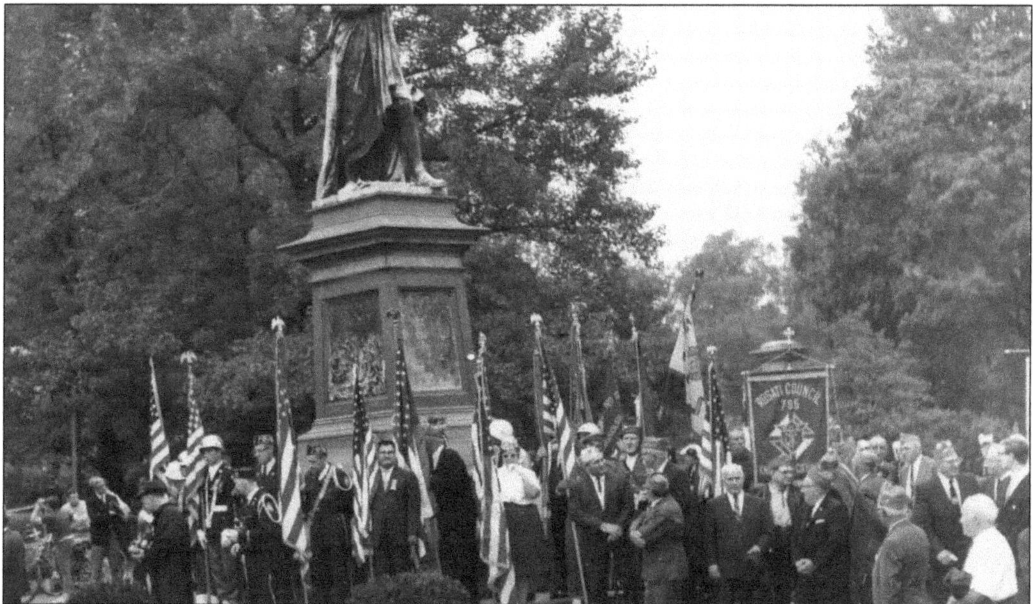

This is a Columbus Day parade at Tower Grove Park in the early 1970s. The parade was a combined effort by the Knights of Columbus and the Fratellanza Society, which began the parade in 1867. The procession started downtown and ended at the Christopher Columbus statue in Tower Grove Park. (Courtesy of Gino Mariani.)

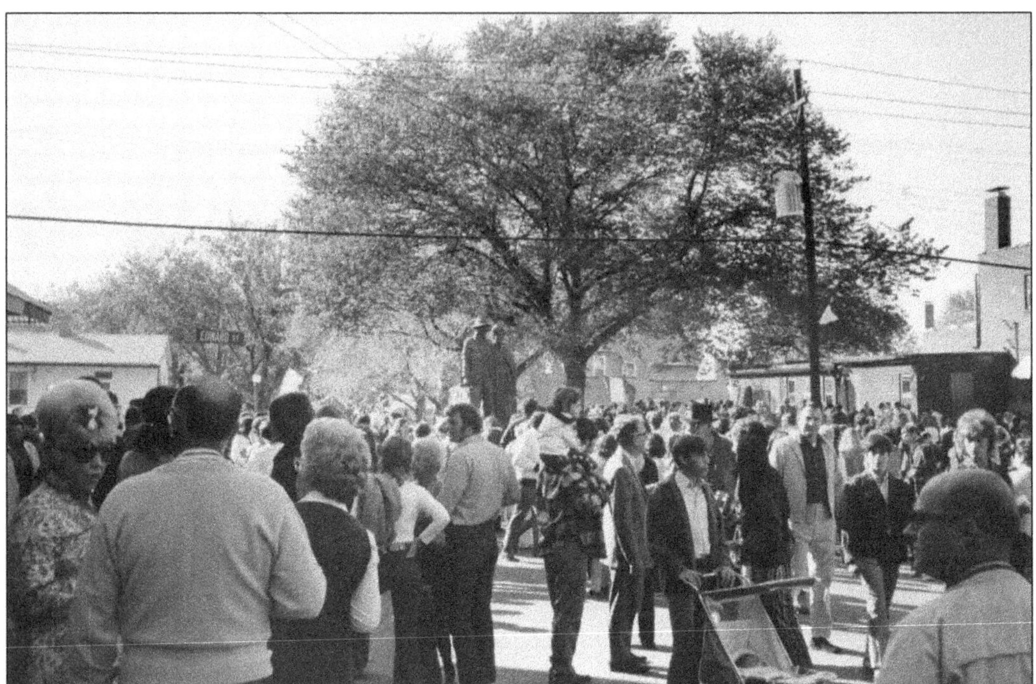

The crowd at Hill Day in 1971 gets its first chance to view the model of the statue *The Italian Immigrants* at the corner of Wilson Avenue and Edwards Street. The idea for the monument came from Msgr. Salvatore Polizzi in the late 1960s. After this prototype was displayed, momentum for the project grew. The model was brought to several other locations on the Hill, and the project quickly received neighborhood approval. (Courtesy of Gino Mariani.)

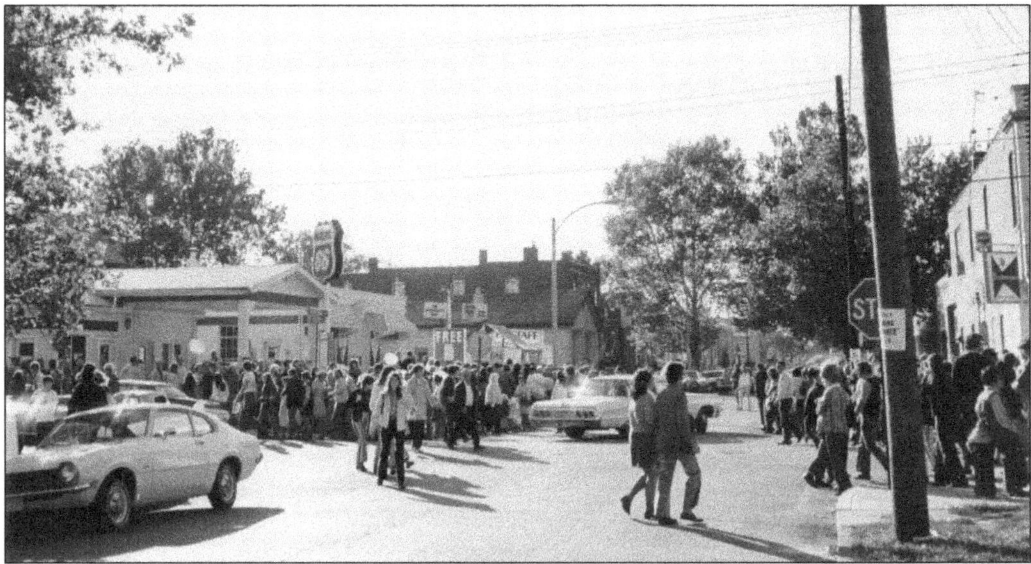

Phillips 66 was one of the few service stations built in a residential area on the Hill. It is now Fairmount Service LLC., which offers state automobile inspections and service. Owned by Harry Berra, it stands only a few steps from St. Ambrose Church. It is also the hangout for the Roundees, a group of men who congregate around the station and talk about the old days. Pictured here is Hill Day in 1971. (Courtesy of Gino Mariani.)

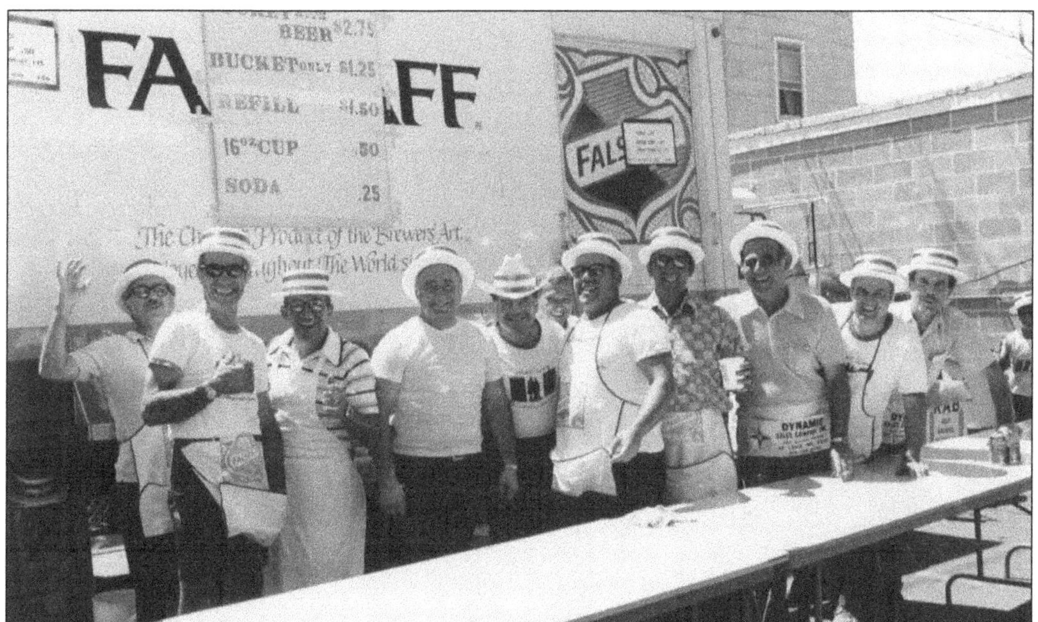

These men of the Hill are enjoying their volunteer work on Hill Day. Beer was sold in tin buckets, much like the ones that were used in years past. These buckets are taken home as keepsakes and proudly displayed by residents. (Courtesy of Gino Mariani.)

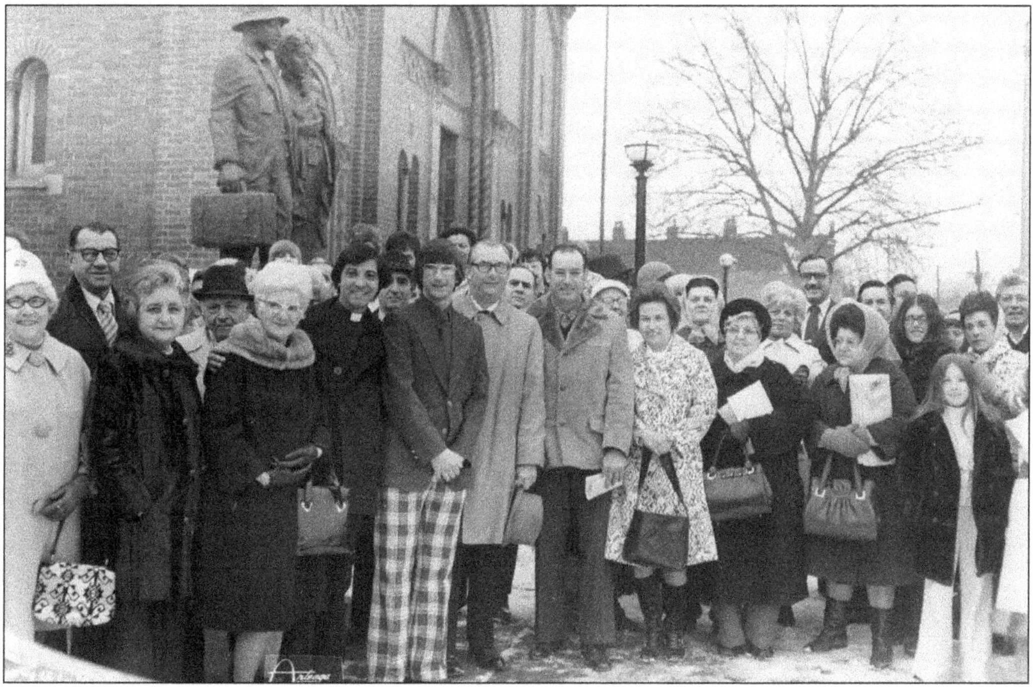

The Italian Immigrants, sculpted by Rudy Torini, stands next to St. Ambrose Church. Here, members of the parish gather for a photograph after the unveiling. The statue brings to mind the sacrifice of the brave men and women who left their homeland to create a better life. Dignity and determination can be seen in their eyes, and hope is represented by their suitcase. The future can also be seen in the infant being held in the woman's arms. (Courtesy of Gino Mariani.)

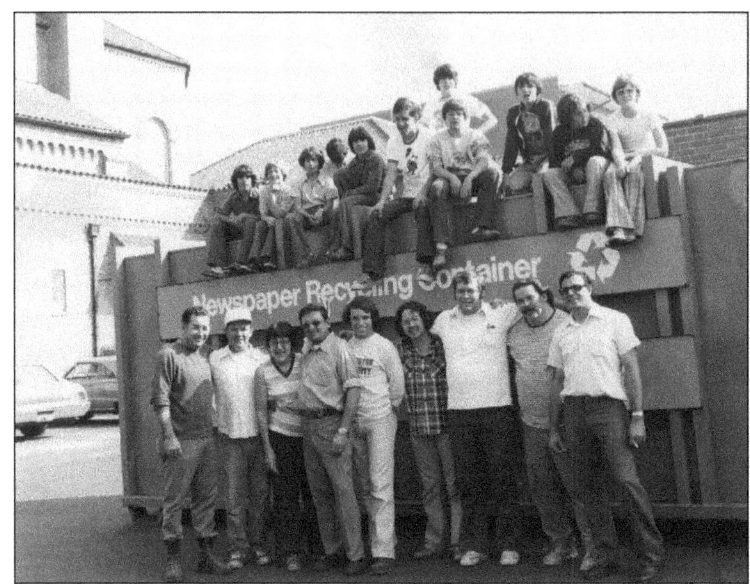

The youth of St. Ambrose pitch in to clean, work, and volunteer for projects, much like their parents and grandparents did. Summer programs keep them busy, and they learn how to stay productive and provide needed services to the community. (Courtesy of Gino Mariani.)

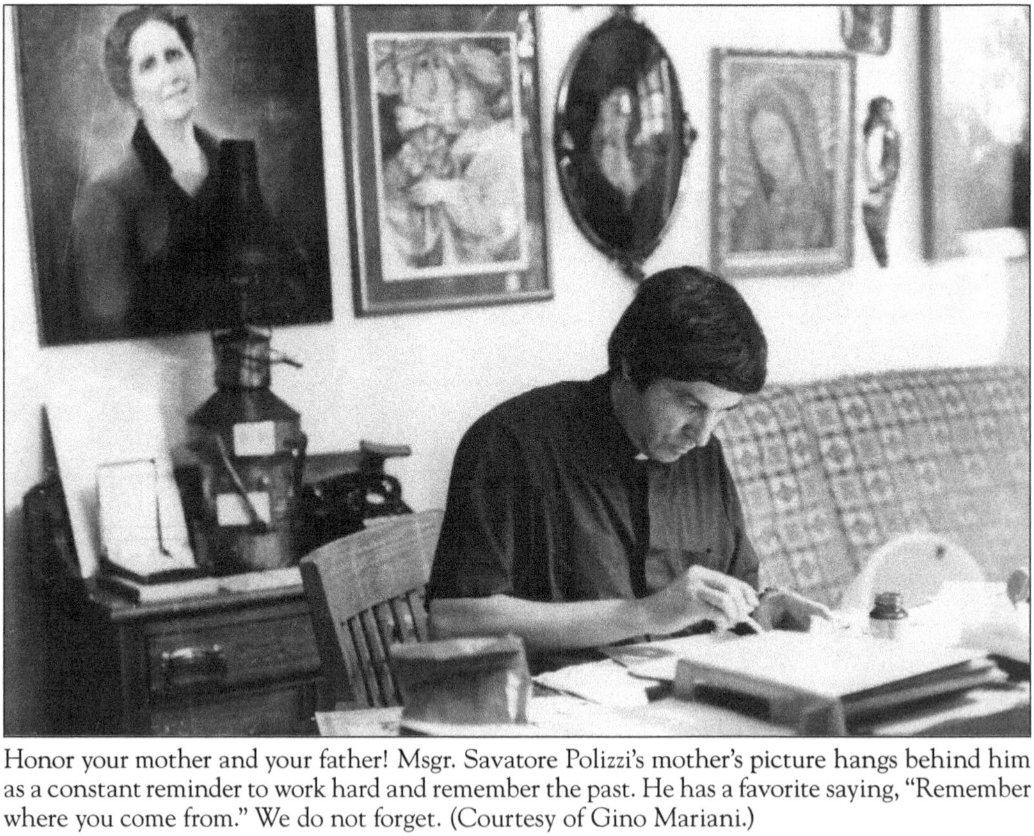

Honor your mother and your father! Msgr. Savatore Polizzi's mother's picture hangs behind him as a constant reminder to work hard and remember the past. He has a favorite saying, "Remember where you come from." We do not forget. (Courtesy of Gino Mariani.)

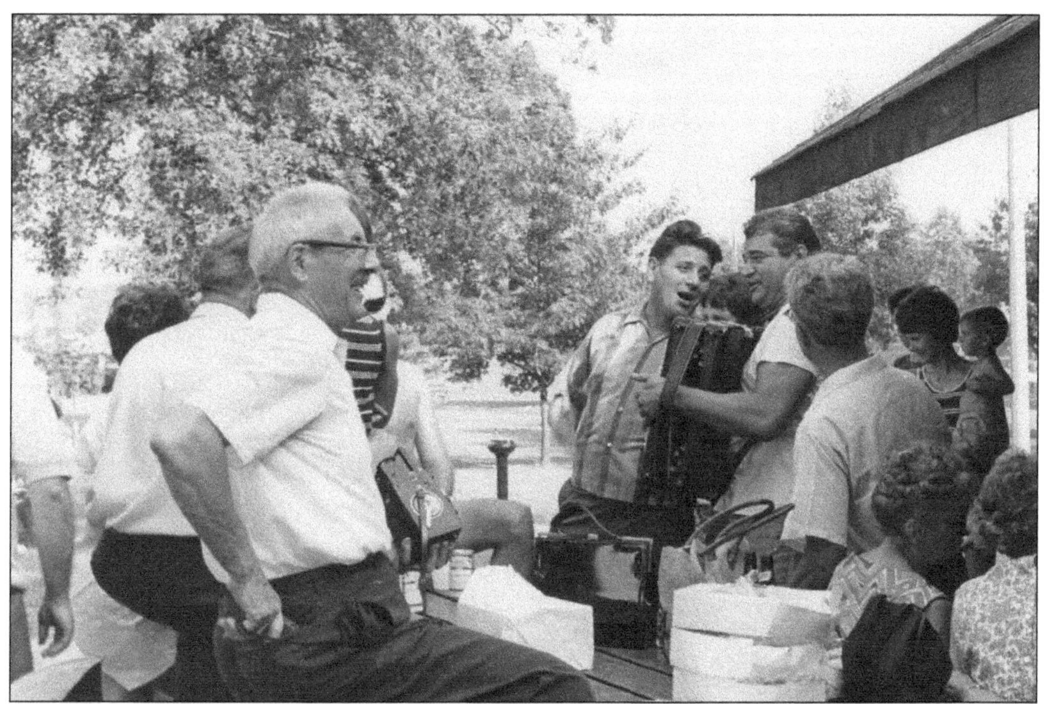

At one of the annual picnics of the Fratellanza Society, Gino Mariani, "The Roving Photographer" (left), sings with Aldo Della Croce (left of the accordion player). Music, food, drink, and bocce continue to be among the picnic's most popular activities. (Courtesy of Gino Mariani.)

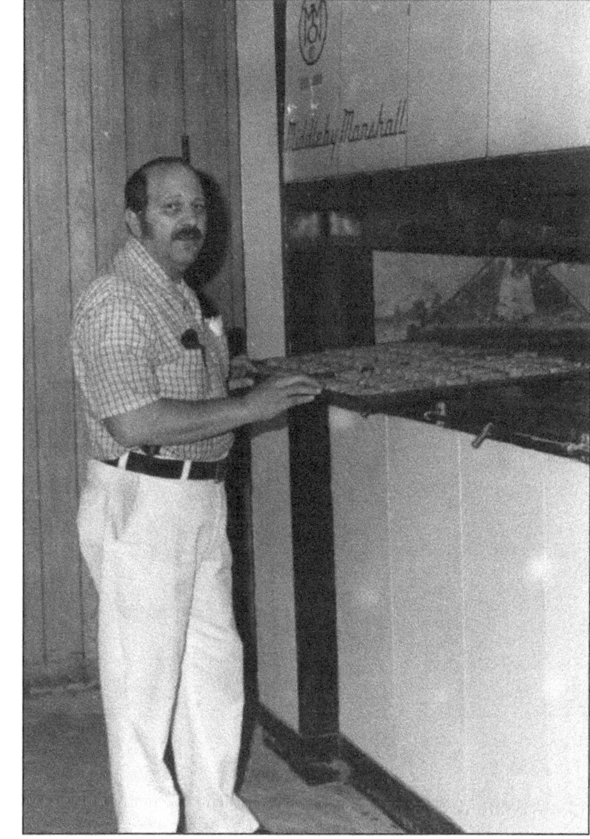

Pete Vitale learned the trade of baking from his father-in-law, Peter Bommarito, in downtown's Little Italy. Pete and his wife, Grace, opened Vitale's Bakery on the Hill in 1975, at 2130 Marconi, where it remains today. (Courtesy of Gino Mariani.)

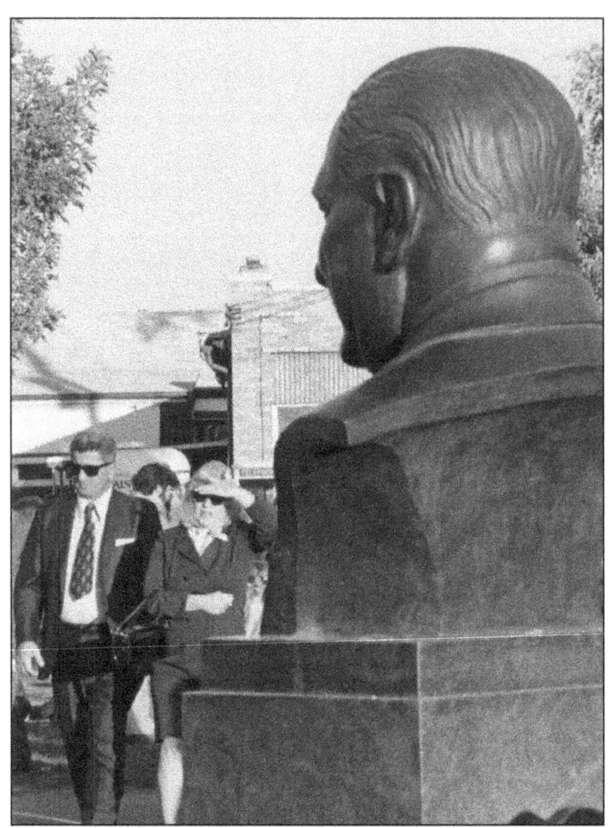

Lewis "Midge" Berra was elected alderman of the 24th Ward in 1939. He married Louise in 1926 in her hometown of Herrin, Illinois. He felt that the young people of the Hill should develop an interest in politics, and was instrumental in organizing the 24th Ward Democratic Juniors Club. This bust of him is located in Berra Park, which is named after him. (Courtesy of Gino Mariani.)

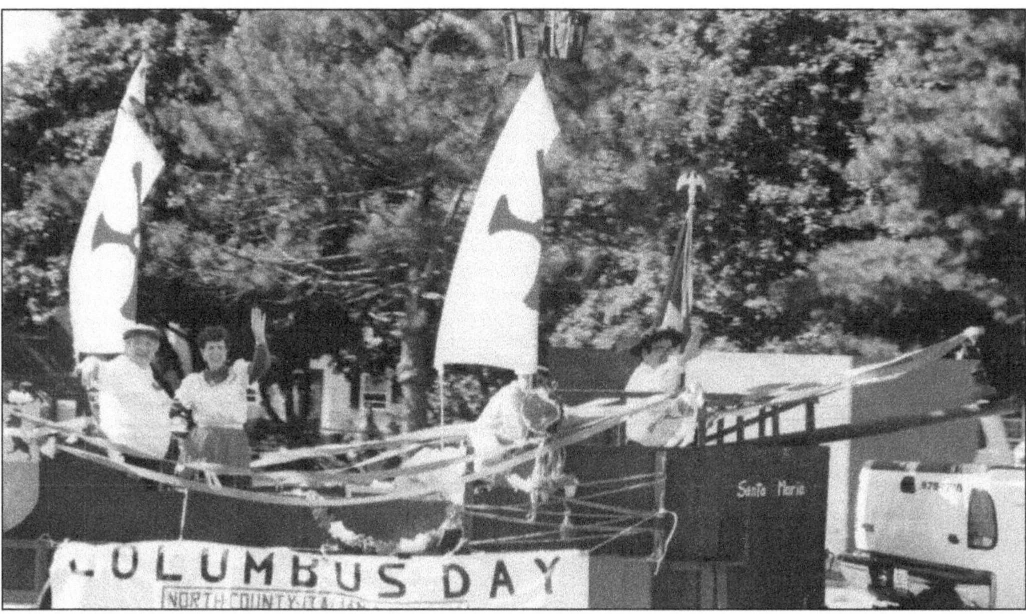

In the 1980s, the Columbus Day Parade and Festa were moved from Tower Grove Park to the streets of the Hill. The parade winds through the streets and past St. Ambrose Church, ending at Berra Park. The Festa follows, where all can enjoy Italian culture, food, and sweets. It is also a chance to honor those who came before. (Courtesy of Marianne Peri-Sack.)

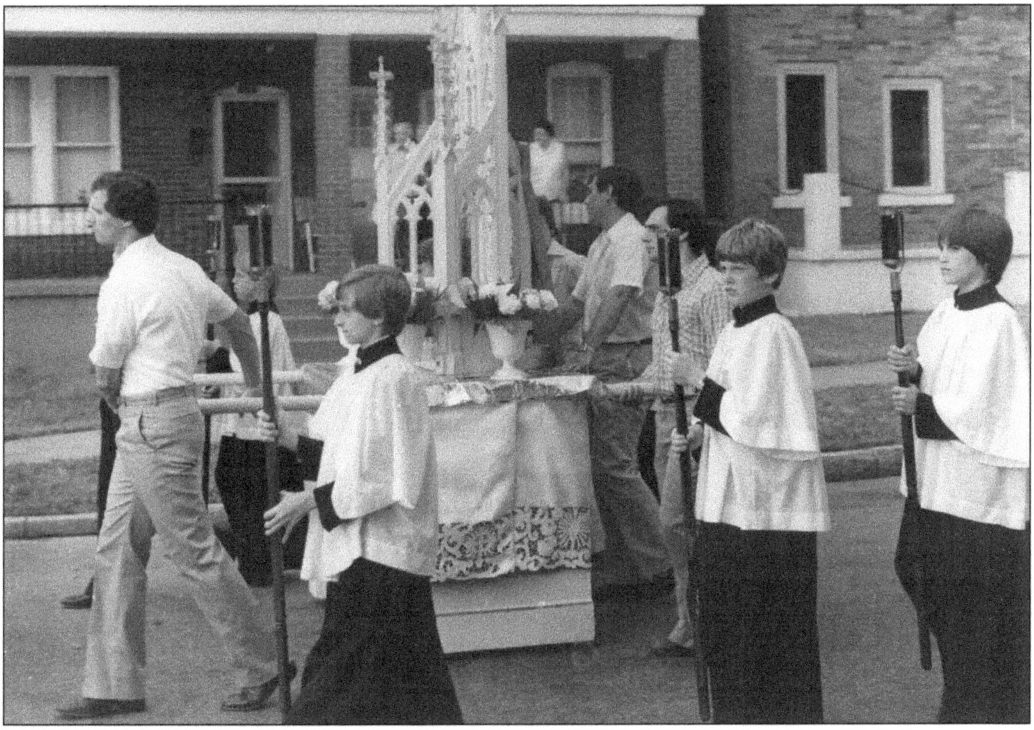

The Corpus Christi Procession is a tradition that continues today. Residents make sure that the lawns are freshly cut and the streets are clean. If a home is not prepared, the owners can expect a phone call from the St. Ambrose Rectory. (Courtesy of Gino Mariani.)

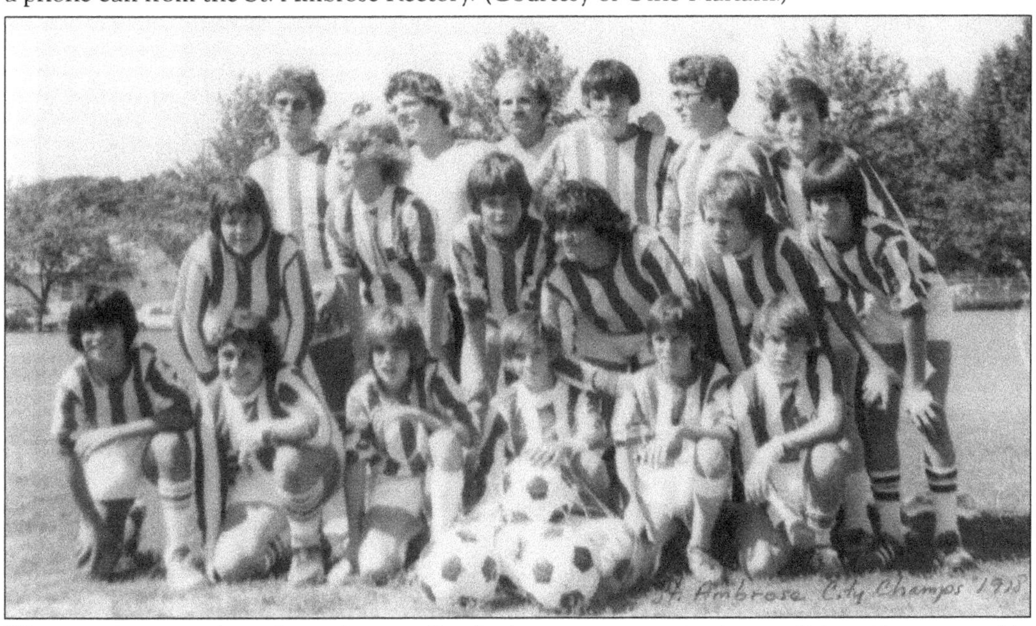

Winning teams and good coaching at St. Ambrose are a continuing tradition. Sportsmanship and professional coaching are the most important virtues. The St. Ambrose Athletic Association continues to provide the best possible equipment and facilities for the youth of the neighborhood. (Courtesy of Gino Mariani.)

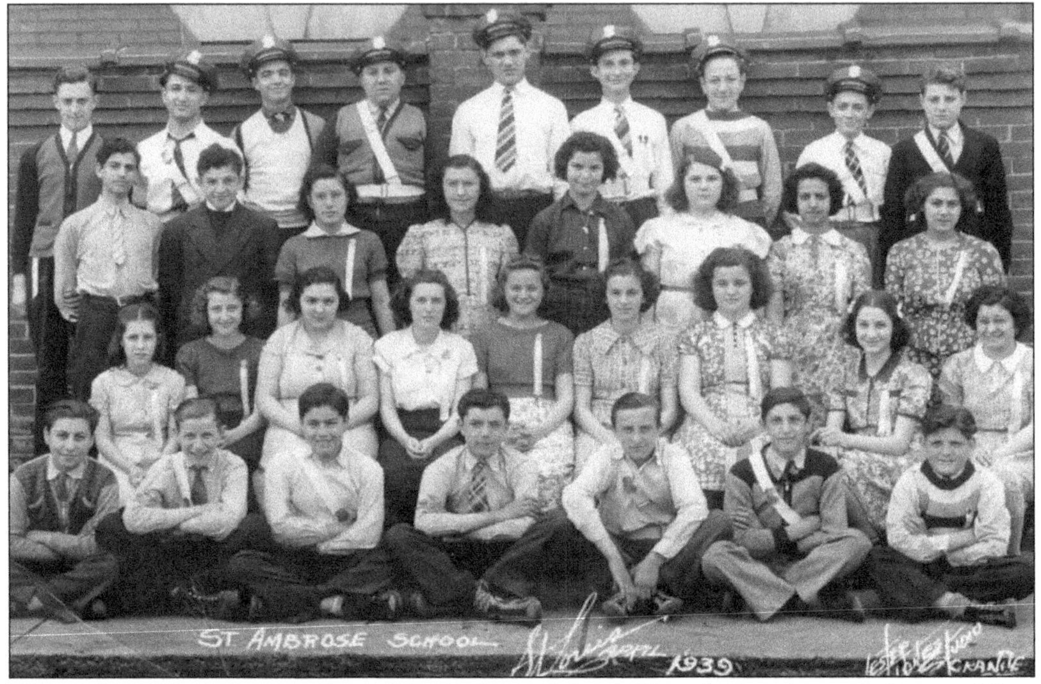

This is the 1939 graduation class of St. Ambrose School. This class and many others to follow would work tirelessly for the Hill and in their professions. (Courtesy of Robert Garagiola.)

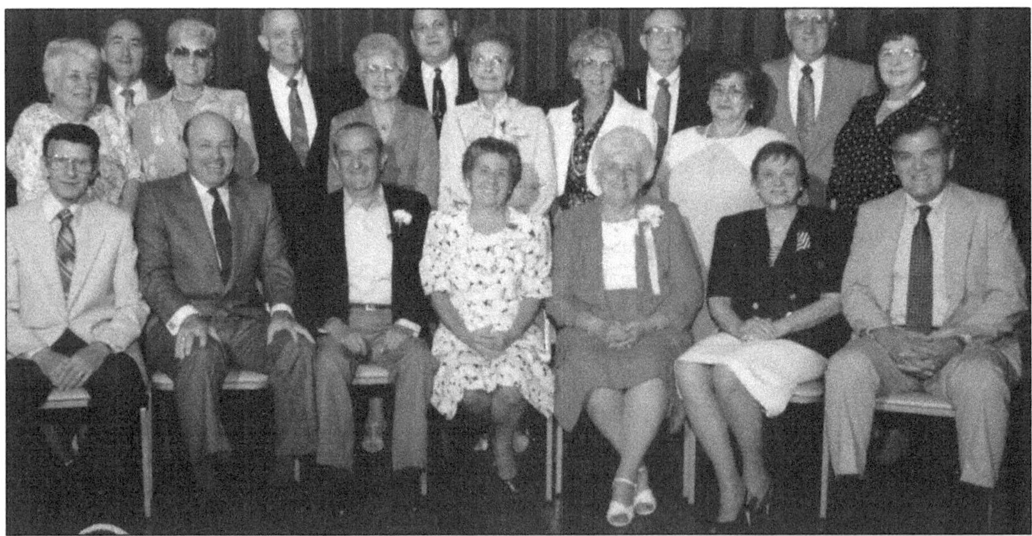

Shown here are attendees of the 50th reunion of St. Ambrose's class of 1939. Many of the students pictured in the photograph above were in attendance at the reunion. Each year, St. Ambrose School celebrates with an alumni breakfast that is very well attended. (Courtesy of Anne Garavaglia Agusti.)

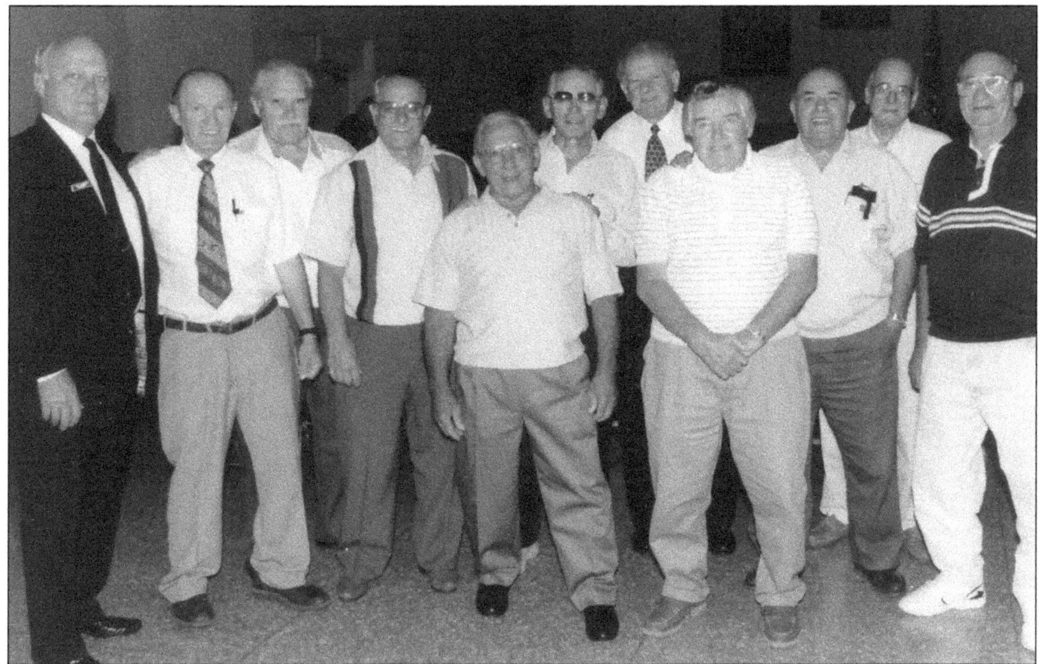

The Ravens are now a group of men from "the Greatest Generation," and they continue to cling to the principles that they learned as first-generation Americans from their immigrant parents. They value hard work, family, friendship, faith, and service to the community. They are a remarkable group of men who not only grew up together, served their country, and raised their families, but also remained true to their friendships. (Courtesy of Faye Berra Venegoni.)

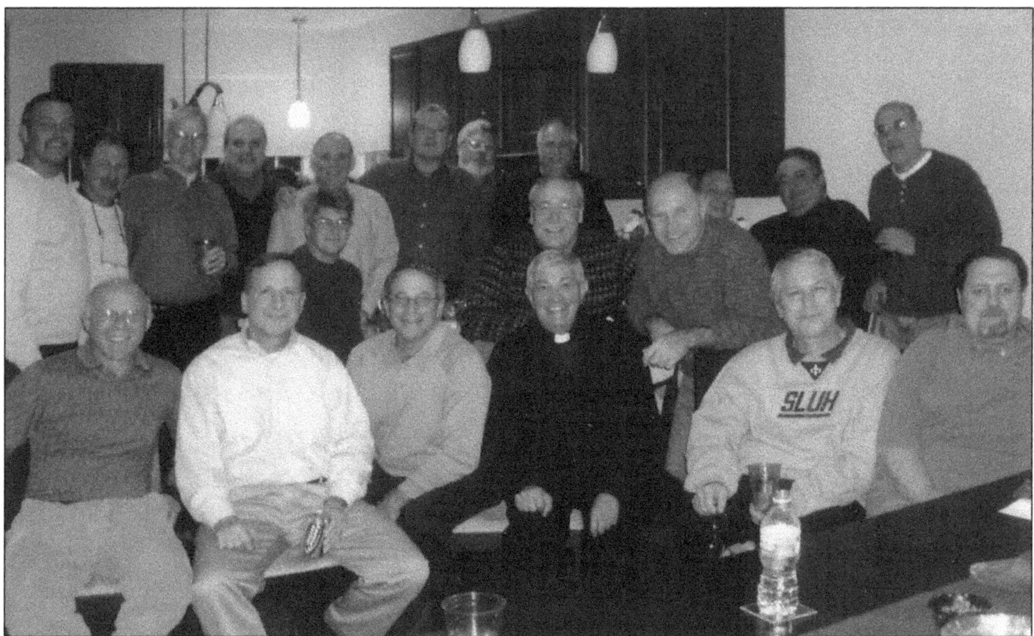

The last and youngest of the clubs, The Hill Boys, was founded in 1970. They were sponsored and mentored by Reverend Polizzi, who attends each reunion. This club, still active in the community, provides an annual scholarship to St. Ambrose School. (Courtesy of Robert Saffo.)

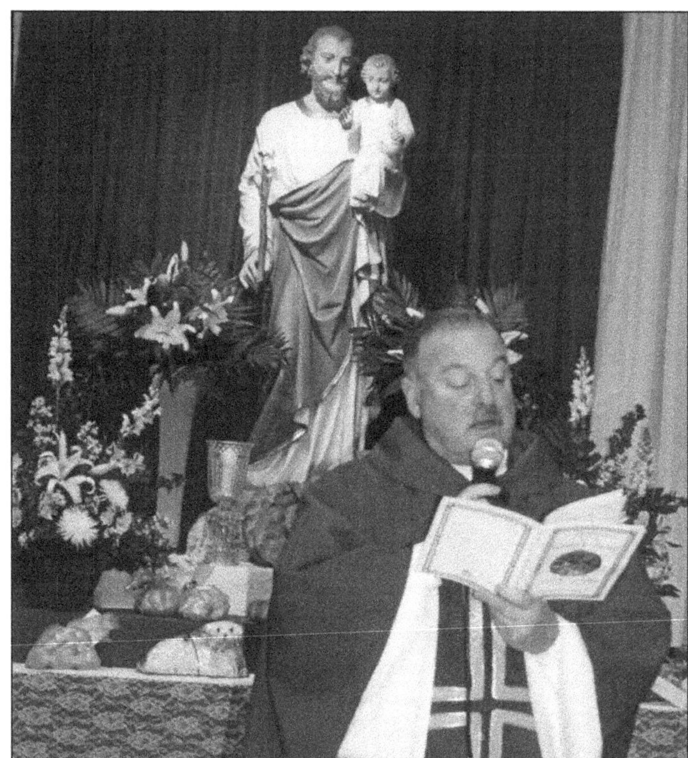

St. Joseph's Day is celebrated in the cafeteria of St. Ambrose School. Msgr. Vincent Bommarito is the current pastor of St. Ambrose Church. This celebration, mainly a Sicilian tradition, gives thanks to St. Joseph (San Giuseppe) for preventing a famine in Sicily during the Middle Ages. People of Sicily prayed to St. Joseph for rain during a drought. The rain came, and a crop of fava beans saved the population from starvation. For information on St. Ambrose, visit www.stambroseonthehill.com. (Courtesy of Rosemary DiGregorio Parentin.)

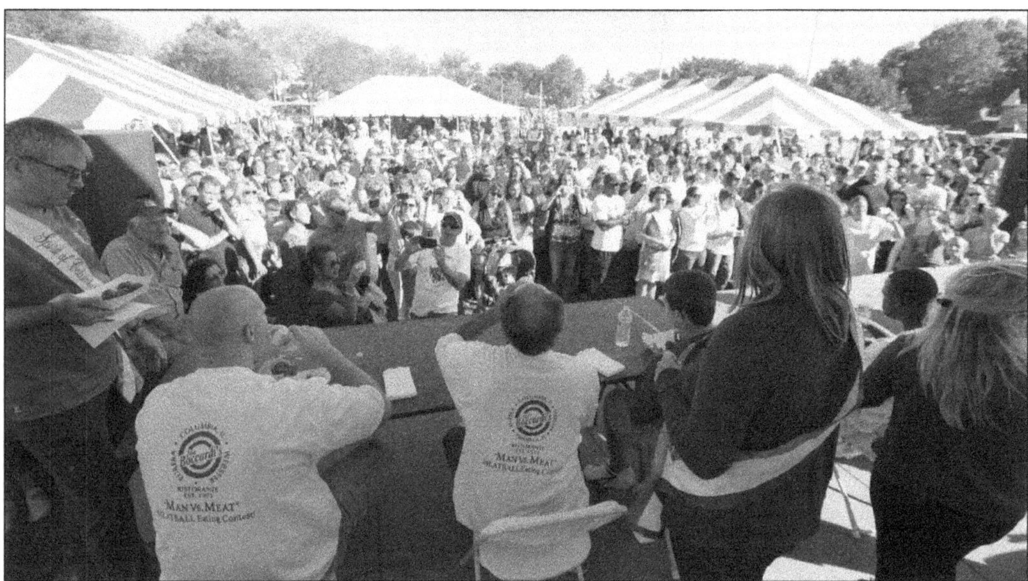

The crowds are watching a meatball-eating contest at Berra Park following the Columbus Day Parade in 2013. Pictured judging (wearing sashes) are Chris Stephens, 2013 Spirit of Columbus Award winner, and daughter Teresa Stephens, 2013 Junior Miss Italian St. Louis. They are third and fourth generation descendants of Lombard immigrants. The parade and festival continue to attract large crowds that enjoy Italian food, music, and dancing. La Festa in May is another popular event that is held at St. Ambrose Church. For information on Columbus Day, see www.stlcolumbusday.com. (Courtesy of the Italian American Heritage Corporation, St. Louis.)

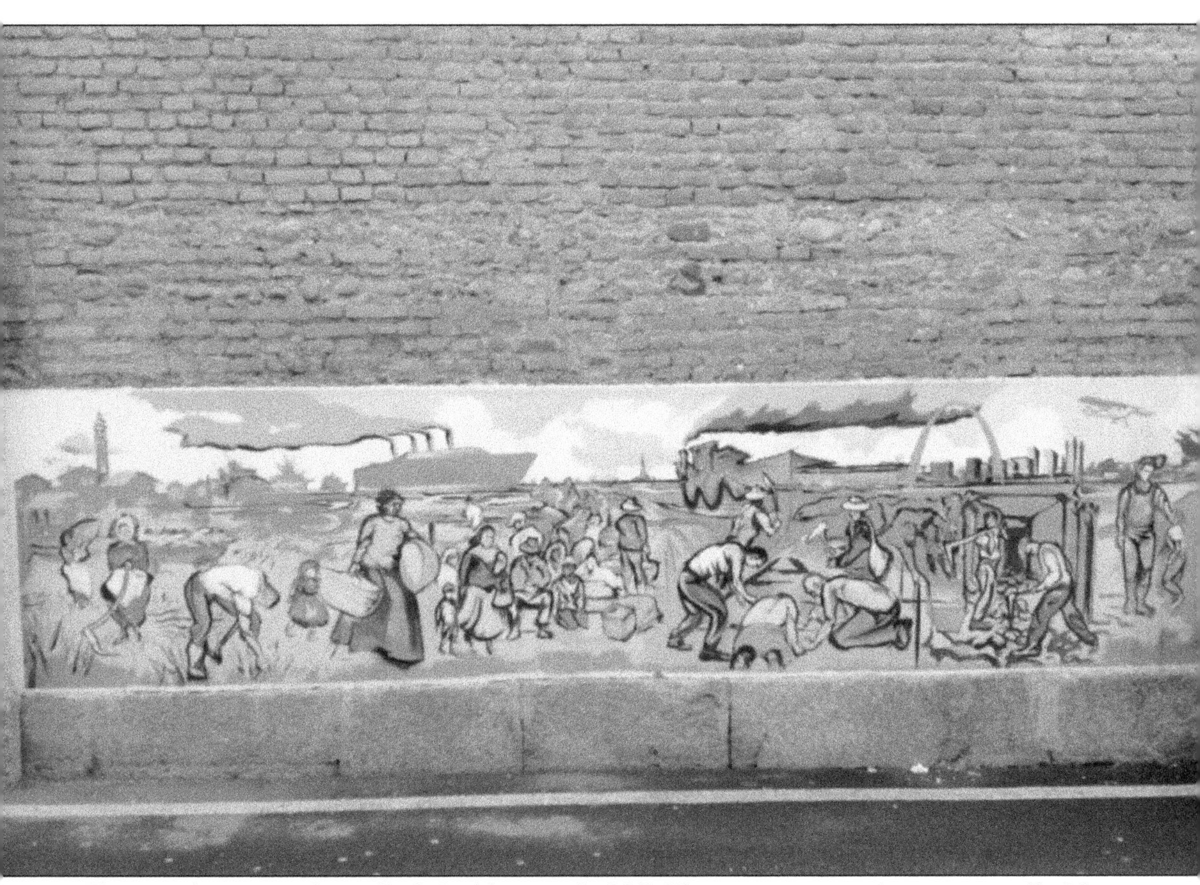

This mural is not on the wall of a building on the Hill. The painting is on the exterior wall of the Le Radici e le Ali emigration museum in Cuggiono, Italy. From the surrounding towns, thousands came to the United States, leaving their homeland. They crossed oceans through ports unknown for a new life of hard labor and high hopes in the United States and other countries. Note the Gateway Arch and the *Spirit of St. Louis* in the background on the right. For information on the museum, see www.cuggiono.org. (Author's collection.)

www.ingramcontent.com/pod-product-compliance
Lightning Source LLC
LaVergne TN
LVHW060626110826
845147LV00015B/948
* 9 7 8 1 4 6 7 1 1 2 2 1 5 *